D1321370

Art and Authority

Art and Authority

*Moral Rights and Meaning
in Contemporary Visual Art*

K. E. Gover

OXFORD
UNIVERSITY PRESS

OXFORD
UNIVERSITY PRESS

Great Clarendon Street, Oxford, OX2 6DP,
United Kingdom

Oxford University Press is a department of the University of Oxford.
It furthers the University's objective of excellence in research, scholarship,
and education by publishing worldwide. Oxford is a registered trade mark of
Oxford University Press in the UK and in certain other countries

First Edition published in 2018
Impression: 1

Published in the United States of America by Oxford University Press
198 Madison Avenue, New York, NY 10016, United States of America

British Library Cataloguing in Publication Data
Data available

Library of Congress Control Number: 2017954800

ISBN 978-0-19-876869-2

Printed and bound by
CPI Group (UK) Ltd, Croydon, CR0 4YY

Contents

1

Introduction

On your way to these words, you probably skimmed past a few pages containing the usual perfunctory text that begins any book, what publishers call the 'front matter.' Within the familiar blur of fine print sits a striking statement: "The moral rights of the author have been asserted." There, amid the formulaic language announcing publisher's address, assertions of copyright, ISBN, and other essential pieces of legal boilerplate, the book makes a quiet demand of its reader. It asks him to recognize that the author of the book has certain rights with respect to its content. Moral rights protect the special interests that an author has in her work insofar as it is her personal creation and expression, and they are maintained even when the author has surrendered her economic rights to it. Under the doctrine of moral rights, the work—be it an artwork, a novel, or even a piece of academic scholarship—serves as a distal extension of the author as it leaves her hands and passes into yours. She is thereby entitled to retain a certain degree of control over its disposition, presentation, and treatment.

Considered in these terms, authorship seems to entail a strange and powerful bond between creator and work. This is particularly the case with art, which in contemporary Western culture is seen as primarily if not purely the personal expression of the artist. And yet we tend to take the concept of authorship for granted. People engage with authored works all the time. They buy paintings, read books, and download songs. They might even be artists themselves. The basic idea that an artist as author maintains some kind of claim to his creation, even as it circulates in the world at large, seems natural. In our familiarity with the functions and trappings of authorship, we pass over the book publisher's front matter unless some reason compels us to consult it. Similarly, we accept without question the fundamental concepts upon which those legal declarations are based—authorship, copyright, moral rights—unless an unusual set of circumstances, such as a lawsuit or controversy, brings them to our attention.

My interest in moral rights and the nature of authorship began in 2007, when a bitter dispute between an artist and a major museum located thirty miles from my home turned into a lawsuit that attracted international attention. Put simply, the case hinged on the question of who had the right to determine the fate of an abandoned, unfinished work of installation art in the museum's largest gallery. The museum wanted to show it to the public; the artist insisted that it be dismantled and discarded without the unfinished work being shown. As I began to follow the case closely, I realized that both sides were claiming ownership over the same set of physical objects, but in different respects: the artist was asserting that the unfinished installation was, in an important sense, *his* insofar as it was an artwork that he conceived and designed, whereas the museum, which had provided all of the financial and logistical support for its construction, claimed that it had the right to show the abandoned objects assembled on its property. The museum owned the materials, but their presence was largely the result of the artist's choices. To that extent, they embodied something that belonged only to him: his artistic vision, his intentions. While the installation was left unfinished and unrealized, it was nevertheless in many respects his creation. But who had the right to decide the fate of these 'materials,' as the courts, in an attempt at neutrality, called them? How do we parse the competing claims over the corpse of this unfinished work of art? Does it matter that the artist never gave the work the carapace of completion by declaring it 'done'? As art experts, journalists, and judges weighed in on the fiasco, I realized that the dual nature of the artwork, as both a material object, and an authored creation, is a metaphysical distinction that can lead to some very concrete battles.

My fascination with the case between the artist and the museum also became a turning point in my thinking about philosophical aesthetics. I noticed that the dispute generated a lot of impassioned claims by the litigants and by commentators about the nature of art and what it means to be an artist. What seemed to be a legal wrangle over contracts and property became a charged debate about ontology, ethics, and the nature of artistic authorship. These are subjects that philosophers of art have considered in great detail for some time. But when I turned to the scholarly literature to help clarify my thinking about the case, I noticed that very little of it addressed my questions directly. Certainly, there is no shortage of theoretical material addressing the same general areas of interest that this case touched on. Philosophers have devoted a great deal of attention in the past fifty years to the definition of art, its nature, and ontology. Arthur Danto revolutionized the field by making some of the twentieth century's most challenging artworks the centerpiece of his philosophical reflections on art and aesthetics. And in literary circles, the concept of authorship has come under a great deal of scrutiny in recent decades, inspired by Barthes' and Foucault's notorious and highly influential polemics against it. All of these were highly relevant to the issues raised by the case.

As I continued to think and write about the seemingly dual character of the artwork as a physical embodiment of the artist's immaterial ideas, choices, and expressions, however, I soon found myself at a loss. I discovered that there was very little written about the nature of the relation between artist and artwork, and what rights or obligations might follow from that relation. The messiness and high stakes of the lawsuit gave the philosophical ideas a new kind of urgency and potency that are often missing from the theoretical treatments of these topics. But it became increasingly difficult to find genuinely philosophical reflection on the questions raised by the case amid the rhetorical posturing of the players involved.

Hence the book you hold in your hands. It is a philosophical essay on artistic authority: its sources, nature, and limits. Unlike many works of academic philosophy, however, this inquiry draws upon real-world cases and controversies in contemporary art. Artworks, it is widely agreed, are the products of intentional human activity. And yet they are different from other kinds of artifacts; they are understood to be fundamentally and primarily the expression of some meaning intended by their makers. For this reason it is often presumed that artworks are an extension of their authors' personalities in ways that other kinds of artifacts are not. This is manifest in our recognition that an artist continues to own his or her creation even once the art object belongs to another. If I buy a handmade wooden table, I can do whatever I wish to the artifact in my possession. I can leave it outside in the rain, use it for firewood, or paint it purple. Not so with a wooden Martin Puryear sculpture. The Visual Artists' Rights Act (VARA), which is the US statute governing the moral rights of artists, protects artworks of "recognized stature" from intentional destruction.[1] It also enjoins the owners of artworks from mutilating, distorting, or falsifying the authorship of the works in their possession. Copyright prevents the owner from making and selling derivative works such as facsimiles of the artwork or coffee mugs adorned with its image. The law thereby grants artists a degree of control over their creations that the producers of other kinds of artifacts do not enjoy.

But it is far from clear how or why artists acquire this authority, and whether it originates from a special, intimate bond between artist and work, as the traditional justification of artistic moral rights would have it. These questions are particularly pointed in our contemporary culture. The legal doctrine of artistic moral rights has gained international recognition and strength. And yet the rhetoric of postmodernism, which has been so influential in both art and theory, criticizes and even disavows the Romantic ideology of authorship that valorizes the solitary creator-genius, upon which that doctrine is based. This tension becomes particularly pointed in recent controversies involving contemporary visual art, because that is where these two worlds collide most explosively: the legal and the ideal.

Thus, our understanding of the nature and extent of artistic authority is significant for many reasons. It has philosophical importance insofar as it bears on ontological questions concerning the relation between the art object and the artwork. Where does the object end and the work begin, such that the artist can legitimately claim authority and ownership over the work, even as the object that embodies it belongs to a museum or collector? It is also relevant to the problem of how the art object expresses the intention of its maker. How and to what extent does artistic authority extend beyond the boundaries of the artwork and to its interpretation? How does this shift in the case of ontologically innovative works, in which we are unusually dependent on statements from the artist to indicate what, precisely, constitutes the features of the work that are relevant to interpretation? And how do we reconcile our recognition of the authorship rights of artists with the advances in contemporary art

---

[1] While the precise definition of "recognized stature" has never been clarified for the purposes of this law, Puryear's work, which is widely collected by and exhibited in major international art museums, would most certainly qualify.

that have sought precisely to problematize, deny, and challenge the very assumptions that ground those rights?

The concept of artistic authority also demands our philosophical attention because it entails provocative metaphysical and ontological assumptions about the nature of authorship. These claims in turn shape the legal landscape surrounding copyright and artistic moral rights. And yet, as I have mentioned, it has gone largely unexamined in the philosophical literature on art and aesthetics. Perhaps this is because the foundational ideas surrounding the nature of authorship are assumed to be the proper province of one or the other of two alien tribes: on the one hand, cultural and literary theorists have long expounded the theory of the 'death of the author.' On a purely theoretical level, at least, they have sought to dismantle the concept of authorship. On the other hand, scholars of intellectual property and copyright law deal in the legal manifestations of authorship. The postmodern critique of the concept of authorship seems not to have touched the legal realm in any significant sense. In this latter body of literature, we find many impassioned advocates for artists' rights, but the authors do not always submit their arguments' assumptions to critical reflection.

Against the backdrop of this scholarly landscape, some argue that philosophers have no place on either terrain. They are usually not qualified to comment on matters requiring legal expertise.[2] And analytic philosophers do not generally have much patience for or interest in the post-structuralist attacks on the concept of authorship that have been inspired by Foucault.[3] It may seem as though there is no useful philosophical work to be done on the concept of artistic authorship, and that we are better off continuing to focus on its end product: art and artworks. However, as Darren Hudson Hick points out, the foundational ideas underpinning the rights of authors in their works are most definitely philosophical, and the conceptual confusion that surrounds them is

[2] Roger Shiner, "Ideas, Expressions, and Plots," *Journal of Aesthetics and Art Criticism* 68, no. 4 (2010).

[3] See Peter Lamarque, "The Death of the Author: An Analytical Autopsy," *British Journal of Aesthetics* 30, no. 4 (1990). See also the debate between John Searle and Jacques Derrida surrounding the latter's attempt to deconstruct copyright in Jacques Derrida, *Limited Inc*, trans. Jeffrey Mehlman and Samuel Weber (Northwestern University Press, 1988).

precisely the kind of 'housekeeping' (in the Wittgensteinian sense) that philosophy is good for. As Hick puts it:

Copyright law is rife with metaphysical assumptions about its objects—beginning with the principle that authored works are abstract rather than material objects. The law goes further in suggesting that ideas are things themselves *embodied* in authored works. These are ontological distinctions, and in opening the door to ontology, the law invites in the philosopher. Introducing into copyright law a central distinction between ideas and expressions is like embossing the invitation in gold. And when the law is conceptually confused, whether about its own technical concepts or those of ordinary usage, I would argue not only that the door is open, but also that it is the philosopher's *duty* to step through it.[4]

The legal domain is a fertile site for theoretical investigation of artistic authority because it is the meeting point of the metaphysical and the everyday. And it is there, where these two make contact, that a better account can be given.

In cases of legal contest regarding the rights of authors in their works, the hitherto implicit values, norms, and assumptions surrounding artistic authority are rendered explicit. The role of the philosopher with respect to artworld controversies is not necessarily to take sides, particularly when such cases hinge on legal judgments. The philosopher can, however, critically examine the arguments given in support of each side and determine whether they are coherent or confused. She can also examine concepts such as 'artistic freedom' that are both rhetorically loaded and semantically vague in order to seek greater clarity about the principles they uphold. Moreover, the philosopher has the ability to suspend judgment on the specific legal questions that arise in a given case so as to focus on the larger principles or cultural values at stake in the conflict.

Some might argue that organizing one's inquiry around real-world cases may deflect energy and attention from the philosopher's proper task of pure conceptual analysis. But while analytic aesthetics is not concerned with simply providing a descriptive account of the artworld's activity, it cannot ignore actual art works and the cultural norms and practices surrounding art in the name of pure theory, either. I share the view of philosophers such as Amie Thomasson, Sherri Irvin, and David Davies that artistic practice is foundational to any adequate philosophical

---

[4] Darren Hudson Hick, "Expressing Ideas: A Reply to Roger A. Shiner," *Journal of Aesthetics and Art Criticism* 68, no. 4 (2010): 407.

reflection on art. As Irvin puts it, "only by looking carefully at particular, real works can we develop adequate theories of contemporary art, and, indeed, of art in general."[5] The same is true for artistic authorship—a concept that is assumed by all philosophers of art as a necessary condition for something to be an artwork, but which generally goes unexamined. This book seeks to fill that gap.

In Chapter Two, I consider the nature of artistic freedom and moral rights. I show that these concepts have their source in a conception of authorship that is assumed but incorrectly accounted for in both the legal and philosophical literature. I then present my 'dual-intention theory' of authorship. I argue that artistic authorship entails two orders of intention: the first, 'generative' moment, involves the intentions that guide the actions that lead to the production of an artwork. The second moment is the evaluative moment, in which the artist decides whether or not to accept and own the artwork she has made as 'hers.' This second moment often goes unnoticed in the theoretical accounts of authorship because it only becomes explicit when challenged: hence the importance of using real-world controversies as a lens through which we can better understand the nature of artistic authority.

In Chapter Three, I look at the relation between the second moment of authorship, in which the author ratifies the work as his or her own, and another crucial but often overlooked aspect of authorship, which is artwork completion. These two moments are logically separate but often collapsed, both in theory and in practice. I explain what is at stake for authors, audiences, and philosophers in determining whether an artwork is finished or not. Clement Greenberg's controversial decision to strip the paint from five of the late David Smith's unfinished sculptures serves to illustrate how unfinished works complicate any claims to a moral right of integrity with respect to artworks. Finally, I turn to the philosophical debate surrounding the necessary and sufficient conditions for artwork completion. While I find much to agree with in their work, I find that both Hick and Livingston, the chief interloctors in this debate, commit a fundamental error in ontology when reasoning about artwork completion. Because being finished is a relational property of an artwork

---

[5] Sherri Irvin, "The Artist's Sanction in Contemporary Art," *Journal of Aesthetics and Art Criticism* 63, no. 4 (2005). See also David Davies, "The Primacy of Practice in the Ontology of Art," *Journal of Aesthetics and Art Criticism* 67, no. 2 (2009).

that is tied to the potentially vacillating attitudes, beliefs, and dispositions of the artist, there is no single moment when a work can be said to cross the threshold from incomplete to complete such that its formal features are irrevocably locked in. Artwork completion is ultimately provisional.

In Chapter Four, I provide an analysis of the aforementioned controversy between the Massachusetts Museum of Contemporary Art (Mass MoCA) and the artist Christoph Büchel. This case provides a clear example of a situation in which the second, evaluative moment of art authorship is thrown into high relief, as the artist refused to recognize as 'his' a work that he nevertheless saw himself as having authored in the generative sense. This explains the seemingly paradoxical situation that arose, in which he claimed that the unfinished artwork was not a 'Büchel,' and yet he nevertheless insisted on his right as author to determine its fate. In my view, the Mass MoCA case represents a significant challenge to the widespread artworld intuition that the creative freedom of the artist should be given virtually absolute precedence in decisions about the creation, exhibition, and treatment of artworks. I argue that this view is incorrect: respect for the artist's moral rights does not require deferring to the artist's wishes in every case. I show that the distinction between artifactual ownership and artistic ownership that underlies the notion of artistic moral rights also serves to establish limits on those rights.

In Chapter Five, I reconsider Irvin's theory of the 'artist's sanction,' which articulates the authority of artists to determine the boundaries of ontologically innovative works of art through their public declarations. While this theory shares some similarities with my 'dual-intention theory' of art authorship, it is importantly different in scope. I argue that this principle effaces the boundary between the artist's authority to determine, on the one hand, the disposition of the work as an object-to-be-interpreted and, on the other hand, the proper interpretation of the work. I turn to the example of site-specific artworks to illustrate the theoretical and practical difficulties that can arise when artists use their authority to bestow features of an artwork through their declarations.

Chapter Six examines the problem of appropriation art as a seemingly paradoxical renunciation and reinforcement of artistic authority. I then turn to the established philosophical debate surrounding interpretive intentionalism in light of the 2008 lawsuit between photographer Patrick Cariou and the contemporary appropriation artist Richard Prince. This case illustrates the essential role that intentionalism plays in deciding copyright suits. I then consider the philosophical problems surrounding the legal status of appropriation art. A number of scholars have proposed ways for the courts to accommodate appropriation art without eroding copyright protections for authors. I consider some recent proposals and reject them. I then argue that appropriation art should be considered derivative and hence presumptively *unfair*. This is actually more in accord with appropriation art's theoretical purpose to undermine originality as an ideal of authorship.

In the Conclusion, I argue that the challenges to artistic authority by contemporary art practice have certainly enlarged our sense of what kinds of things count as artworks, and by extension they have altered our sense of who artists are and what they do. However, while the landscape of art has changed, these ideal or rhetorical challenges to the modernist ideology of artistic authority have not in fact penetrated our most deeply held cultural beliefs and practices surrounding the artist's special relationship to his or her work. The concept of the artist serves as a regulative ideal, and the gestures by the avant-garde to demystify or destroy this ideal serve a largely rhetorical function. However, this is not a condemnation of contemporary artists as hypocrites or charlatans, as some might have it, but rather an acknowledgement that our current system for recognizing and valuing artworks depends on the conception of artworks as primarily the expression of their makers, and hence as uniquely tied to them. Truly ontologically innovative works that do not accommodate themselves to this conception risk not being recognized as artworks at all.

In the chapters that follow, I do not offer an abstract, universal definition of authorship, nor do I attempt a sociological 'thick description' of authorship as it functions in the artworld context. My approach stakes out an intermediate position between the rarefied air of the high-altitude theorist and the boots-on-the-ground descriptivist in order to provide a philosophical account of the basic structure of the moment in which authorship emerges.[6] I intend for this book to be an example of the kind of reflective equilibrium between description and analysis that a robust, culturally relevant philosophy of art aims to cultivate.

---

[6] On the aim and methodology of analytic aesthetics, see also Nicholas Wolterstorff, "Philosophy of Art after Analysis and Romanticism," *Journal of Aesthetics and Art Criticism* 46 (1987); Lydia Goehr, *The Imaginary Museum of Musical Works*, Revised ed. (New York: Oxford University Press, 2007).

2

Art, Authorship, and Authorization

A large part of our practice is, and quite commonly through the history and tradition of Western art (to which we are constantly adjured to attend) has been, precisely not to treat visual works as physical objects.[1]

I. The Drama of the Gifted Artist

In December 1897, *The New York Times* reported that the lawsuit between artist James McNeill Whistler and Sir William Eden had ended in what the artist declared a "triumph": the Paris Court of Appeal determined that Whistler could not be forced to hand over a commissioned portrait of Lady Eden against his wishes. The dispute arose over Whistler's piqued response to Eden's payment for the picture. They had agreed that the price for the portrait would be between 100 and 150 guineas, but Whistler was insulted when Sir Eden gave him a "valentine" on February 14, 1894 containing 100 guineas for the picture, the minimum amount. The *Times* article points out that "Whistler is a peculiarly sensitive personality, as everybody knows."[2] The artist refused to hand over the painting, Eden sued, and the appellate court ruled that Whistler could be made to pay Eden damages, but could not be forced to give Eden the painting, which Whistler in any case had altered by painting over Lady Eden's face.

---

[1] Frank Sibley, *Approach to Aesthetics: Collected Papers on Philosophical Aesthetics*, ed. John Benson, Betty Redfern, and Jeremy Roxbee Cox (Oxford: Clarendon Press, 2001), 266.
[2] "Whistler's Paris Suit Ended: He May Keep the Picture of Lady Eden and Declares His Triumph," *The New York Times*, December 18, 1897.

The artist's lawyers argued that the breach of contract was an instance of the artist's absolute right to refuse to deliver his artwork, for any reason. As l'Avocat Général Bulot put it, "what he protests against in the name of personal freedom, the freedom of the artist, the independence and the sovereignty of art, is the judgment which condemns him to deliver the picture in its present state." The case is taken by French scholars to be a landmark decision in the artist's moral right of disclosure.[3] (The first technical use of the French term '*droit moral*', or moral right, occurred just twenty years before *Eden v. Whistler*).[4] The right of disclosure, also referred to as the right of divulgation, protects the artist's right to decide when or whether to release an artwork to the public.[5] Moral rights are a collection of rights designed to recognize and protect the non-economic rights of artists in their works. In addition to the right of disclosure, these rights typically include the right of integrity, which is the obligation not to distort or dismember an artwork, and the right of attribution or 'paternity', which is the right of the artist to have his or her name attached to the work. In Europe, it has included the right of withdrawal, which under certain conditions entitles the artist to alter or take back an artwork that has entered the public sphere.

Just over a century later, in another *New York Times* article, art critic Roberta Smith expressed her outrage at the Massachusetts Museum of Contemporary Art (Mass MoCA) for attempting to show Swiss artist Christoph Büchel's art installation against his will.[6] The exhibition was supposed to have opened in December 2006, but foundered over

---

[3] Cyrill Rigamonti, "Deconstructing Moral Rights," *Harvard International Law Journal* 47, no. 2 (2006): 373. While pointing out that it has been interpreted as a foundational case for the artist's right of disclosure in the French scholarship on moral rights, Rigamonti argues that this case is better understood more simply as arising from a general rule about service contracts.

[4] Cyrill Rigamonti, "The Conceptual Transformation of Moral Rights," *The American Journal of Comparative Law* 55 (2007).

[5] One of the ironies of this case is that Whistler had exhibited the painting at the Salon du Champs de Mars, so it had in that sense already been disclosed to the public. What was at issue in the lawsuit was whether he could be compelled to hand over the painting to Eden once he decided that 100 guineas was too low a price (though he had cashed Eden's check). John Henry Merryman, "The Refrigerator of Bernard Buffet," in *Thinking About the Elgin Marbles: Critical Essays on Cultural Property, Art, and Law* (Alphen aan den Rijn: Kluwer Law International, 2009), 407.

[6] Roberta Smith, "Is It Art Yet? And Who Decides?," *The New York Times*, September 16, 2007.

disagreements between the artist and the museum over the budget and construction, eventually leading to Büchel's abandonment of the project. The museum, which had invested over $300,000 of its own money and nine months of labor in the work, was unwilling simply to discard the assembled objects that filled its football-field sized Gallery 5. It sought permission in federal court to show the unfinished work to the public. At issue in the lawsuit was whether the 1990 Visual Artists' Rights Act, a subset of US copyright law that protects the moral rights of artists, applied to unfinished works of art. Unlike *Eden v. Whistler*, the outcome of this case was not triumphant for either party. After an appellate court partially overturned the district court's ruling in favor of the museum, the two parties settled quietly, and the assembled objects of Gallery 5 were never shown to the public.

In the 110 years between these two lawsuits, our understanding of what art is, what it can look like, how it is made, and its proper role and function in society has undergone a profound transformation. Whistler was a virtuoso easel painter who made portraits of wealthy patrons' wives, whereas Büchel is an installation artist who makes edgy, politically charged environments using assemblages of junk. And yet there are some telling similarities to the cases. Both artists reneged on their verbal agreements to deliver an artwork and yet claimed that they, not the commissioners, were the victims in the transaction. Whistler and Büchel were cast by their supporters as making a principled stand for their freedom as artists not to be bound by prior contracts or agreements. Just as Whistler had a reputation for being 'sensitive,' Büchel was known to have a difficult, mercurial personality, which was treated by some as a sign of his authenticity. As Smith put it: "Maybe Mr. Büchel was behaving like a diva. But what some call temper tantrums are often an artist's last, furious stand for his or her art."[7]

Like Whistler's lawyer, Smith saw a deeper significance in what, on the surface, might seem to be a simple contract dispute. This was not a matter of failed communication or unmet expectations: what was really at stake was the absolute respect for Büchel's artistic freedom that the museum failed to heed. This view implies that the nature of artistic creation is something special, out of the ordinary, such that artists cannot

---

[7] Ibid.

be required to produce artworks in the same way that other kinds of fee-for-service labor is carried out. The unspoken premise in both cases is that the demands of art supersede venal concerns over money, contracts, or professional obligation. The doctrine of artistic freedom permits the artist to operate outside of the usual rules and obligations entailed by such economic arrangements. This is undoubtedly related to the ideals that we have inherited from the Romantic tradition, in which art and artists generally are seen to operate outside of rules and convention.[8] But while a great deal of effort has been expended both within artistic movements and in theoretical circles to reject this Romantic heritage, our beliefs and behaviors surrounding art and artists show that this disavowal has in many respects been more rhetorical than real.

II. Artistic Freedom and Moral Rights

On a cultural level, there is a widespread intuition that the creative freedom of the artist should be given virtually absolute precedence in decisions about the creation, exhibition, and treatment of artworks. But the concept of artistic freedom, like that of academic freedom, is as slippery as it is potent. Its indeterminacy may in fact lend the concept some power, since it can be uncritically applied to many different kinds of situations involving artists and their creations. Philosopher Paul Crowther has observed that the prevailing conception of artistic freedom is essentially negative in character: it is based "purely on the absence of ideological or conceptual restraint."[9] This ideal of artistic freedom stems from the conception of the artist as outsider, visionary, sufferer, and rebel that was consolidated in the late nineteenth century and which, I will argue, we are still in thrall to today.[10]

In some cases, the notion of artistic freedom is taken to mean that an artist should be able to dictate his creative vision for a work no matter

---

[8] Kant's definition of genius is the *locus classicus* for the expression of this idea. Adorno's understanding of art as having a fundamentally dual character, in which it participates in and yet is distant from the social world, is also an important outgrowth of this tradition. His idea that artistic freedom is a vehicle for critical reflection fits with his understanding of art's liminal status. Theodor Adorno, *Aesthetic Theory*, trans. Robert Hullot-Kentor (Minneapolis: University of Minnesota, 1997).

[9] Paul Crowther, "Art and Autonomy," *British Journal of Aesthetics* 21 (1981): 12.

[10] See Alexander Sturgis et al., *Rebels and Martyrs: The Image of the Artist in the Nineteenth Century*, ed. National Gallery (London: Yale University Press, 2006).

how much it costs, who is paying, and whom it affects.[11] In reality, most artists who try to make a living from their creations struggle with the very real constraints of budgets, commissions, and gallery fees. They must constantly compete for clients, the attention of curators, and publicity in a densely crowded field of would-be Whistlers and Büchels. In all likelihood, only the tiny minority of artworld superstars can really be said to enjoy creative freedom in any practical sense.[12] Nevertheless, the rhetoric surrounding artistic freedom in both the popular culture and in the legal system can have powerful effects. For example, despite initially winning its suit to unveil Büchel's abandoned, unfinished installation to the public, Mass MoCA decided to dismantle it, in part from fear of the backlash that was stoked by the artworld's outraged editorials. A museum devoted to the production of new works of contemporary art cannot be seen by the public and its donors as an enemy to artists.

The phrase 'artistic freedom' often calls to mind the problem of censorship, that is, cases in which artists are not free to express controversial ideas publicly with their art. This is the main aspect of artistic freedom that philosophers have given their attention to, presumably because it involves ethical and political questions about the nature of free speech and the right of the state to limit that speech.[13] In the mass media, as well, the idea that artistic freedom is primarily a problem of censorship is reinforced whenever contemporary artists provoke popular outrage with the content of their works. The Corcoran Gallery's cancellation of a Mapplethorpe retrospective in 1989 due to his incendiary photographs of nude gay men, Senator Jesse Helm's outrage over Serrano's *Piss Christ* (1987), which features the photograph of a crucifix submerged in the artist's urine, and Ofili's *Holy Virgin Mary* (1996), which incorporated pornographic images and elephant dung, and was denounced by New York mayor Rudy Guliani, are three notorious cases

---

[11] For a detailed and wonderfully entertaining autopsy of such a case, see Steven Bach, *Final Cut: Art, Money, and Ego in the Making of Heaven's Gate, the Film That Sank United Artists*, updated ed. (New York: Newmarket Press, 1999).

[12] See Henry Finney, "Mediating Claims to Artistry: Social Stratification in a Local Visual Arts Community," *Sociological Forum* 8, no. 3 (1993).

[13] See Haig Khatchadourian, "Artistic Freedom and Social Control," *Journal of Aesthetic Education* 12, no. 1 (1978); E. Louis Lankford, "Artistic Freedom: An Artworld Paradox," *Journal of Aesthetic Education* 24, no. 3 (1990); Julie Van Camp, "Freedom of Expression at the National Endowment for the Arts: An Opportunity for Interdisciplinary Education," *Journal of Aesthetic Education* 30, no. 3 (1996).

from the past few decades in which the artist's freedom to express controversial content in a public forum was called into question.

While censorship of the arts is certainly an important issue, it is not the dimension of artistic freedom that I am concerned with here. The question of the artist's right to show obscene or offensive artworks in public involves ever-shifting popular standards of decency, as well as governmental tolerance for artistic expression that it deems inappropriate or threatening. In short, it has to do with artistic expressions that challenge the norms of what can and can't be said in public. But this aspect of artistic freedom leaves untouched the questions of what it means to author an artwork in the first place, what the nature of the relation is between artist and work, and in what ways artworks have expressive content akin to verbal utterances.

The Whistler and Büchel cases involve what I see as a deeper, more fundamental sense of artistic freedom, because they involve the artist's assertion of his right not to produce or deliver a promised work of art. Rather than touching on the political question of a community's response to an artwork's content, these cases hinged on the notion that artists retain a special degree of control over their creations precisely because they are *artworks* and not some other kind of commissioned artifact, such as a table or a shed. These cases are powerful illustrations of the cultural value that we attach to artists, the fascination that they hold for us as personalities, and the difficulties that can arise when we try to understand the nature of artistic labor—assuming we should understand it as labor at all. When Whistler insists that he has the right to withhold his painting of Lady Eden from the man who commissioned it, or Büchel claims that he has the right to not only abandon his unfinished art installation in Mass MoCA's largest gallery, but to insist that they remove and discard it at their own expense, their arguments are premised on the idea that artworks are special creations. Artistic freedom in this context does not concern objectionable content, but rather points to the notion that artworks have a unique status as extensions of their makers insofar as they are their personal expressions. The principle of artistic freedom suggests that such expressions cannot be compelled, even when the artist had previously indicated that he would produce the work.

This basic idea—that artworks, unlike other kinds of artifacts, are extensions of the artist's personhood—is the premise that underlies the legal recognition of artistic moral rights.[14] Behind this strange-sounding phrase (how can an object be an extension of its maker? how literally are we supposed to take this expression?) lies the recognition that 1) in the Western art world, artistic reputation is a form of wealth; 2) artworks are seen as the expression of their makers, over which they have total control and responsibility; 3) artists should therefore have the right to control how and when those expressions are permitted to circulate because 4) their reputations depend on how those artworks are seen and understood. To take an example from theater, Samuel Beckett was notoriously sensitive to any deviation from his directions in the production of his plays. He brought legal action against a Dutch theater company for mounting a production of *Waiting for Godot* with an all-female cast, because he felt that it misrepresented his intentions.[15] In another case, he denounced an American production of *Endgame* because it was set in a subway station rather than the "bare interior" he specified in the stage directions.[16] In both episodes, he was objecting to a perceived violation of his moral rights as an author to have his artistic intentions accurately represented in the plays that bore his name.

While moral rights and copyright both protect the interests of authors, they are conceived as protecting different kinds of interests. As conventional wisdom has it, copyright protects the economic interests of authors in the production and distribution of copies, versions, or reproductions of artworks. Copyright is alienable: it can be waived, exchanged, or transferred. Moral rights, on the other hand, are understood as rights of personality: according to the orthodox view, they are inalienable because they follow from the "presumed intimate bond between artists and their works."[17] (In practice, the legal alienability of moral rights differs by country.) There are differing accounts of this bond in the theoretical literature, but the basic idea is that the artwork is not just a fungible property of the artist, but an extension of his or her

---

[14] For comprehensive treatments of moral rights in case law and in non-Western countries respectively, see Elizabeth Adeney, *The Moral Rights of Artists and Performers* (Oxford: Oxford University Press, 2006); Mira Sundara Rajan, *Moral Rights: Principles, Practice and New Technology* (Oxford: Oxford University Press, 2011).

[15] *Moral Rights: Principles, Practice and New Technology*, 366–7.

[16] Charles R Beitz, "The Moral Rights of Creators of Artistic and Literary Works," *The Journal of Political Philosophy* 13, no. 3 (2005): 340.

[17] Rigamonti, "Deconstructing Moral Rights," 355.

very self.[18] This unique bond entitles artists to a certain degree of control over their works, even when the artifacts that embody those creations have been sold to another. The Whistler and Büchel lawsuits happen to bookend the century-long development of the legislation surrounding these rights that began in Continental Europe and which has become the global norm.[19] The designation of these rights as 'moral' (as opposed to economic—there are no 'immoral' rights) points to the idea that an artist retains a special authority over her works as a matter of her autonomy, because they are seen as an extension of her personality.

Hence, if we are to understand the concept of artistic freedom in its most fundamental sense, we need to have some grasp on the nature of artistic authorship. Of course, it is not immediately clear why an artist should have a special interest in his artwork as opposed to other things he might make, like breakfast, a doghouse, or a shopping list. We can begin by pointing out the widespread philosophical agreement that artworks are intentional objects.[20] By this I mean that artworks are deliberately made so as to communicate or express some form of meaning. This excludes from consideration as art such things as naturally occurring phenomena, or paintings made by elephants.[21] But since the designation 'intentional objects' covers non-art artifacts—the shopping list also communicates a content—we must seek further clarification if we are to understand the nature of the special bond between artist and artwork that gives rise to the legal recognition of moral rights. We seek to understand what makes an artwork a different kind of thing from other kinds of communication, such that artists

---

[18] "The moral right of the artist is usually classified in civil law doctrine as a right of *personality*, and in particular is distinguished from patrimonial or property rights. Copyright, for example, . . . is a patrimonial or property right which protects the artist's pecuniary interest in the work of art. The moral right, on the contrary, is one of a small group of rights intended to recognize and protect the individual's personality. Rights of personality include the rights to one's identity, to a name, to one's reputation, one's occupation or profession, to the integrity of one's person, and to privacy." Merryman, "The Refrigerator of Bernard Buffet," 408.

[19] Rigamonti, "The Conceptual Transformation of Moral Rights."

[20] Christy Mag Uidhir, *Art and Art-Attempts* (Oxford University Press, 2013), 2–3.

[21] This necessary condition of intentionality does not entail that the object was made with the intention that it be an artwork in our modern sense of the term, for this would exclude premodern, non-Western, or Outsider artifacts that we value as artworks.

are presumed, both culturally and legally, to have a special interest in their works. Such a line of inquiry threatens to lead us down the philosophical rabbit hole of the 'what is art?' question, which I decline to do. My theory of artistic authorship does not depend on any particular definition of art, and the reader is invited to supply whichever account she finds most plausible.

In what follows, I give a brief overview of the history of our contemporary understanding of authorship as a form of intellectual property. I then turn to the two dominant accounts of art authorship in the relevant scholarship pertaining to artistic freedom and moral rights: the legal and the philosophical. Each captures something important about our intuitions and values surrounding art authorship, but both ultimately fail to account for the nature of the bond between author and work. I then present my dual-intention theory of artistic authorship, in which I argue that authorship entails two moments of intention. The artwork is not only intentionally made, but must also be ratified and affirmed by the author as fulfilling her artistic and expressive intentions. It is in this second moment that artistic freedom and the ownership relation that grounds moral rights can be found.

III. The Modern Author

As Hick has pointed out, authorial rights rest on a metaphysical distinction between two kinds of property that can inhere in one and the same object: the material artifact and the immaterial, intellectual content that it expresses.[22] We find this material/immaterial distinction repeated yet again within the legal realm of authors' rights: while copyright is said to protect the economic rights of artists in their creations, moral rights are frequently understood as non-economic rights of 'personality.'[23] And yet it is far more difficult to disentangle the economic and the non-economic aspects of artworks than the distinction between copyright and moral rights would make it seem. In fact, they are practically, conceptually, and

---

[22] Hick, "Expressing Ideas: A Reply to Roger A. Shiner," 407.
[23] John Henry Merryman, Albert E. Elsen, and Stephen K. Urice, *Law, Ethics, and the Visual Arts*, Fifth ed. (Alphen aan den Rijn, The Netherlands: Kluwer Law International, 2007), 422.

historically bound together. As Rigamonti explains, moral rights legislation has always been linked to copyright:

The decision [by France, Germany, Italy] to insert moral rights into the copyright statutes was not a simple accident or a matter of pure legislative convenience, but instead the expression of the idea that moral rights are rights of authors in their works and therefore ought to be formally regulated as a part of copyright law... It is precisely the formal and conceptual unity of moral and economic rights as rights of authors in their works that is the essence of the 'droit d'auteur' approach to copyright, which is generally viewed as the defining feature of Continental European copyright theory.[24]

Copyright laws arose at a time when a growing market for printed books made it possible for authors to make a living from their work.[25] But in addition to these economic and social changes, the conception of authorship upon which copyright is based required a theoretical shift as well. While we may take it for granted now, the idea of intellectual property is a relatively recent development. As Woodmansee puts it, "The notion that property can be ideal as well as real, that under certain circumstances a person's ideas are no less his property than his hogs and horses, is a modern one."[26] It affirms the idea that authors' contributions, even when ideal and immaterial, are nevertheless substantive. It transformed the understanding of authors as passive vehicles, either of divine inspiration or of traditional skills, and replaced it with the notion that authorship involves the unique contribution of the author's self in the work.[27] As another historian of copyright puts it, "The attempt to anchor the notion of literary property in personality suggests the need to find a transcendent signifier, a category beyond the economic to warrant and ground the circulation of literary commodities."[28] In other words, the claim that authors had a right to economic compensation for their intellectual labor required a transformation in the understanding of what that labor was. Both copyright and artistic moral rights are rooted in the idea of intellectual property.

[24] Rigamonti, "Deconstructing Moral Rights," 360.
[25] Martha Woodmansee, *The Author, Art, and the Market: Rereading the History of Aesthetics* (New York: Columbia University Press, 1994), 36.
[26] See ibid., 42.   [27] Ibid., 36.
[28] Mark Rose, *Authors and Owners: The Invention of Copyright* (Cambridge: Harvard University Press, 1993), 128.

Scholars frequently point to the theories of authorial rights advanced by Kant and Hegel as the philosophical origin of the idea that a literary or artistic work is its author's intellectual property. In his 1785 essay, "On the Wrongfulness of the Unauthorized Publication of Books," Kant argued that a book as a material object is distinct from the book as the vehicle of the author's speech. One can own the material object without thereby owning the communication contained therein. Some see Kant's remarks on authorship as the basis for modern-day copyright law.[29] Others claim that Hegel's theory of property, in which he asserts that the appropriation of the external world through one's will is necessary for an individual's self-actualization, is the true foundation for a personality-based theory of moral rights.[30] However, Hegel's follower Fichte appears to have had the most developed theory of authorship in the modern sense. In his 1793 essay "Proof of the Unlawfulness of Reprinting," Fichte claimed that a book consisted of three parts: the material object, the content, and the form. The content consisted of the communicated ideas, but the form was the way in which this content was expressed, and it was the form that belonged solely to the author.[31]

While we can find in Kant, Hegel, and Fichte ideas about authorship and property that appear to prefigure our contemporary ideas about the nature of authorship as the foundation for moral rights, it is not clear

[29] See Anne Barron, "Kant, Copyright, and Communicative Freedom," *Law and Philosophy* 31 (2012); Adeney, *The Moral Rights of Artists and Performers*, 25.

[30] G. W. F. Hegel, *Elements of the Philosophy of Right*, ed. Allen Wood and trans. H. B. Nisbet (Cambridge: Cambridge University Press, 1991), secs. 44–53. Lee points out that Margaret Jane Radin's 1982 *Personality and Personhood*, a seminal work in bringing the personality theory into debates about moral rights, was based on Hegelian notions of property, though there is some doubt as to whether her understanding of Hegel on this point was accurate. Brian A. Lee, "Making Sense of 'Moral Rights' in Intellectual Property," *Temple Law Review* 84 (2011): 91.

[31] As Woodmansee puts it, "In his central concept of the 'form' taken by a thought—that which it is impossible for another person to appropriate—Fichte solves the philosophical puzzles to which the defenders of piracy had recurred, and establishes the grounds upon which the writer could lay claim to ownership of his work—could lay claim, that is, to *authorship*. The copyright laws enacted in the succeeding decades turn upon Fichte's key concept, recognizing the legitimacy of this claim by vesting exclusive rights to a work in the author insofar as he is an *Urheber* [originator, creator]—that is, insofar as his work is unique or original [*eigentümlich*], an intellectual creation that owes its individuality solely and exclusively to him." Woodmansee, *The Author, Art, and the Market: Rereading the History of Aesthetics*, 51–2.

whether these early philosophical articulations of a theory of artistic property were *in fact* directly influential in the development and consolidation of moral rights law and the conceptual articulation of the orthodox theory of moral rights that followed.[32] When we compare their theories of authorship with the contemporary justifications for moral rights that they supposedly ground, we find some significant discrepancies among their own theories and with the contemporary articulation.

First, Kant's theory concerns the authorship of books as speech acts; he would not have regarded non-linguistic art forms such as painting or sculpture as embodying an utterance in the same way that a text does. The contemporary point of view, on the other hand, treats all works of art as intentional utterances. As for the Hegelian argument that human beings only become self-actualized when they appropriate and transform the material world through their work, it is not clear on this basis what the difference is between artworks and other kinds of products that result from human labor, and why one would be more the extension of the laborer's personality than another. Fichte's idea that the form of expression belongs solely to the author even as its content is public and cannot be owned is the closest that we have to our contemporary intuitions about the nature of authored works. However, his theory does not suggest that there is something qualitatively different about artistic expression as opposed to other kinds of authorship, which the orthodox theory of moral rights assumes. Nevertheless, what is important about their theories is that they articulated an understanding of authorship as immaterial expression that derives from and belongs to its creator. This metaphysical distinction serves as a foundation for copyright and moral rights legislation, but it does not address the question of whether artists have a unique bond with their works that other kinds of authors do not have, and which deserves legal recognition and protection.

---

[32] Rigamonti argues that the patchwork of laws came first, and the conceptual justification of moral rights as rights of personality followed after. If he is right (and his detailed historical overview is very convincing), his argument would refute the assumption that Kant and Hegel were foundational theorists for moral rights legislation, unless what is meant by tracing moral rights back to them is not an empirical claim regarding lines of influence, but simply an observation that the theoretical seeds had already been sown by the two most important Continental philosophers of the Romantic era. Rigamonti, "The Conceptual Transformation of Moral Rights."

IV. The Emotivist Account

Insofar as we are seeking an account of the theoretical foundations that ground the century-long development of artistic moral rights legislation, we might expect the legal scholarship on the subject to yield an answer. It is therefore surprising to find in that literature a prevalence of uncritically neo-Romantic accounts of the nature of art authorship, in which the legal advocates for moral rights appeal to a kind of primal emotional and spiritual identification between the artist and work.[33] This serves as a deontological justification for moral rights legislation, in which it is argued that the law has a duty to protect artists' works just as it has a duty to protect their personhood from harm. The special legal category of artists' moral rights is seen as a kind of moral or natural right in the more general sense.

Let us call this the 'emotivist' account, because of its emphasis on the artwork as a spiritual extension of the artist. One of the more vehement articulations of this idea is given by Susan Liemer, who argues that the artwork is such an intimate expression of the artist that any harm to the work is sure to do serious psychological damage to its maker. I quote her here at length because it is a representative sample of the kind of account that one often finds in the legal literature on moral rights:

The unique relationship between an artist, the creative process, and the resultant art makes an artist unusually vulnerable to certain personal harms. The art an artist produces is, in a sense, an extension of herself. The artists' [sic] connection to herself is much more personal and simply qualitatively different from the relationship of most other people to other objects and activities.

When an artist creates, she produces something that allows others a glimpse into her individual human consciousness. The medium may be clay or choreography, the message may be silly or serious, but the mental process is surprisingly similar. The artist allows herself to take a very personal risk, opening up

---

[33] See for example Francesca Garson, "Before That Artist Came Along, It Was Just a Bridge," *Cornell Journal of Legal and Public Policy* 11 (2001); Roberta Rosenthal Kwall, *The Soul of Creativity: Forging a Moral Rights Law for the United States* (Stanford University Press, 2009); Lee, "Making Sense of 'Moral Rights' in Intellectual Property"; Susan Liemer, "Understanding Artists' Moral Rights: A Primer," *Boston University Public Interest Law Journal* 41 (1998); Alina Ng, "The Author's Rights in Literary and Artistic Works," *John Marshall Review of Intellectual Property Law* 9 (2009); Burton Ong, "Why Moral Rights Matter: Recognizing the Intrinsic Value of Integrity Rights," *The Columbia Journal of Law & the Arts* 26 (2003); Sundara Rajan, *Moral Rights: Principles, Practice and New Technology*; Lior Zemer, "Moral Rights: Limited Edition," *Boston University Law Review* 91 (2011).

something of her view of the world to others and showing others what is going on in her head, whether emotional, intellectual, or spiritual. That view is available for others to experience, over and over again, potentially forever.

Everyday life does not require such openness. The artist stands uniquely open to attack upon her psyche because she is so closely connected to the creative process and the creative product. A blow to either the process or the product may be a blow to her personally. Because the artist infuses her work with her own personality, a harm to the work or her relationship to the work may well harm the artist herself. The artists' [*sic*] reaction may even resemble her reaction to a physical injury to herself or someone very close to her.[34]

Liemer presents artistic creation as such a vulnerable emotional endeavor for the author that any slight to the process or the product could result in serious psychological trauma.[35] But in her attempt to capture the unique character of the connection between artists and their artworks, Liemer assumes that artworks are primarily emotional expressions of their authors. While this may be the case for some people, there is no logical necessity that artists be psychically or emotionally invested in their creative endeavors.[36] Nor is it clear why a personal investment of the kind she describes would entitle artists to legal protection of their feelings. One is tempted to say that if making artwork and putting it into the world represents such an emotional risk for the author, then he or she would be better off finding a different occupation.

To that some would say that artists cannot help but undergo such vulnerable acts of creation. In her book on moral rights, *The Soul of Creativity*, law professor Roberta Kwall has a similarly Romantic account of artistic authorship. She argues that artistic creativity originates from deeply personal and uncontrollable forces. She describes the creation of artworks somewhat paradoxically as the product of a tremendous amount of labor and suffering, and at the same time as the result of an uncontrollable urge on the artist's part to make his art, come what may. This is the artistic-creation-as-childbirth model of art authorship. As Kwall describes it, "this inner labor embodies a drive to create emanating from powerful forces within the soul of the author."[37] It combines what

---

[34] Liemer, "Understanding Artists' Moral Rights: A Primer," 43.

[35] And yet, oddly, selling the work presumably poses no psychological complications for the artist under this account.

[36] See also Beitz, "The Moral Rights of Creators of Artistic and Literary Works," 343.

[37] Kwall, *The Soul of Creativity: Forging a Moral Rights Law for the United States*, 12.

are actually two separate lines of thought concerning the foundation of artistic moral rights: the Lockean view that authorship is labor that deserves legal recognition, and the Hegelian construal of the work as an extension of self.[38] Like Liemer, Kwall characterizes artistic creation as fundamentally different from other kinds of making or expression, because it issues from a deeper, more personal place. Hence, she argues, artists are entitled to legal recognition of their moral rights because of the personal risk and sacrifice that they make in providing us with their creations.

I suspect that there are a couple of things motivating this surprising tendency in the legal literature to portray the artist–artwork bond in such sentimental terms. First, the authors are writing primarily in an American legal context that has been inhospitable to the idea of artists' moral rights compared to Europe. On the occasions when the United States has granted rights to authors, as in Article 1, Section 8 of the Constitution, it has generally been with an eye to the public good, not because authors are seen to have a natural propriety over their works. Thus, the high-flown rhetoric about the special bond between artist and work may be an attempt to compensate for the United States' utilitarianism. Second, these accounts are an attempt to capture the immaterial aspect of intellectual property. The artist can sell the object in which the work inheres and yet still identify himself—or some version of himself—with its essential, immaterial element that he designed and created. The pseudo-metaphysical, emotivist accounts make a case for why we must recognize the immaterial aspect of an artwork as inalienably belonging to its author even when the artifact that embodies it becomes the property of another.

Nevertheless, the emotivist account of art authorship suffers from some obvious problems. While Kwall implies that her account of creativity has a universal validity, the idea that authorship is the result of powerful urges deriving from the soul of the maker only began to be consolidated in late eighteenth-century Europe.[39] Just as premodern

---

[38] See Jeanne Fromer, "A Psychology of Intellectual Property," *Northwestern University Law Review* 104, no. 4 (2010): 1451. Both of these duty-based approaches to moral rights contrast with the utilitarian tradition in the US, in which the Constitution grants artists and inventors authorship rights so as to incentivize their productivity, which in turn benefits the public.

[39] For a historical account of the genesis of authorial rights, see Woodmansee, *The Author, Art, and the Market: Rereading the History of Aesthetics*.

accounts ascribe art authorship to divine inspiration, Kwall mystifies the creative act in order to justify the uniqueness of the bond between author and artwork. She simply transfers the mysterious source from an external Muse to a vague set of "powerful forces" in the maker's soul. Furthermore, Kwall and Liemer both commit the genetic fallacy by arguing that the conditions under which an artwork is created are relevant to its value as an artwork. On the basis of these accounts of moral rights, it remains unclear how an artwork, unlike other forms of communication, is an extension and externalization of the artist's personality, even though that is a key premise of the arguments. Indeed, it is hard to understand what sort of ontological account of personality would enable us to understand it as extended into material objects in the first place.[40]

It is ironic that we find the most lyrical versions of the psycho-spiritual account of artistic creation in the arena of legal scholarship, just where we might expect a narrow focus on the more tangible realities of contracts, property, and material expenditures. As we can see, the emotivist account of artists' moral rights is questionable for a number of reasons: it presupposes that artists' works are their spiritual offspring, and it characterizes the nature of this investment as profoundly emotional in nature. As an empirical claim, it is highly unlikely that all or even most artists experience the level of psychological vulnerability described here. But if we take it as a normative account—that artists *should* feel this level of emotional attachment to their works (as we expect that parents should feel a high degree of attachment to their children)—the argument also fails because it presupposes that artworks, above all else, are the outward expressions of their makers' inner selves.

Some might pejoratively label this view 'Romantic' and assume that it serves as sufficient refutation. But the problem with the emotivist account is not that its origin can be traced to a certain historical moment, nor is it that all ideas associated with the Romantic movement are ipso facto wrong or bad. The problem is that it tries to capture the source of an artist's unique interest in her work with a psycho-spiritual account that does not necessarily hold, either as a description of the artist's experience, or as a universal account of art. For to say that an artwork is an intentional utterance, signifying some content, does not entail that

---

[40] See also Beitz, "The Moral Rights of Creators of Artistic and Literary Works," 339–40.

this be an expression of the artist's emotions, nor does it imply that the artist has strong emotions about whatever the artwork signifies, or about her creation as such.

Yet another irony surrounding the emotivist account's neo-Romanticism is that the philosophers originally associated with this movement did not themselves characterize the bond between author and work in terms of psychological exposure and attachment. Presumably, the legal scholars who paint such a dramatic picture of artistic creation are trying to capture what is different and special about artistic author- ship as opposed to other kinds of authorship. They want explain why an artist should retain a degree of control over her work even after it becomes another's property, and they want to do so without appeal- ing to economic interests, since moral rights protect an artist's non- economic interests in her work. But they founder on their appeals to a spurious psycho-spiritual bond between author and work.

Despite the obvious shortcomings of the emotivist account, it never- theless captures something important about the modern conception of artistic authorship that persists throughout the many permutations that art has taken in the past century. Artworks are understood first and foremost as the expression of their authors, and as expressions for their own sake. Other kinds of authored works, like a corporate memo or a physics textbook, may no less be the result of the author's creativity and insight, but their form of expression is determined to some extent by the information they intend to convey.[41] But in a work of art, the artist generates both form and content. The proponents of the emotivist account are right to emphasize that artists are personally tied to their works, but they fail to recognize that this connection is rooted in our (historically and culturally contingent) conception of artworks as pri- marily the intentional expressions of their makers, rather than in a psycho-spiritual bond that arises from the creative process. Furthermore, this understanding of artworks as intentional expressions is a value that is held by society at large and not just by the artist and her heirs. Artistic

---

[41]   See Fromer, "A Psychology of Intellectual Property." She points out that psychological studies confirm that inventors have just as much emotional investment in their creations as artists do, yet the legal bar for obtaining a patent—novelty, nonobviousness, and utility—is much higher than the standard for copyright, which is that the creation be original to its author and demonstrate at least a minimal degree of creativity.

moral rights serve the interests of the public, which has an interest in preserving artworks in their intended form. As Merryman puts it, "we yearn for the authentic, for contact with the work in its true version, and we resent and distrust anything that misrepresents it."[42] Both artists and their public have an interest in ensuring that artworks accurately present the intentions of their makers.

V. The Responsibility Account

It may seem from our opening examples of the Whistler and Büchel cases that the concept of artistic freedom involves a total abdication of responsibility to anyone or anything except the demands of one's Muse. But in fact artistic freedom derives its potency as a principle precisely from a certain kind of responsibility that it entails: in an absolute sense, the artist just is the one responsible for the work being what it is, and for being the way it is. Because the artwork serves primarily as the expression of the author, the artist is entirely responsible for the work's final form. Like the turtles in the joke about what holds up the Earth, artistic authorship goes all the way down. Because artworks, unlike shopping lists and chainsaws, are ends in themselves, the fact of their having been intentionally authored is their most salient feature.[43]

Recent philosophical accounts of art authorship do not invoke a putative emotional bond between creators and their works: instead, they coalesce around the concept of responsibility. Sherri Irvin, for example, claims that "the artist's authorship is defined by the fact that she bears ultimate responsibility for every aspect of the objectives she pursues through her work, and thus every aspect of the work itself."[44] This identification of authorship with responsibility is true for all kinds of authorship, but, as Irvin indicates, it is particularly heightened in the case of artworks. Whereas the authors of a textbook on Special Relativity may demonstrate considerable creativity in the way that they express the

---

[42] Merryman, "The Refrigerator of Bernard Buffet," 423. For a psychological account of this yearning, see G. E. Newman and Paul Bloom, "Art and Authenticity: The Importance of Originals in Judgments of Value," *Journal of Experimental Psychology: General* (2011).

[43] Peter Lamarque, "The Uselessness of Art," *Journal of Aesthetics and Art Criticism* 68, no. 3 (2010).

[44] Sherri Irvin, "Appropriation and Authorship in Contemporary Art," *British Journal of Aesthetics* 45, no. 2 (2005): 134.

concepts that they are trying to explain (what Fichte called the "form"), they are nevertheless constrained by the content and the aims of such a textbook. The success of their choices will be measured by how well the book conveys the information. The artist, on the other hand, must determine both what she wants to express and how her artifact is to accomplish that expression. The price of this artistic freedom, however, is total responsibility for the finished product.

In his account of the role that intentions play in determining what constitutes an artwork, Christy Mag Uidhir emphasizes the ontological dimension of this responsibility: "To be an artist is to be directly responsible for a thing being an artwork, and to be directly responsible for a thing being an artwork just is to be the source of the intentions directing the activities constitutive of the successful art-attempt of which that thing being art is the product."[45] Like Irvin, Mag Uidhir focuses on the concept of responsibility, rather than spirituality, when articulating what an artist is. He cannily avoids the difficult task of providing a definition of art. Instead he argues that, given any viable theory of art, artworks are robustly intention-dependent, and the artist simply is the one directly responsible for the manner in which an artifact fulfills the conditions by which it not only acquires its features as an artifact, but by which it acquires art-status, whatever those conditions may be.[46]

Paisley Livingston's pragmatic account of authorship in *Art and Intention* is congruent with Mag Uidhir's account, but he emphasizes the semantic nature of authorship: an author is one who intentionally communicates or expresses something by means of her action. As an ordinary language concept, authorship for Livingston takes many forms. One can author a conventional greeting of "good morning," or one can author original and innovative poetry. Again, the core of this more general concept of authorship is responsibility. This may seem to be at odds with the legal concept of authorship, which is based on originality,

---

[45] Mag Uidhir, *Art and Art-Attempts*, 85.

[46] The responsibility account is very similar to Becker's sociological account of artistic authorship, who says that a work of art can be understood "as a series of choices [...] The choice could always have been made differently and everyone who works in these trades knows what the range of possibilities was and what might have motivated the particular choice that was finally made. Even if many or most of the choices are made in a conventional or routine way, they are still choices." Howard S. Becker, "The Work Itself," in *Art from Start to Finish*, ed. Howard S. Becker, Robert R. Faulkner, and Barbara Kirshenblatt-Gimblett (Chicago: University of Chicago Press, 2006), 26.

but in fact they are compatible: the law does not require that a work be original in an absolute sense to merit copyright protection, only that it have originated from its author. (This means that a work may be indistinguishable from an already-existing work, yet the author can still obtain copyright so long as she can show that her work did not derive from the other.)

Artistic authorship provides an answer to the question of who is responsible for the artwork being what it is, which also means the one responsible for it saying what it says. As Livingston puts it, "behind the question of authorship lies the interest we take in knowing who, on a specific occasion, has been proximally responsible for the intentional production of a given utterance."[47] For Livingston, as for Irvin and Mag Uidhir, the difference between the author of a mundane email and the author of an artwork has nothing to do with the degree of emotionality or vulnerability with which an artist produces her work. It is simply that the artist is the one responsible for the object being an artwork with artistically relevant properties.[48] Note that this does not entail that the artist must be the one who personally fabricates the art object, only that he be the source of the intentional actions that determine its production. Nor does it entail the claim that the artist must have consciously intended every interpretation that is plausibly ascribed to the object.[49] But it does mean that we hold the artist responsible for its features, and we assume these to be the result of the intentions and choices of the person who claims to have authored it.

The philosophical 'responsibility account' of artistic authorship avoids problematic appeals to the psychological and spiritual aspects of artistic creation. Instead it focuses on the artist as the source of the intentions that are both ontologically and semantically causal.[50] The accounts of artistic authorship given by the philosophers just mentioned are not motivated by the desire to argue on behalf of moral

---

[47] Paisley Livingston, *Art and Intention: A Philosophical Study* (Oxford: Oxford University Press, 2005), 68.

[48] Ibid., 89–90. Hick's account is also based on the concept of responsibility. See Darren Hudson Hick, "Authorship, Co-Authorship, and Multiple Authorship," *Journal of Aesthetics and Art Criticism* 72, no. 2 (2014): 151.

[49] Livingston, *Art and Intention: A Philosophical Study*, 150.

[50] See also Risto Hilpinen, "Authors and Artifacts," *Proceedings of the Aristotelian Society* 93 (1993).

rights legislation, and perhaps for this reason they do not attempt to make a case for the putative special bond between artist and artwork. However, while they are right to focus on artists as the source of the intentions that guide the activities resulting in the final nature and disposition of artworks, the philosophical accounts overlook a key aspect of the intentionality that defines artistic authorship by collapsing the artist's ontological intentions into his expressive aims. It is possible, even commonplace, for artists to succeed in their intentions to make an artwork but to find that it falls short of their desired intentions for it to do or say what they want. It seems trivial to point out such an obvious fact about the creative process.[51] And yet philosophical theories of artistic authorship do not make explicit the idea that simply being responsible for making an artwork is necessary but not sufficient for artistic authorship in the fullest sense of the term. In section VI, I present my 'dual-intention theory,' in which I argue that we must distinguish the intentions that govern the making of an artwork from the artist's intention to ratify the work as 'hers.'

VI. The Dual-Intention Theory of Authorship

In a recent review of a show featuring the works of the late color-field painter Helen Frankenthaler, *New Yorker* critic Peter Schjeldahl remarks, "There's a provisional, close-call air to each painting, which I think owes less to her spontaneous method than to her appraising taste: the long look afterward to decide if something had worked or not."[52] Schjeldahl's observation suggests that Frankenthaler's painting process involved two distinct steps: the first involved the generation of paintings, which in Frankenthaler's particular technique involved pouring paint directly onto unprimed cotton canvas laid flat on the floor. The second step involved the appraisal of each canvas, the "long look," after she had finished with it: did she like what was there? Was there anything worth keeping? Did the composition work? The suggestion that Frankenthaler

---

[51]   Again, this is true for other kinds of authored works as well. The difference is that our conception of what an artwork is and what it does is more tied to the expressive intentions of its maker than other kinds of works.

[52]   Peter Schjeldahl, "When It Pours: Works by Helen Frankenthaler and Morris Louis," *The New Yorker*, September 22, 2014, 111.

would decide if a painting had "worked" once she had stopped working on it (and perhaps even once it had dried and could be viewed vertically) reminds us of something important about the creative process generally. It shows that artists do not always know what they have made until after they have made it (just as writers do not always know what they mean to say until after they have said it). One does not have to subscribe to a view of artistic creation as an Ion-like divine madness to recognize that, for at least some artists, it is useful to temporarily suspend critical judgment while in the generative phase of making work. With apologies to Yogi Berra, you can't think and make art at the same time.

Let us imagine Frankenthaler in her studio, taking that "long look," perhaps bringing over associates, such as the critic Clement Greenberg or sculptor Anthony Caro to look with her at the completed canvases and make some decisions (Figure 2.1).[53] Some are selected as good, or good enough, and are sent off to the framer. The others are rejected on the basis of whatever visual calculus the artist uses to determine that the drips, stains, and scribbles on a given canvas fail to work as a composition. Perhaps some are edited or reworked and evaluated again.

What is the authorial status of the rejected paintings in Frankenthaler's studio? Surely they are 'hers' in at least a couple of senses: they are her material property; she can dispose of them however she wishes. They are also 'her' paintings in the sense that she is responsible for having made them.[54] Ontologically speaking, the rejected paintings are artworks just as much as the successes are. In one sense, Frankenthaler is undoubtedly their author. But in another, important sense, she has withheld authorship from the paintings that she deems to be failures. They issued from her hand, yes, but she does not endorse them as works worthy of her name and reputation. She perhaps views these rejects as an inevitable by-product of the creative process. And yet these rejected paintings are not unintentional products of her artistic activity in the same way that drill-bit shavings or breadcrumbs from one's morning toast are the

---

[53] Anecdotal accounts from artists who knew Frankenthaler, Greenberg, and Caro indicate that such conversations were a regular feature of the artistic process.

[54] By asking who 'made' the work, I am not concerned with who actually wielded the brush. (Caro rarely did the physical construction of his own sculptures—he directed a team of assistants to do the welding.) I mean only that, however they actually come to be fabricated, the artist is the one who determines their disposition.

Figure 2.1. Helen Frankenthaler in her studio, 1961. Andre Emmerich, photographer. André Emmerich Gallery records and André Emmerich papers, 1929–2008. Archives of American Art, Smithsonian Institution. © 2017 Helen Frankenthaler Foundation, Inc. / Artists Rights Society (ARS), New York.

unintentional results of one's carpentry or breakfasting.[55] They are the direct products of her intentional art-making activity. But just because she made them, does not mean that she wants to—or should have to—claim them as part of her artistic corpus.

An essential element of artistic authorship consists in the artist's freedom to disavow the work as 'hers' in this final sense. She can, as it were, withhold her signature from the piece even though it undeniably issued from her in the genetic sense. While it is a successful attempt to create *a* work of art—it fulfills the ontological conditions of an art-attempt, to use Mag Uidhir's term—it turns out not to be *the* work that the artist wanted, or thought she wanted. The philosophical accounts of authorship assume but do not make explicit the notion that the artist's responsibility extends beyond the simple fact of creation

---

[55] Cf. Hilpinen, "Authors and Artifacts," 156.

to her affirmation that the work fulfills her intentions. They tend to over-emphasize the genetic moment of authorship: it answers the question of who made the work, without bringing into relief the fact that this making involves both generation *and* evaluation.[56]

Both the 'emotivist' and the 'responsibility' accounts, as I call them, elide the essential second moment of artistic authorship, in which the artist accepts the work as hers. It is perhaps not surprising that the previous accounts of artistic authorship tend to conflate these two moments. The evaluative moment is easily overlooked in theoretical accounts of authorship because most rejected artworks never see the light of day. Nevertheless, there are actually two moments of intention implied in the creation of a work of art: the first-order intentions that determine the production of the work, and the second-order intention that what was produced in the first moment be accepted and approved as a work 'of' that artist. I call these two moments the 'generative' and the 'evaluative' moments of authorship. By 'moments' I mean that they are logically separate, not necessarily that they are separated in time.

While both moments involve intention and responsibility, the philosophical accounts do not articulate the fact that they are logically distinct from one another, and can, in fact, come apart. It is the difference that we hear in the distinction between 'being responsible for' and 'taking responsibility for.'[57] Under this account of artistic authorship, the second implies the first—an artist can only claim authorship of an artwork whose genesis she is responsible for, but the first does not imply the second.[58] Artists do not have to officially recognize as 'theirs' all of the

---

[56] Another example of the philosophical over-emphasis on the generative moment can be found in David Davies' ontology of art as performance. He argues that the artwork is fundamentally a creative act, a performance of the artist: "Works themselves are neither structures nor objects simpliciter, nor are they contextualized structures or objects. They are, rather, intentionally guided generative performances that eventuate in contextualized structures or objects (or events, as we shall see)—performances completed by what I am terming a focus of appreciation." David Davies, *Art as Performance* (Malden, MA: Blackwell, 2004), 98. But he does not take into account the artist's intentional relation to what she has generated as an essential aspect of authorship.

[57] I thank an anonymous reviewer for this observation.

[58] The case of appropriation art, discussed in Chapter Six, appears to be precisely this: ownership without generative authorship. Strictly speaking, it is not, but it defies expectations surrounding the generative moment by replacing the act of generating a new object or image with the act of selecting and appropriating an object or image that already exists. I elaborate on the nuances of this problem more fully in that chapter.

works that they happen to make.[59] The ontological conditions of artistic creation are fulfilled in the generative moment. But the artist's freedom as an author resides in the moment where he (either literally or metaphorically) steps back from the work and decides whether to take ownership of it as a work he has authored.

The Frankenthaler example above illustrates this as a literally two-step process, but that is in part due to her particular style and painting technique. I do not mean to suggest that all artists first produce work in an intuitive flurry and then at some later point return to the work to see and judge what they have done. The making and the judging may take place simultaneously for some artists, such that it is, practically speaking, impossible to distinguish generation from evaluation. The point is that, with all works of art, no matter how they come into being, we are interested not just in the question of whether the work issued from the hand or mind of a particular artist, but also what his attitude was toward that work—did he regard it as a success or a failure, according to his own standards of evaluation?[60] Authorship is not purely a matter of recognizing historical origins, of determining that a certain person, and not someone else, made something.[61] Think, for example, of the protectiveness with which some authors treat their drafts: an author can claim ownership of the work's content but not be ready to 'own up' to it, so to speak. Purely genetic accounts of authorship are incomplete

---

[59] In terms of moral rights legislation, this is an area on which the law is silent. The right of attribution protects the artist's right to be associated with works that he made, and to not be associated with works that he did not make. But it does not address the question of the artist's right not to be associated with works that he *did* in fact make, but does not want to claim as his.

[60] While I am expressing it as a binary, this is not to suggest that artists' attitudes regarding the relative success of their works is not in fact more nuanced. As Auden puts it in the preface to his 1945 edition of collected poems, "In the eyes of every author, I fancy, his past work falls into four classes. First, the pure rubbish which he regrets ever having conceived; second—for him the most painful—the good ideas which his incompetence or impatience prevented from coming to much (The Orators seems to me such a case of the fair notion fatally injured); third, the pieces he had nothing against except their lack of importance; these must inevitably form the bulk of any collection since, were he to limit it to the fourth class alone, to those poems for which he is honestly grateful, his volume would be too depressingly slim." W.H. Auden, *The Collected Poetry of W.H. Auden* (New York: Random House, 1945).

[61] In the case of famous artists, particularly those no longer living, we do take an interest in their sketches and discarded works. Even then, however, we want to know whether the artist accepted the work as fulfilling his or her intentions.

because they do not tell us whether the artist recognizes the work as one that fulfills her expressive intentions.[62]

In his examination of the rights of private owners to cultural treasures, law professor Joseph Sax identifies this evaluative moment as essential to artistic autonomy:

> Every writer and artist has made efforts that he ultimately decides are unworthy of him and consigns to the trash. Certainly inferior work can diminish one's reputation. A creator should be allowed to implement his own judgment about what is worthy of him. (To be sure, some artists have carried this privilege to an extreme, like Soutine, or Whistler, who had the notion that he could just take back a painting he had sold and keep reworking it until—if ever—it satisfied him.)
>
> There are of course competing considerations. No doubt there is biographical and critical interest in knowing as much as possible about an eminent artist, and for those purposes every scrap of information is precious, and discarded work may be especially revealing to the art historian. That is not a trivial consideration by any means, but neither is it sufficient, I think, to overcome the claim for self-determination: Renoir or Rubens is what Renoir or Rubens presents to the world as his art.[63]

There is very little practical risk to most living artists that their cast-offs will be published and attributed to them against their will, though famous artists do have to guard against this. Sax's point is important because he underscores the idea that artists cultivate and curate their reputations through the works they present.[64] This complicates the notion that artistic

---

[62] There is also a third sense of responsibility that could be to added to the discussion of authorship, which is moral responsibility in the more common sense of that term. We might ask, for example, whether it was morally correct for the artist Kim Jones to burn three rats alive as part of his *Rat Piece*, performed February 17, 1976, at Union Gallery at California State University, Los Angeles. The moral dimension of authorial responsibility, apart from causal or artistic responsibility, is beyond the scope of this discussion. I thank Paul Voice for raising this point.

[63] Joseph Sax, *Playing Darts with a Rembrandt* (Ann Arbor: University of Michigan Press, 1999), 42–3.

[64] Howard Becker echoes Sax's point when he observes, "Since artists know that other art world participants make reputational inferences from their work, they try to control the work that becomes available for making such inferences. They destroy work they don't want considered, or label it 'unfinished'; if they are lucky, a court may (as French courts can) prevent the circulation of work they don't want publicly attributed to them. They distinguish categories of work, as contemporary photographers sometimes distinguish their 'commercial' work (not to be considered in assessing them as artists) from their 'personal' work (to be so used), according to the seriousness of their intentions in making it. They

moral rights are rooted in 'personality' interests. Artworks are not simply emanations of the self that are injected into the public realm, like a squid squirting its ink; rather, the artist *curates* what she authors. This means that she not only chooses to make an artwork, but that she chooses whether to accept it. Artistic authorship in its fullest sense implies authorization.

VII. Evaluation, Completion, and Alienation

As we have seen, the emotivist account of artistic creation focuses entirely on artistic expression as an irrational, emotive act in order to make the case that artists have inalienable ownership rights over their works. But it ignores the fact that the artist has the ability to step back and make the rational, evaluative decision whether or not to ratify the work as 'hers.' The putative special bond that exists between artist and artwork, and which is the foundation of moral rights legislation, does not come from the simple fact that the artist made the work. It rests on the assumption that she has endorsed it as a work that bears her name and stands as her creative expression. In other words, authors can alienate themselves from their own works; unlike with their human offspring, artists can deny paternity of their art if they do not like what they have made.

This idea, which is so fundamental to our understanding of artistic freedom, is actually at odds with the orthodox doctrine of moral rights, which regards those rights as inalienable.[65] Charles Beitz has argued that the alienability restriction on moral rights actually serves to limit the options of authors with respect to their works, even as the intention is to protect them from exploitation.[66] His is a utilitarian critique of the alienability restriction. But, in light of the two orders of intention that artistic authorship entails, there is also a logical problem with the view that artists' moral rights are inalienable. If artistic authorship were absolutely inalienable, then artists would not be able to deny, reject, or

revise their work when they can, as Stravinsky and Henry James did." Howard S. Becker, *Art Worlds*, 25th Anniversary ed. (Berkeley: University of California Press, 2008), 357.

[65] The United States' Visual Artists' Rights Act does allow artists to waive their moral rights, but the orthodox doctrine of moral rights holds that they are inalienable, which helps to underscore the distinction between an artist's moral rights and economic rights in the work.

[66] Beitz, "The Moral Rights of Creators of Artistic and Literary Works," 350–2.

disapprove of works that they generated but do not want to ratify as theirs. One cannot consistently hold that artists have a primal bond with their creations, simply in virtue of their status as personal expressions that arise out of a powerful urge to create, but at the same time insist on their right to disavow those same creations. The idea that artistic authorship is inalienable rests on the idea that while the economic rights to a work can be transferred to another, the fact of authorship, of who is responsible for its creation, cannot be. That seems true, insofar as the question of authorship is a purely empirical matter. However, what goes unmentioned and unexamined is the fact that artists first have the right to alienate themselves from the things they have made by refusing to endorse them.

Another reason why this second moment of ratification has received so little attention is that the mechanisms by which this occurs are so thoroughly embedded in artistic practice that they are easy to overlook. Signing a painting, sending a sculpture off to a gallery, showing a work-in-progress, or putting the finishing touches on an installation before the show opens are all ways in which the artist indicates his acceptance and approval of the work as 'his.' The evaluative moment of artistic authorship does not typically occur with the same degree of fanfare that accompanies the paradigm cases of speech acts, like the christening of a ship, or the pronouncement of a couple as man and wife. In fact, it is made most apparent only when it is publicly withheld or contested. Nevertheless, when we consider what it means to attribute an artwork to someone in light of the philosophical 'responsibility account' of artistic authorship, a robust, dual-order sense of intention is in play. We tend to forget that the artist's signature is not merely a historical statement about who caused the artwork to come into being; it does not just say, "I made it"—but also "I mean it", or "I like it," or, more pragmatically, "it's good enough."

Contrary to the existing theories of authorship that emphasize the artist's role as creator, artistic freedom actually resides in the second, evaluative, moment of authorship. It consists in the artist's ability to decide whether or not to recognize the work she has made as hers, as fulfilling her expressive intentions. It is only then when the artist takes full ownership of the content of the artwork. Another way to say this is that artistic creation involves both generation and evaluation, but that the evaluative moment tends to be overlooked or under-theorized. These logically distinct moments may or may not be temporally separated from each other in the artist's practice. The responsibility accounts of authorship are basically correct in understanding that authorship is essentially an attribution of intentional agency, but they are unable to distinguish among rejected and accepted works by the same author. Similarly, the emotivist account offers no theoretical means for the artist to distance herself from the experiments gone awry, the bloopers, the mistakes, and the rejects that issue from her just as authentically as the good ones: such accounts would have to say that they are all equally extensions of their maker's personality. This is a particularly ironic outcome, since these accounts are often given as an attempt to argue on behalf of artists' legal rights. But surely it would be an infringement on artists' freedom if they were required to recognize such a bond even with those works they deem to be failures.

As we have seen, 'artistic freedom' can mean different things in different contexts. For example, it can mean the freedom to make artworks with offensive content, to violate the established norms and expectations of art, to follow one's expressive vision in the face of a hostile and uncomprehending public, or the freedom to insist that one's authorship not be misrepresented, either through false attribution or the distortion of the artwork itself. But artistic autonomy begins with the artist's right to determine which works are to be identified as 'hers.' In order to forestall any potential confusion, I should say here that an artist's decision that she is satisfied with a work she made does not of course mean that the audience will find it satisfying in any aesthetic or artistic sense. Nor does it guarantee that the audience will agree that the artwork expresses what the artist claims she intended to express. It might seem as though there are actually three, nested moments of intention involved in artistic authorship: the intention to make a work; the intention to ratify the work as good enough to bear the artist's name; and the intention to express something by means of that work. Depending on how you want to approach it, however, this third category of intention can either be subsumed under the first two moments or set aside as a separate issue. *That* the work is an intentional expression of the artist is covered by the second moment. *What* the work says, its correct interpretation, if there is one, is a separate issue. (I address the fraught questions surrounding the relations among the artist's endorsement of the work, its intended meaning, artist's statements about work meaning, and audience interpretation in Chapters Five and Six.)

VIII. Conclusion

Artistic authorship is different from other kinds of authorship only because the authored artifact is an artwork and not something else. This sounds viciously circular. But what I mean by this is that artworks in our culture are understood first and foremost as the expressions of their authors. This does not make them inherently different from other kinds of authored works, but it does place them at the extreme end of a continuum of authored utterances in which their status as expression is foregrounded and hypostatized. As sociologist of culture David Brain puts it,

> the 'artful' quality of the object depends on the practical rhetoric with which the inscription of the author's status is effected. [. . .] The modalities of authorship inscribed in artifacts focus our interpretive attention, organize our capacities for self-conscious cultural creation, and embed our creations (as well as the act of creation) in a social world. They make it possible to recognize objective possibilities for subjective action in the world of artifacts. At the same time, they represent an inscription of a moral order, a configuration of relations between author and audience, and an authorization of an agent to undertake responsibility for a certain kind of representation. [. . .] Aside from its function as a means of social distinction, art is a ritualized and abstracted enactment of a form of agency that can be transposed to other practices—not just those related to making social distinctions between the classes, but to the construction of other forms of cultural agency.[67]

I take Brain's point here to be that artworks are not essentially different from other kinds of created artifacts insofar as they are the results of an agent's rational intent. What makes artworks different is that the fact of their being authored is, as he says, 'ritualized and abstracted' so that its status *as* an intentional object becomes its most salient feature.

The artwork symbolically represents agency, authority, and responsibility *as such* through its embodiment of the artist's choices. The fact of those choices is highlighted because they take precedence over any function that the art object might serve. Thus, the reason why artists are presumed to have a special interest in their works is not because of a prima facie unique spiritual bond between artists and their art as opposed to other kinds of intentional utterances. Rather, it is due to

---

[67] David Brain, "Material Agency and the Art of Artifacts," in *The Sociology of Art: A Reader*, ed. Jeremy Tanner (London: Routledge, 2003), 138–9.

the culturally determined and historically contingent status of artworks as the personal expressions of their authors. For this reason, the first- and second- order intentions of the artist to both generate and ratify the work are particularly important, because the artwork is so tightly identified with its author's intentions for what it is to be, how it is arranged, and what it is to say.

Sax noted above that Whistler represents an extreme example of an artist asserting his continued ownership over works that he had sold or released to the public. In the Lady Eden case with which this chapter begins, what was at issue was not Whistler's aesthetic satisfaction with his painting, but rather his insult at being paid the minimum agreed-upon amount. The court's agreement with Whistler that he could not be compelled to hand over the painting—even though Eden had respected the terms of the commission's contract—is remarkable because it so dramatically illustrates the extent to which a distinctly modern view of the artist had coalesced in the cultural and legal imagination.[68] It shows how far we are from the view of an artist as a craftsman doing labor-for-hire, such that even in the case of a commissioned work like the portrait of Lady Eden, the artist can claim a kind of exceptionalism by appealing to his freedom as an artist. This is rooted in the understanding of the work as an extension of his personhood. Whistler's rebellion was a play for authority, and it worked.

The Büchel case, on the other hand, was not about the artist's payment, but about the artist's aesthetic dissatisfaction with the museum installation that was taking shape under his direction and in his name. As I will argue in Chapter Four, we can understand the artist's seemingly contradictory assertions of ownership over the unfinished work—on the one hand, his refusal to accept it as 'his,' and on the other hand, his insistence on his right to prevent disclosure of the work to the public—once we see that this was a case of authorship that was stalled between the genetic and evaluative moments. In other words, the artist recognized that he was, at least to a significant extent, responsible for authoring the work in the genetic sense, but his aesthetic dissatisfaction led him to

[68] Cf. Baxandall's observation that paintings in the Renaissance were generally not made freely—either in the creative or economic sense—but were done under contract at the behest of commissioning patrons. Michael Baxandall, *Painting and Experience in Fifteenth-Century Italy* (Oxford: Oxford University Press, 1988).

abandon the project as unfinished and to withhold his sanction from the work. This led to his seemingly illogical treatment of the work as both his and not-his. With the dual-intention theory of authorship in place, we can reconcile this apparent contradiction by recognizing this as a case in which the genetic and evaluative moments of authorship dramatically—and catastrophically—came apart.

Before we turn to that case, however, I must first establish the relation between authorized works and completed or finished works. It is the artist's prerogative to determine both when (or whether) his work is finished, as well as whether he ratifies it as fully 'his.' These two elements of artistic authorship are fundamental to our understanding and appreciation of artworks, and they are often collapsed: we often use the one as shorthand for the other. In the cultural imagination, the moment when the artist affixes his signature to the work is both the sign that it is finished and the indication that he takes ownership of it as his authored work. Conversely, the artist's claim, "it's not finished!" can be another way of saying, "I'm not happy with it yet." Because the Büchel case concerns an installation that was both unfinished and unauthorized, I want to dwell on what it means to call a work 'finished' in some detail so that we can understand its relation to the second moment of authorship with which it is often—and sometimes wrongly—conflated: ratification.

3

When the Work Is Finished

Authority is control over ends, very often in the direst sense of having control over life and death. Authority resides in being able to say when something is done and enforcing that claim. An author has traditionally been understood as someone who knows the endings, someone who puts an end to something.[1]

I. Completion and Ratification

In eighteenth-century Britain, the artist's studio was a room in a domestic house called the 'Painting Room.' It was the place where the painter did his work and sitters had their portraits painted.[2] The painting room was the workspace and the private, inner sanctum for the creative labor of the artist. The production of the artwork was kept hidden from its eventual consumers, much as the kitchen is separated from the dining room in a restaurant. A second room, the 'Show Room,' was the place of publication; it was where completed works were displayed to viewers. These two aspects of the artistic process—the making of the work and its endorsement as complete and ready for public viewing (which are often, but not necessarily, the same thing)—were kept physically separate with these two designated rooms.

In Chapter Two, I presented my dual-intention theory. I argued that artistic authorship consists of two moments of intention: the generative moment, in which the artist deliberately produces the work, and the evaluative moment, in which she evaluates whether to endorse it as her

---

[1] Michael Joyce, "How Do I Know I Am Finnish?," in *Art from Start to Finish*, ed. Howard S. Becker, Robert R. Faulkner, and Barbara Kirshenblatt-Gimblett (Chicago: University of Chicago Press, 2006), 71.

[2] Giles Waterfield, "The Artist's Studio," in *The Artist's Studio*, ed. Giles Waterfield (London: Paul Holberton Publishing, 2009).

own creation, or to disavow it. Contrary to theories of authorship that understand the work simply in terms of what the artist has made, the dual-intention theory recognizes that artists curate the works that they author. Artistic freedom is grounded in the artist's authority to own or reject the artworks that she makes, and what is at stake in this decision is the artist's personal satisfaction with the works that bear her name as well as her public reputation.

Unless we happen to be an artist, art teacher, or a critic who makes a lot of studio visits, most of the artworks we encounter are finished; hence we tend to overlook the significance of and ambiguity surrounding the artwork's transition from 'unfinished' to 'finished.' But the question of what determines the work's passage over that threshold is not as simple as it might first appear. Moreover, because finished artworks are so ubiquitous—are indeed the norm—the stakes involved in this distinction often do not become apparent until the boundaries between unfinished and finished are contested.

One of the difficulties with understanding the second, evaluative moment of authorship is that it is often combined, in both theory and practice, with the artist's assessment that the work in question is finished. The paintings that get moved from the studio to the Show Room (literally or metaphorically) are presumably those that the artist has deemed both complete *and* worthy of his name. It is easy to see how the moment of ratification can be conflated with the artist's decision that a work is done, since a natural reason to stop working on a piece and deem it finished is that one finds it satisfactory in this deeper sense. Conversely, the artist can label 'unfinished' those works that are not, or not yet, acceptable to him. We often assume, with good reason, that 'complete work' means that the artist both regards the work as finished *and* endorses it as his own.

But these are not the same decision, not necessarily. An author can go so far as to finish a work and still decide that it is bunk. So what does finishing mean in such a case, if not bringing the work to the point where the artist is willing to endorse it as 'hers'? It might mean that the artist has made the work she planned to make, but only upon its completion can she see that the idea failed. In some sense the work has reached what the artist regards as an endpoint, and yet the artist nevertheless rejects it. Conversely, an artist can choose to put out into the world a work that she regards as unfinished. In such a scenario, the artist is permitting her name to be associated with the work, and tacitly endorsing it, even as it is still a work in progress. The point is simply that while completion and ratification often coincide—the work continues until the artist finds it acceptable—they are not logically the same moment in the artistic process.

Nevertheless, it is easy for theorists to assume that a work is complete if and only if it is ratified by the artist, not only because most of the works we encounter are both complete and endorsed, but because our conception of what an artwork is, in the fullest sense, assumes this easy equivalence. A useful illustration of the ease with which completion and ratification can be conflated is found in a salient philosophical theory of artwork completion. Livingston and Archer identify the condition for work completion as the artist's practical, effective decision to stop making alterations to the work because some pragmatic level of artistic satisfaction has been reached:

An effective completion decision turns out, then, to be a psychological event in which the artist acquires a compound attitude that includes a retrospective *assessment or evaluation* of the results of prior work—which are deemed at least *good enough* for the artistic purposes on hand—and the formation of a forwarding-looking intention, namely the intention to refrain from making any further artistically relevant changes to the work.[3]

I discuss their theory of artwork completion later in this chapter. What I want to highlight here is the idea that completion entails the artist's 'assessment' that the work is 'good enough' for his purposes. Livingston and Archer are right to acknowledge that artists do not have to be thrilled with their creations in order to deem them complete. It can be a utilitarian decision rather than the sign that some ideal has been reached. This is true for ratification as well. But by describing the artist's attitude in this way, the authors of the theory suggest that the completion decision is reached when the maker reaches some degree, however provisional and pragmatic, of artistic satisfaction with the work.

This natural tendency to conflate completion and satisfaction is tricky. Indeed, one can read Livingston and Archer's description of the artist's attitude in two different ways. Under one interpretation, the

---

[3] Paisely Livingston and Carol Archer, "Artistic Collaboration and the Completion of Works of Art," *British Journal of Aesthetics* 50 (2010): 445. Emphasis added.

artist's assessment that the work is finished when it is 'good enough' means that she also accepts the work and ratifies it as hers. And yet surely Livingston and Archer understand that artists can finish an artwork and decide that it is nevertheless an irredeemable failure. Another way to understand the meaning of 'good enough' in this passage quoted above is to see the completion decision as separate from the ratification decision. Suppose an artist decides to try making a portrait using only dried pasta and glue. He might regard a work as finished because it has reached the fulfillment of his intentions for this particular work, and in that sense, it is 'good enough,' and yet this assessment is separate from his evaluation whether it is 'good enough' in the larger sense of something he wants to add to his corpus. It is not clear from the way it is phrased what theoretical work "good enough" is doing in Livingston and Archer's description, and I suspect it is because they have not made explicit, as my theory does, the fact that completion and ratification are logically separate moments. The language of their account leaves it ambiguous whether they assume that the artist's completion decision is also an endorsement of the work, or if they have some other kind of psychological satisfaction in mind that they are trying to capture there.

Another example of the tendency to confuse the moment of completion with the moment of ratification can be found in a later article on artwork completion by Trogdon and Livingston:

the [complete/incomplete] distinction has practical significance in the world of art. It figures, for example, within intellectual property legislation in many national jurisdictions. The legal category of 'derivative' works depends on the category of previously completed works, those works on which derivative works are based. In ordinary circumstances, a work is to be displayed or distributed in its completed condition, and doing otherwise can constitute a violation of the artist's rights.[4]

In this passage the authors conflate completion and ratification when making the case that the work's completion status is relevant to the artist's copyright and moral right of divulgation. First, it is incorrect to say that the category of derivative works "depends on the category of previously completed works." US copyright law says that the work must

---

[4] Kelly Trogdon and Paisley Livingston, "The Complete Work," *Journal of Aesthetics and Art Criticism* 72, no. 3 (2014): 225.

be fixed in a tangible medium, but it does not say that the work has to be complete in any absolute sense. One might argue that the word 'fixed' in the statute just means complete. While in practice it seems likely that the works submitted for copyright protection are viewed by the artist as finished, the law itself takes no position on the completion status of the work. It simply means that the work has been stabilized in a physical object, either as a painting or sculpture, or as a text, musical score, dance notation, or video recording, so that the courts have some object to which they can refer when comparing the original against putative cases of infringement. But this fixed object does not necessarily have to be a finished work, either in the artist's eyes or anyone else's. Let us take *The Pale King*, the novel that David Foster Wallace was working on when he committed suicide. It was published in its unfinished state. His heirs own the copyright, which means they have the right to enjoin against the unauthorized creation of derivative works. The ultimate completion status of the novel is irrelevant from a copyright standpoint; the published work has still been 'fixed' in a tangible medium of expression. What matters is the decision by the artist—or in this case his estate—to put the work into circulation as an authored work. In other words, what is relevant here is endorsement, not completion.

Second, the authors allude to the right of divulgation, which refers to the moral right of the artist to decide when to display or publish a work, as relevant to completion. As Trogdon and Livingston acknowledge, it is linked to completion by common custom: we assume, unless there are indications to the contrary, that the work is complete if published. The right of divulgation protects artists from having their unfinished works displayed against their will, but it equally protects their finished works from this fate. Hence it would be more correct to see the right of divulgation as protecting the second moment of endorsement—of ensuring that only those works that the artist wants to be associated with are allowed to circulate in public. Even this does not fully capture the extent of the right of divulgation, because an artist could conceivably finish *and* ratify a work but for some reason nevertheless decline to publish it. (Perhaps the artist has created a series of erotic drawings that are for private consumption only). While Trogdon and Livingston are right that "in ordinary circumstances, a work is to be displayed or distributed in its completed condition," we must be careful not to confuse the norm with logical or legal necessity.

Since some works are finished and then go straight to the rubbish pile, it is clear that completion does not imply ratification. But does ratification imply completion? It would seem that an artist cannot know whether he wants to fully endorse the work as his own unless he first has a whole, finished work to evaluate. The idealized scenario might unfold as follows: the painter first completes the canvas in the Painting Room, steps back, decides that it is good enough to present to the world, and then moves it to the Show Room for display and sale. In practice, of course, these moments are not necessarily divided into two literally separate moments, two separate decisions. We can think of many cases where works are put on display before they are complete, even at the risk of making an unsatisfying work in public. *Plein air* painters in European city squares, muralists, and some contemporary installation artists, for example, might allow the public to see their works in progress, with no concern that their honor or reputation might be damaged by the publication of a work that they may end up regretting. (Just as some restaurants have open kitchens.) In these instances, the generative and evaluative moments of artistic authorship are to some extent collapsed, since the artists have chosen to put the generative process of their work on display. They effectively renounce the possibility of taking that long evaluative look that Frankenthaler enjoyed in her studio, of stepping back and curating which of their works they want to affix their name and reputation to. Nevertheless, in such cases of tacit endorsement of the incomplete work, it still lacks an essential property, and one that only the artist can give it: the designation that it is done; the fixing of its boundaries as the work that it is.

It might seem strange to claim that unfinished works are problematic, since they are products of their authors just as much as their finished counterparts. Both have been generated by the artist, and so have been intentionally authored in the first sense outlined by the dual-intention theory. The problem is that unfinished works are still caught in that first moment of generation, and so their status as the author's expression is uncertain and unstable. In the next section, I describe a controversy over the late David Smith's (1906–65) unfinished sculptures and its connection to both the dual-intention theory and moral rights. In section III, I describe in more detail the cultural and philosophical stakes in determining whether a work is complete. Then, in section IV, I turn to the philosophical debate between Darren Hick and Paisley Livingston et al.

concerning the question of when an artwork is finished. There I argue that Hick and Livingston are mistaken in their understanding of the nature of artwork completion. Finally, in section V, I return to the relation of artwork completion to ratification.

II. The David Smith Controversy

One of the most notorious moral rights disputes concerning unfinished art played out not in a court of law, but in the editorial pages of *Art in America*, and on behalf of an artist—sculptor David Smith—who had been dead nearly a decade. This controversy brings into sharp relief the unique problems that unfinished works can pose for artists, their estates, and their publics, and yet it has not been discussed in the philosophical literature on the subject.

Smith's death following a car crash left some of his sculptures in a liminal state of incompletion. The question of how to release them for circulation, both for sale and display, in a way that would honor the artist's unrealized (and forever unrealizable) intentions became particularly fraught because there was no clear answer regarding the proper disposition of the works. The ensuing contest for authority ostensibly centered on the question of how best to represent Smith's artistic vision for the incomplete works. The dual-intention theory is an important lens through which we can understand what was at stake in this case; while the sculptures were undoubtedly generated by David Smith, they lacked the second moment of ratification for two reasons: they were left incomplete, and they were subsequently altered by the estate.

In 1974, the art historian Rosalind Krauss published an essay, "Changing the Work of David Smith," in which she accused the estate of violating the integrity of Smith's work by removing paint from several sculptures, and negligently allowing the paint on others to erode.[5] She argued that this denied the artist's right to determine the appearance of his works. Clement Greenberg, acting as an executor of Smith's estate, had indeed authorized the removal of the white paint covering five of his unfinished

---

[5] Rosalind Krauss, "Changing the Work of David Smith," *Art in America*, September/October 1974, 30–4. A companion essay immediately following Krauss's essay put her accusation into context as a moral rights issue. Carl Baldwin, "Art & the Law: Property Right Vs. 'Moral Right'," *Art in America*, September/October 1974, 33–4.

large-scale metal sculptures. He then had the bare metal coated in a layer of protective varnish. Krauss implied that Greenberg's primary motivation for the removal had been taste. Greenberg had been publicly critical of Smith's painted sculptures because they contravened his ideas about the 'purity' of the medium, which included a preference for raw metal. Krauss acknowledged that the prevailing fashion might not judge Smith's painted sculptures kindly. Unpainted metal was in favor at the time, as opposed to the polychromatic treatments that Smith was fond of applying to some of his sculptures. Nevertheless, Krauss argued, stripping the paint from the form was an unacceptable violation of Smith's moral rights as an artist:

> The situation may indeed represent a concession to some idea of contemporary taste—a taste for the monochrome of unadorned metal. But leaving aside all speculation about motive the fact remains that these pieces reveal an impairment of the integrity of the oeuvre of a major artist—an aggressive act against the sprawling, contradictory vitality of his work as Smith himself conceived it—and left it.[6]

Krauss accused Greenberg of altering his sculptures and thereby misrepresenting his artistic intentions. Her position was a moral one: even if one finds Smith's painted sculptures to be suboptimal from an aesthetic standpoint, the artist's intentions for his work must be respected.[7] Apparently, this was not the first time that the paint on a Smith sculpture had been altered. She quoted from a letter that Smith had written in which he complained bitterly about the "vandalism" of one of his painted sculptures by a collector, declaring, "I renounce it as an original work and brand it a ruin. My name cannot be attributed to it [...]."[8] In the letter, Smith explicitly disavowed authorship of the altered work, claiming that it was no longer authentically 'his.' Krauss pointed to Smith's anger at the alteration of the paint on his sculpture while he was living, as

---

[6] Krauss, "Changing the Work of David Smith," 32.

[7] This is not to say that Krauss did not have extra-moral motivations of her own in taking such a public stand against him. (Greenberg himself accuses her of "bad faith" in making it). Krauss's doctoral dissertation was on David Smith, and she edited the catalogue raisonné of his work. By "plucking at [his] wreath," as Nietzsche's Zarathustra asked of his students, it may be that she was asserting her authority over that of Greenberg, her former teacher, perhaps in a bid for professional advancement, as well as staking a claim for a new generation of art critics against the establishment. *Quaeritur.* Nevertheless, her argument is a moral one in letter if not in spirit.

[8] Krauss, "Changing the Work of David Smith," 32.

evidence that Smith would also have disapproved of Greenberg's choice to strip the white paint from his sculptures after his death.

Note the key role that the second, evaluative sense of authorship set out by the dual-intention theory plays here. We see the all-or-nothing character of this second authorial moment: one aspect of the sculpture, its color, was modified against the artist's wishes, but Smith wanted to withdraw his authorship from it entirely. One might argue that a coating of paint is a minor element of a complicated metal sculpture, and that, from the perspective of its generation, it is still accurate to say that Smith is responsible for having designed the sculpture, and hence was its author. But the evaluative moment trumps these kinds of calculations. The artist either accepts it as his, or he does not. The modification of its color was a significant enough alteration—to him— that Smith felt justified in disowning it. Krauss argued that Smith would have regarded the posthumous alteration of his sculptures in exactly the same way. They issued from him (generative moment), but by removing their white paint they were no longer of him (ratification). The fact that Smith was no longer alive to make the complaint himself added to the pathos.

What makes the posthumous case of paint removal more complicated is that Smith's death left the sculptures in a liminal state of incompletion. As a result they were caught in a permanent limbo between the two moments of authorship, leading *Art in America's* editor to ask the riddling question, "Is a Smith of another color still a Smith?"[9] In the case of the paint removed by a collector during his lifetime, Smith's answer to this question was clearly "no." The editor's question efficiently recognizes the two moments of artistic intention: the nearly finished sculptures are clearly artworks generated by the artist, and so they are unequivocally 'Smiths' in that sense, but the removal of the white underpainting contravened his ultimate vision for the work, and so by implication they may not be fully 'his' any more.

In Krauss's initial essay, and in the unsigned editorial commentary by *Art in America* that introduced it, little mention was made of the idea that the works altered by the estate were unfinished. In fact, the rhetoric of her complaint and that of the accompanying editorial made it sound

---

[9] Editorial, "Issues and Commentary," *Art in America*, September/October 1974, 30.

as though the works were complete. Krauss says that Smith "had carefully placed multiple layers of white paint over a yellow undercoat," the word "carefully" signaling the care and intention with which these layers were applied by the artist. She briefly raised the possibility that more layers of paint were intended for them, but noncommittally left it "in the realm of conjecture." But the language with which she characterizes the alterations, i.e., "a direct intervention to change the work," an "aggressive act," made it sound as if the changes were to finished pieces.[10]

The suggestion that the estate had violated Smith's finished works was also carried out rhetorically by the aesthetic judgments included in the descriptions of the pieces before and after alteration. The *Art in America* editorial accompanying Krauss's accusation complained that the stripping of the paint "transforms the crisp, assertive, light-reflecting white or yellow painted shapes and surfaces into dark, light absorbing forms."[11] It went on to describe the formerly bright sculptures as having a "chocolaty look" upon which a "gravylike slipcoat" of varnish masks the sharpness of the metal planes. The implication was that the artist himself had left behind aesthetically pleasing, "carefully" painted white and yellow sculptures, which were then made ugly by the inappropriate intervention of the estate that altered them. Hence the insult to Smith's sculptures was not only moral, but aesthetic. Greenberg, for his part, also participated in this contest of aesthetic judgments, denying the validity of the descriptions and comparing the look of the white paint instead to "chicken down."[12] Technically speaking, of course, aesthetic considerations should not be relevant to questions of violations against artwork integrity. The question is not whether a given act of unauthorized alteration improves or impairs the work from an aesthetic perspective, but whether the artist's intentions for the work have been respected.[13] We can see in these moves, however, that there is a strong temptation to conflate the artist's completion decision with the work's having reached a level of aesthetic satisfaction that is apparent not only to the artist but to the knowing viewer.

[10] Krauss, "Changing the Work of David Smith," 32.
[11] Editorial, "Issues and Commentary," 30.
[12] Clement Greenberg, *Art in America*, May/June 1978, 5.
[13] See Paisley Livingston, "Counting Fragments, and Frenhofer's Paradox," *British Journal of Aesthetics* 39, no. 1 (1999).

Greenberg's primary defense, which engaged in its own form of rhetorical combat (mainly by insulting Krauss), was that the sculptures in this case were unfinished. He pointed out that the white paint served merely as the primer layer for some unknown and undetermined future chromatic topcoat. He said it was well known that Smith did not like white sculptures, so it was better to remove it than to let them stand permanently in a condition that he would not have accepted. Furthermore, Greenberg claimed, the white alkyd paint was starting to rub off when touched. Its removal was simply a restoration of the unfinished sculptures to their pre-primed condition, which had two advantages: it respected Smith's aesthetic preference not to make white sculptures, and it stabilized the physical object.[14] Museum of Modern Art director William Rubin, among others, wrote letters to *Art in America* in support of Greenberg's position.[15] They confirmed Smith's avowed dislike of white sculptures and pointed out that Smith chose Greenberg as the executor in charge of his art because of the trust and understanding they developed during twenty years of friendship.[16]

In her response, Krauss conceded that the works were unfinished, something that she had insisted earlier was unknown: the white paint was intended to serve as an undercoat for a final layer of color. This was an important admission, because she could no longer suggest that the integrity of a completed work had been destroyed. We were in the murkier waters of negotiating what artwork integrity means for *unfinished* works. But she maintained, however, that the paint's removal effectively misrepresented Smith's intentions:

Stripping the sculptures . . . is to take them one step further backward in the process of finishing, *not* in some mysterious way to complete them. And worse, because it effaces the evidence that these works were meant to be painted, *were in fact already painted*—since primer, whether it is "alkyd," oil-base, or metallic, or whatever, is still paint—this action misrepresents the original esthetic intentions of the artist.[17]

---

[14] Clement Greenberg, "P.S.," *Art in America*, March/April 1978, 5.

[15] William Rubin, "More on David Smith," *Art in America*, May/June 1978, 5.

[16] Hamill points to some evidence suggesting that this might not have been entirely accurate, and that Smith did have some completed white sculptures: Sarah Hammill, "Polychrome in the Sixties: David Smith and Anthony Caro at Bennington," in *Anglo-American Exchange in Post-War Sculpture, 1945–1970*, ed. R. Peabody (Getty Online Publications, 2011), 103, fn 11–13.

[17] Rosalind Krauss, "Rosalind Krauss Replies," *Art in America*, March/April 1978, 5.

Krauss astutely argued that even if Smith would not have wanted to leave behind white sculptures, the presence of the primer signaled his future intention to paint the work some other way. The white primer should be seen by viewers of the work not in terms of its aesthetic effect, but as a sign that the sculptures had already been set on a path toward becoming chromatic. Stripping the paint misrepresented the *telos* that Smith had intended.

Greenberg countered that leaving the sculptures white would *also* contravene Smith's aesthetic intentions and preferences, and hence would be an even greater misrepresentation of his authorial intentions than stripping them back down to steel. Both sides agreed that the sculptures were unfinished and that Smith intended to paint them further. The question was, which treatment would bring the sculptures closer to Smith's authentic artistic intentions? For Krauss, the white primer would serve as a sign of Smith's final intentions for the work; it would point to his "original" future intention to finish the sculptures by painting them in some unknown (and forever unknowable) manner. On the other hand, others insisted that Smith would never have wanted his work to be presented in white paint as its final resting (if unfinished) state. As Greenberg said, "I'll take it upon myself to speak for a dead artist: Smith would hate to know that those seven [*sic*] sculptures stayed covered with that alkyd white."[18]

Even if Greenberg were right, however, it is not clear whether Smith's avowed aesthetic distaste for finished white sculptures would apply to *unfinished* sculptures left white after his death. What we do not know, in addition to Smith's ultimate plans for their finished look, is what Smith would have wanted his permanently unfinished sculptures to look like. In other words, the question is not simply, did the living David Smith want white sculptures? But rather: how would the deceased David Smith want his permanently unfinished, primed works to be left for posterity? Covered in white primer, taken back to bare metal—or perhaps destroyed entirely? In the absence of any written statement by him on the matter it is open to speculation and dispute by those who knew him. In the breach come squabbles over aesthetic judgments, claims and

---

[18] Greenberg, *Art in America*, May/June 1978, 5. The seven sculptures that Greenberg is referring to here are the five whose primer was removed, plus two that were sold with the primer still on.

counterclaims of expertise, accusations, and personal insults. While the finished works of an artist's estate are not immune from these, either, the charge that a work's integrity has been violated becomes exponentially more complicated when it has no final finished form.

The David Smith controversy vividly illustrates the central insight of the dual-intention theory, which is that artistic authorship entails two conceptually separate moments of intention, and hence of authorial responsibility. The mere fact of the artist having generated a work of art is not enough to guarantee that he or she authored it in the fullest sense of the term. The fact that Krauss, Greenberg, and their respective supporters were arguing about what the artist would have wanted for the final disposition of the sculptures shows their recognition that Smith's artistic intentions were paramount in making this determination. And yet in this case, as with other artworks whose completion is arrested permanently by the artist's death, ratification, too, is forever withheld. As a result, it is much less clear what our obligations and responsibilities are with regard to the unfinished work. Furthermore, we can see in the arguments on both sides that other concerns, such as taste, the stability of the material object, and historical preservation of the object just as the artist left it, threaten to override that authority once the artist is no longer able to declare his intentions.

III. The 'Work Itself'

The fundamental claim of moral rights legislation, and contemporary Western culture's basic understanding of what artworks are generally, is that they are the personal expressions of their authors.[19] Hence, one reason why unfinished works are so problematic is that their perpetually provisional status renders it difficult if not impossible to know which elements of the work are to be seen as embodying the artist's ultimate intentions. When faced with an unfinished work, we do not know what aspects of it would have received final approval from the artist as

---

[19] "In retrospect, the most important right sought by artists from the time of the Renaissance was that of authorship and the protection of their individuality, including the protection of a work as the expression of that individuality." John Henry Merryman, Albert E. Elsen, and Stephen K. Urice, *Law, Ethics, and the Visual Arts*, Fifth ed. (Alphen aan den Rijn, The Netherlands: Kluwer Law International, 2007), 419.

comprising the 'work itself.' Authorship entails a series of choices, of decisions made against the backdrop of various constraints, conditions, and expectations. In the case of an unfinished work, however, one cannot be certain how to assess any of the author's choices, because they remain provisional. Insofar as they are or would have been in principle subject to revision, alteration, or even destruction, none of the work's formal features have been fixed *as* final choices. Artwork completion is important to artists because only they have the authority to decide when it is done.

The status of the work as complete or finished is equally important to a work's audience. Trogdon and Livingston say it well: "There can be no experience of the artwork as a discrete and intended, appreciable whole unless the work is complete. Hence, it is constitutive of artwork appreciation that its overall aim is the appreciation of a complete artwork."[20] The open-ended nature of artwork interpretation requires a stable foundation, and the presence of this foundation is indicated by the work's status as finished. Even a critic or observer's judgments about the aesthetic completeness of a work requires an ontically complete work to begin with. Consider, for example, the observation that a given work seems either underdeveloped or overworked. These are aesthetic judgments that only become meaningful when directed at a work that is actually finished in a more fundamental sense. If such criticisms were made of an unfinished work, we would either be stating the obvious or wasting interpretive energy on an artwork whose formal properties were not yet fixed. (An exception would be cases when a critic is shown a work-in-progress by the artist and asked for help in deciding whether it is done yet, which happened frequently in Clement Greenberg's studio visits, for example).

Both artists and audiences have an interest in the completion status of a given work. Artists may be concerned that the audience know that they are looking at a work in progress as opposed to a finished work. Audience members are equally interested in knowing whether the artist considered a given work to be finished or not. Sociologists of art point out that the norm of the finished work is a generally unexamined but nevertheless essential condition of its circulation as an artwork. Only when it is recognized as a bounded whole can the artwork be

---

[20] Trogdon and Livingston, "The Complete Work," 225.

recognized as the 'work itself,' as a discrete individual, and completion is constitutive of that status. As Pierre-Michel Menger observes:

A work of art is usually conceived, in the fine arts, as a finished, lasting reality, complete, never changing—a part of material and cultural eternity. Thus what happens to it later is separate, something completely formed being pulled into a turbulent future. Diverse viewpoints, readings, and competing interpretations give it multiple meanings. Diverse formats of exhibition, 'publishing,' and diffusion create new connections and put the work into changeable contexts where its meanings will be seen from new perspectives. Reproduction in media that may not transmit all its original characteristics as well as restoration will subject it to unforeseeable manipulations. The work is what, in this Heraclitean flux, remains the same, still itself, with its name, its title, its inventoried characteristics, and the list of its physical movements and transfers between owners.[21]

Under this account, completion solidifies the artwork's status as a stable, fixed object that persists through time. When accompanied by the artist's endorsement, the finished work can also be regarded as the authentic expression of its maker, and serve as a stable ground for interpretation. And yet the idea that the artist moves the artwork teleologically to its completion, fixing it forever and releasing it to the world at the moment when it reaches fulfillment of his expressive aims is recognized by artists, philosophers, art historians, and sociologists to be, essentially, an idealized fiction that conceals a much more complicated reality.[22] Menger calls it a "protective illusion" that the author maintains both for his benefit as well as the work's audience.[23]

Nevertheless, the notion that artists fix the formal features of their artworks upon completion is an assumption that drives much of the current philosophical debate about artwork completion. While the participants in this debate disagree about the necessary and sufficient conditions for artwork completion (and whether there are any), they

---

[21] Pierre-Michel Menger, "Profiles of the Unfinished: Rodin's Work and the Varieties of Incompleteness," in *Art from Start to Finish*, ed. Howard S. Becker, Robert R. Faulkner, and Barbara Kirshenblatt-Gimblett (Chicago: University of Chicago Press, 2006), 31. For a philosophical argument about why it is wrong to modify finished works of art that is based on this point of view, see for example David E. W. Fenner, "Why Modifying (Some) Works of Art Is Wrong," *American Philosophical Quarterly* 43, no. 4 (2006).

[22] See Kelly Baum, Andrea Bayer, and Sheena Wagstaff, "Unfinished: Thoughts Left Visible," ed. The Metropolitan Museum of Art (New Haven: Yale University Press, 2016).

[23] Menger, "Profiles of the Unfinished: Rodin's Work and the Varieties of Incompleteness," 42.

agree that the artwork's status as 'finished' is significant because it effectively 'locks in' the work's formal properties and makes it numerically distinct from other artworks. Under this view, any subsequent alteration by the artist to a finished work results in a new work, whereas an alteration to an unfinished work is merely part of the generative process.[24] As Hick puts it,

the process of art making leads to a finished work, and the many stages leading to this state do not identify different *works*, but different stages in the development of the *same* work. Two finished works, however, will be distinguishable and identifiable as *different* works.[. . .] I take it that a work of art's being finished is a *terminal* condition—that if a work of art is, in fact, a finished work, then any changes made to it following its having been finished will result in a *new* work.[25]

Under this view, unsanctioned or illicit alterations to finished works result in vandalism of the physical object but do not alter the work itself, whereas unwelcome alterations to an unfinished work may violate the artist's rights and wishes, but do not carry the same ontological force. Since the work itself has not yet been fixed, it is not clear what, exactly has happened to it *qua* work.[26] By contrast, the complete work has been sealed off and separated from other objects with what we might call an ontological carapace of completion: this is what distinguishes it from other artworks that it might have been, from other versions that might exist, and from other works by the same artist.[27]

We can see in the quote from Hick above that the norm of the finished work leads to certain assumptions about artwork ontology: that artworks undergo a process of generation which terminates, when all goes well, in

---

[24] See Darren Hudson Hick, "When Is a Work of Art Finished?," *Journal of Aesthetics and Art Criticism* 66, no. 1 (2008): 71; "A Reply to Paisley Livingston," *Journal of Aesthetics and Art Criticism* 66, no. 4 (2008): 397; Trogdon and Livingston, "The Complete Work," 225.

[25] Hick, "When Is a Work of Art Finished?," 70–1.

[26] Lamarque goes so far as to assert that the artwork does not exist until the artist has completed it. In my view this an unnecessarily extreme stance, but it shows just how much ontological significance the moment of completion has for some philosophers of art. Peter Lamarque, "On Bringing a Work into Existence," in *Work and Object* (Oxford: Oxford University Press, 2010). I thank an anonymous reviewer for this point.

[27] Of course, unfinished works are put into circulation, too—usually, but not always, posthumously—Schubert's *Symphony no. 8 in B Minor*, Lord Byron's *Don Juan*, and Gilbert Stuart's portrait of President George Washington, *The Athenaeum*, are prominent examples. In the case of Washington's portrait, it was not the painter but the subject who died before the work's completion. Stuart continued to make and sell copies of the portrait, and it still graces the US one-dollar bill.

a complete work whose formal properties are then permanently fixed. This makes it numerically distinct from all other works, and is what persists even as the object in which the work is embodied degrades over time or suffers unauthorized alteration. Indeed, under this view, not even the artist is able, ontologically speaking, to make changes to her own work once it has crossed the finalization Rubicon: any changes made after the work has been effectively finished will necessarily result in a new work. Trogdon and Livingston share the view that completion is terminal: "we think that once a work shifts from being incomplete to complete there is no going back."[28] Hence the leading philosophies of work completion assume that the passage from the Painting Room to the Show Room is not a swinging door, but a valve through which works can pass but never return. This leads theorists of artwork completion to search for an adequate account of the mechanisms that bring the artwork over this threshold and effectively lock in its features as 'the work itself.' For Hick, uncoerced publication, in the absence of any statement denying completion, is sufficient to ensure that the formal properties of an artwork are fixed.[29] According to Livingston's most recent version of his theory, the artist's acquisition of a 'completion disposition' toward the work is what fixes it.[30] It is important to note that this locking-in principle is asserted rather than argued for by Hick and Livingston. They feel justified in this assumption, I suspect, because they adhere to the principle that artwork ontology ought to reflect art world practice. Since the norm of the finished and fixed work as Menger describes it above is so prevalent, they presume that any adequate account of artwork completion will describe the conditions under which the formal features of a work are fixed.

At the opposite extreme, sociologists of art emphasize the inherently collective, collaborative nature of individual actions. Hence one finds passages in the literature where the high-minded assertion is made that, ultimately, there is no such thing as individual authorship; so too do they deny that there is such a thing as an individual work.[31] In his classic

---

[28] Trogdon and Livingston, "The Complete Work," 231.

[29] Hick, "When Is a Work of Art Finished?"

[30] Trogdon and Livingston, "The Complete Work."

[31] For example, Laermans claims that the individual artist "is not a lonely genius or bohemian outsider but a nodal point in a social network. Without this network, neither artists nor artworks exist as such, that is, as a particular kind of individual and a specific sort

study *Art Worlds*, Howard S. Becker explains that "Works of art, from this [sociological] point of view, are not the products of individual makers, 'artists' who possess a rare and special gift. They are, rather, joint products of all the people who cooperate via an art world's characteristic conventions to bring works like that into existence."[32] But of course, one can give credence to the sociological emphasis on art making and authorship as governed by collective action and social norms while still recognizing that individual artists and artworks exist.[33] I take this demystifying move by the sociologists to be similar to the observation that Newtonian physics has ultimately been superseded by Einsteinian relativity, and yet in most cases the Newtonian paradigm continues to be a viable explanatory model. We can and do speak meaningfully of artists and artworks while still recognizing that these designations might simplify what, upon closer inspection, is much more complicated, and that the concepts of author and work gain their significance within a larger context of historically and culturally contingent norms and practices.

So when philosophers claim that completion fixes the artwork's properties and individuates it from other works, they are accurately representing the prevailing cultural norm for works of fine art, but it is helpful to keep in mind the fact that this status is the result of a social negotiation. It comes about as the result of the artist's participation in certain cultural norms and conventions that signify completion. Recognition of the work as the 'work itself'—complete and individuated—may be initiated by the artist, but it depends on community uptake. Becker calls this anti-essentialist stance toward artwork identity the "Principle of the Fundamental Indeterminacy of the Artwork":

the first contribution of sociology to an understanding of the 'work itself' is the recognition, which should be incorporated into everything else an analyst says, that a work takes many forms and that the 'work itself' is isolated only by virtue

of artefact." Rudi Laermans, "Deconstructing Individual Authorship: Artworks as Collective Products of Art Worlds," in *Art & Law*, ed. Bert Demarsin et al. (Belgium: die Keure, 2008), 51.

[32] Howard S. Becker, *Art Worlds*, 25th Anniversary ed. (Berkeley: University of California Press, 2008), 35.

[33] Just as Becker himself can insist on the inherently collaborative nature of authorship, yet still claim, without contradiction, credit for authoring *Art Worlds*, and even write an advice book for other authors in the social sciences about the writing process. *Writing for Social Scientists*, Second ed. (Chicago: University of Chicago Press, 2007).

of a collective act of definition. This means that what the work is, while in no way arbitrary, is subject to great variation and can never be settled definitively in some way that is dictated by its physical nature.[34]

We tend to regard completion, which is what supposedly finalizes and 'locks in' the work's identity, as a property of the artwork, and we understand the artist to be the sole determiner of its status. Becker does not deny that this is an important aspect of our conception of artworks and authorship. But his disciplinary perspective, which understands authorship and completion as socially constituted, helps us to keep in mind that our usual ways of speaking about and treating artworks as if they were a "finished, lasting reality" as Menger calls it, may mislead us when we begin to give theoretical accounts of artwork completion.

IV. Theories of Work Completion

Picasso claimed that the *Demoiselles d'Avignon* was unfinished.[35] He supposedly said that he didn't know whether *Guernica* was finished or not.[36] How can that be? In every outward respect, the artist behaved as if they were done: he ceased making changes to them; he allowed them to be exhibited; in the case of *Guernica* he authorized a tapestry version to be made for the United Nations. If we recall Livingston and Archer's theory of artwork completion, which defines it in terms of the artist's "effective, practical" decisions to treat the work as complete, it would seem that both artworks satisfy their theory easily and uncontroversially.[37] The art world, for its part, also regards *Demoiselles* and *Guernica* as finished. Monographs are written on the masterpieces under the presumption that their subjects are finished works.

By casting doubt on the completion status of two of his best-known works, Picasso reminds us that artists might feel ambivalent toward the completion status of their works. Nevertheless, they maintain the

---

[34] "The Work Itself," in *Art from Start to Finish*, ed. Howard S. Becker, Robert R. Faulkner, and Barbara Kirshenblatt-Gimblett (Chicago: University of Chicago Press, 2006), 24.

[35] Michael Baxandall, *Patterns of Intention: On the Historical Explanation of Pictures* (New Haven: Yale University Press, 1985), 66. Cited in Menger, "Profiles of the Unfinished: Rodin's Work and the Varieties of Incompleteness," 42.

[36] Trogdon and Livingston, "The Complete Work," 227.

[37] Livingston and Archer, "Artistic Collaboration and the Completion of Works of Art."

authority to determine whether their own works are finished or at the very least treated as such. As Michael Joyce, in the epigram that opens this chapter, points out, authorship entails the right to say when it is done. Philosophers of artwork completion agree: "it is only the artist who has the authority to make such a determination [that it is the definitive and complete artistic artifact]."[38] This authority is now understood to be absolute. Earlier theories of artwork completion emphasized the aesthetic qualities of the work as the driving factor: they depicted the artist as responding to the work's formal integrity and unity, which in turn triggered the recognition that the work was done. Now, however, we grant full authority to the artist to make this determination, no matter what the work looks like.[39]

One might argue that the work is finished just in case it fulfills the artist's intentions in the sense of his plan for the work. If Smith sets out to draw a cat, and he produces a drawing of what is recognizably a cat, then the work is finished whether Smith is pleased with his drawing or not. The endorsement step covers the question of his artistic satisfaction, not the fulfillment of his plans. But such an account relies on an untenably thin, naïve understanding of artistic intention and the creative process. Smith may set out to draw a cat, and he could even announce this fact publicly—he could even sign a contract promising to make a drawing of a cat. But the fact remains that only Smith can decide when his rendering of a cat is finished. An outside viewer cannot decide for Smith when the cat drawing is done. There is more than one way to skin a cat, but there is an infinite number of ways to draw one.

Hence theorists of artwork completion agree that only the artist can decide when her artwork is done. This means that when an artwork has the property 'finished,' it is an intentional property that refers back to and depends on the attitudes and behaviors of the artist with respect to her work, which in turn take place against the backdrop of cultural

---

[38] Ibid., 440.
[39] Livingston, "Counting Fragments, and Frenhofer's Paradox." See, e.g. John Dewey: "The making comes to an end when its result is experienced as good," John Dewey, *Art as Experience* (New York: Minton, Balch, & Co., 1934), 49. Cited in Livingston and Archer, "Artistic Collaboration and the Completion of Works of Art." See also Monroe Beardsley, "On the Creation of Art" (1965), discussed and rejected by Hick, "When Is a Work of Art Finished?," 67.

norms and expectations. But this act of authorship, while so fundamental, is also very peculiar. On the most basic level, it requires the
cessation of behavior. In order to be complete, the artist must *not* do
anything else to the work that would change it.[40] However, because a
work can be abandoned unfinished, the fact that the artist has ceased
making changes to it is not enough to guarantee work completion. An
artist may have any number of works in her studio that she regards as
finished, and they will be in principle indistinguishable from the unfinished ones by the outside viewer. And these attitudes and beliefs
regarding the work can be highly unstable: something that looked to
its maker as finished one day might seem like it needs more work on
another, and vice versa. The question of what sorts of decisions and
behaviors are necessary and sufficient for artwork completion has
turned out to be surprisingly complex.

Since finished works of art are so commonplace in our experience, and
since their status as complete is so important for the reasons I have
spelled out above, I am sympathetic to the view that we ought to be able
to determine when to attach the label 'done' to the artwork, and not just
to the artist. The problem is that the grammar of the phrase 'finished
work of art' misleads us into looking for this definitive point of transformation, as if it were a matter of saying, "when it reaches 165 degrees
Fahrenheit," "when it is christened," or "when the artist signs it." Just as
Kant observes that beauty is not strictly speaking a property of artworks,
but really a complex claim about our subjective state when apprehending
the object, so too is the grammar of 'the finished work' highly misleading.[41] It is really shorthand for a complex claim about the artist's
intentions, decisions, and behaviors regarding the work—the *artist* is

---

[40] I appreciate Livingston and Archers' point that an artist could finish a work while still
anticipating future material changes to it, such as waiting for a topiary to grow, or some
other process out of the artist's control in order for the work to be complete. The artist,
however, would still count as the authority who determines that the work is finished
through what they call the "extended completion decision." Livingston and Archer,
"Artistic Collaboration and the Completion of Works of Art," 446.

[41] Immanuel Kant, *Critique of the Power of Judgment*, trans. Paul Guyer and Eric
Matthews, The Cambridge Edition of the Works of Immanuel Kant (Cambridge:
Cambridge University Press, 2000), 101. I first made this point and several others in this
chapter in my discussion piece, "Ambivalent Agency: A Response to Trogdon and Livingston on Artwork Completion," *Journal of Aesthetics and Art Criticism* 73, no. 4 (2015):
457–60.

done with it—that under certain conditions transfer to the work so that *it* is said to be 'done.'[42] And notice once again that we often conflate completion with ratification, so that sometimes what is at stake when we ask whether a work is done is really a question about whether it is both finished *and* endorsed.

In this section I re-examine the two leading theories of artwork completion in order to show why they are unsatisfactory. I argue that their primary mistake is ontological: they stipulate that there must be a point at which the formal features of an artwork are fixed, such that any subsequent changes to the work by the artist result in a numerically different work. This leads the theories' authors to look for the conditions under which we can say definitively that the work itself is irrevocably fixed and finished. I argue that these attempts fail, and that this supports the sociological view that an artwork's completion status (like its endorsement) is ultimately always provisional. Post-completion changes by an artist to her artwork do not necessarily result in a numerically distinct work, as the locking-in principle would have it, but are best understood as changes to the same work. The determining factor is not when the changes were made, but the amount changed.

It might be objected by Hick and Livingston that the phrase 'post-completion changes to the work' is self-contradictory: if the artist continues to make changes to an artwork, it either was not in fact complete to begin with, or the work was complete and the artist has elected to destroy that work and replace it with a new, perhaps very similar one. Hick considers and rejects the notion that an artist can make changes to her finished work on these grounds. He argues (in part):

> If the artist can always override the state of a work's being finished, it seems, any work is only ever provisionally finished, barring any future decisions by the artist to change it. It would then be, perhaps, only the artist's death that signals the work is more than provisionally finished (though, just as likely, this would place the work in a thereafter permanent superposition of being finished and not-finished.) That a work is never *truly* finished is not an unheard-of claim. Paul Valéry is famously quoted as saying, "A poem is never finished, only abandoned." However, the position that a work is *never* done again certainly contradicts our initial assumption that the given work *is* done.[43]

---

[42] Hick, "When Is a Work of Art Finished?," 70.   [43] Ibid., 71.

Hick rejects the possibility that an artist could make post-completion changes to the same artwork on logical grounds. But to say that artworks are only ever provisionally finished is not the same thing as saying that artworks are "*never* done," for this would deny that there is any meaningful distinction between unfinished works and finished works, which of course there is. One can subscribe to Valéry's skepticism about completion and still understand the difference between the poem in progress and the poem that gets submitted to *The New Yorker* for publication. Hick equates provisional completion with its denial because he assumes that completion means that the artwork has undergone some sort of decisive, irrevocable transformation. This begs the question of what it means for an artwork to be finished. Because artwork completion depends entirely on the attitudes and behavior of the artist, one can recognize the existential possibility that the artist might change her mind, and if given the chance, may well make alterations to her work. To say that completion is provisional does not mean that finished artworks do not exist, but it does mean giving up the locking-in principle.

The belief that completion involves the effective, irrevocable transfer of the property 'done' from the artist to the artwork leads theorists to search—in vain, as I see it—for a satisfactory account of the mechanism that will accomplish this. Two examples from the philosophical debate over work completion will help to illustrate my point. The first comes from Hick, who argues, contra Livingston (2005), that artists do not in fact need to regard their work as finished in order for it to be so. In other words, a completion decision is not a necessary condition for a work to be finished. He gives the imaginary yet plausible example of an artist who puts a work of art in a drawer at the end of the day, thinking it unfinished and expecting to continue work on it later. After some time she opens the drawer, regards the work, and decides that it was in fact complete when she put it in the drawer, even though at the time she did not think it was. As Hick puts it:

So, do we want to say that the work was done when the artist put the work away or when the artist formulated a firm intention to work on it no further? I suspect we want to defer to the artist: that the work was complete when she put it away in the drawer. That is, intuitively, I think we want to say that the work was done when the last change to it was made. The artist might not have been *aware* that the work was done until shortly before she committed her intentional act, but I see no reason to think that the work was not, therefore, done . . . The artist may not be done until she has *decided* that the work is done, but if nothing further has been done *to* the work since it was put in the drawer, it seems that the work was finished when the last change to it was made.[44]

Hick's example presents a scenario in which an artwork can turn out to have had the property 'finished' before the artist realized it—or so it seems. He wants to date the work's completion to the end of the artist's intentional formal changes, and not to the moment of her judgment that it needs nothing else. His scenario has the advantage of seeming to respect the artist's own way of regarding the situation: she recognizes that it was in fact done at the time it was put away. If the artist says that it was done, then who are we to gainsay her authority? This would defeat Livingston's argument that a work is complete if and only if the artist makes an effective completion decision.

This puzzle exploits the folk psychology of artwork completion in order to make its point.[45] The artist in this scenario treats the work as if she were merely recognizing a property of the work that was already present, but she just wasn't 'aware' of it—that is, as if it were a property of the work independent of her attitudes and intentions. But there is a major problem with this strategy. It seems disingenuous to take this way of talking about completion literally, as Hick elsewhere in the same article rejects the idea that artists simply respond to the aesthetic completion of their works in deciding that they are done. His scenario paints the artist as discovering a fact about the work that she had not realized when she put it away initially. This is supposed to show that completion decisions are not necessary, because at *t1* the work was finished, and yet the artist only realized this later at *t2*. But the artist's decision *is* necessary, even in this story. Even if we accept the artist's own experience of realizing after the fact that the work was complete, the artist in this case

---

[44] Ibid., 70.

[45] While Hick's example was fabricated for the sake of argument, the ambiguous status of artwork in a studio drawer is a real phenomenon. In August 2014 Jasper Johns' longtime assistant, James Meyer, pled guilty to stealing and selling twenty-two of Johns' artworks. The artworks were kept in a drawer and were not authorized by Johns: they had not been given inventory numbers and were not part of the official catalog of his work. It is unclear whether these works were actually unfinished, or deemed unfinished by the press simply because they were unauthorized. For an account of the theft, see Robert Kolker, "The Betrayal of Jasper Johns," *New York*, November 17–23, 2014.

still makes the determination that the work is finished.[46] It is indeed tempting, when looking back in retrospect after that judgment, to speak as if the work were already finished when it was put in the drawer. But that does not mean that the work literally had the property 'finished' before the artist judged it to be so, and it just needed to be discovered. What if she had put it in the drawer and never looked at it again? Would it be sitting in the drawer, finished, unbeknownst to her? It seems impossible to hold this view if we are also committed to the view that only artists have the authority to determine that their work is finished. While in common parlance we might be tempted to see the work as being finished when she last made changes to it, it is not as if someone else other than the artist, unless being vested by her with that authority, could have examined the work and made the determination, couched in the language of discovery, that it was finished.

But it is even more complicated than that. The artist not only has to decide that the work is done, but she has to refrain from making further changes to it. Neither Hick nor Livingston, when discussing this case, address the question of what would happen to the artwork's completion status if the artist were to change her mind again and make more changes to the work at $t3$, some point after she took it out of the drawer. It seems that it would no longer have been finished. The work's status is therefore dependent on the potentially vacillating attitude of the artist with respect to its completion. But the goal for theories of artwork completion is to determine when—which really means how, under what conditions—the property of 'finished' transfers definitively from the artist's attitude to the artwork itself.

This is why Livingston, in his theories of artwork completion, empha-sizes that an effective completion decision involves not just an assessment that the work is done, but an intention to refrain from making further changes. On his view, then, we will not be able to determine whether a work has been finished unless and until the artist behaves in such a way that it effectively signals that she really does regard it as done. On this view, we would have to wait a while to know whether the artist really is finished with the work in the drawer, or whether she changes her mind

---

[46] Livingston has the same objection, though he does not discuss it in detail: Paisley Livingston, "When a Work Is Finished: A Response to Darren Hudson Hick," *Journal of Aesthetics and Art Criticism* 66, no. 4 (2008): 398.

and alters it some more. But this strategy also fails to articulate the precise moment when a work of art is finished, because he is unable to say precisely how much time must pass, or under what circumstances, the artist must behave as if the work were finished in order for it to truly become so. And yet because Livingston is also committed to the locking-in principle, his theory also needs to stipulate some tipping point at which the disposition to refrain from changing the work becomes decisive.

Livingston's discussions of Géricault's treatment of the *Raft of the Medusa* fall prey to this strategy. According to the story, after eighteen months of sketching and painting, Géricault arranged to have the *Raft* exhibited at the Salon in Paris, so he had it transported from his studio to the Théâtre Italien. When he saw the painting in the theater before the works were hung for exhibition, however, he decided to make some last-minute changes to the lower right-hand corner. Once he made the changes, he allowed the painting to be shown, and never altered it again.[47] Livingston has discussed this case in two different iterations of his theory of artwork completion, and both times, the question that he expects his theory to answer is, when was the work finished? When Géricault sent it out of the studio, or only after he made his final changes before the Salon opening? In one version of Livingston's theory (co-authored with Archer), they claim that the necessary and sufficient condition for a work to have the status of 'finished' is the artist's effective completion decision. In the Géricault case, it seems that the first completion decision did not transfer to the painting itself, and so was ineffective:

On the highly plausible assumption that Géricault deemed the work good enough to show at the Salon and thought he was done working on it when he had it taken away from his studio, it turns out that his completion decision in this first instance did not suffice for the work to be complete. It would be odd, to say the least, to have to conclude that when he got back to work on *The Raft of the Medusa* in the foyer of the Théâtre Italien what he was really doing was destroying a completed work and using the canvas as material for another, new work to be exposed at the Salon in its place. Instead, what we want to say is that the picture had not really been finished when it was removed from the studio, but was so once the artist finally stopped making changes. Some completion decisions are, then, indecisive.[48]

---

[47] Livingston and Archer, "Artistic Collaboration and the Completion of Works of Art," 444.
[48] Ibid.

Notice that what is important for Livingston and Archer is fixing the moment at which the work acquired the property 'finished.' But their reasoning is held hostage to the assumption that any changes by the artist to a finished work, no matter how minor, will necessarily result in the destruction of the work and the creation of a new and different work. By claiming that the *Raft* was not actually finished when it left the studio, then they can regard Géricault's alteration as a change to the same work rather than commit themselves to the admittedly odd view that the artist's minor alteration to the *Raft* destroyed the work that he spent eighteen months laboring over.

In a subsequent version of his theory, Livingston (with co-author Trogdon) discards talk of completion decisions and judgments and replaces them with the language of disposition. Livingston claims that the disposition theory is superior because it is able to account for artwork completion even in cases where the artist denies that her work is complete, and perhaps even believes that artworks are in principle never complete. And yet Livingston's earlier talk of completion decisions had already accounted for just such ambivalence or skepticism by focusing the artist's "*effective, practical*" decisions. He explicitly denies that artists must hold certain "theoretical attitudes or philosophical beliefs about work completion."[49] So, on this account, one can decide to treat a work as finished without having the occurrent belief that it is finished. By switching to talk of dispositions, he and Trogdon are emphasizing, I think rightly, that the artist's behaviors and not his beliefs are what counts. And yet this was already captured by the earlier theory. In my view, Livingston's theory of the completion disposition collapses into his earlier account of the completion decision. In both cases, however, he makes the mistake of thinking that there is some single moment in time when the artist's decision or disposition causes the work to acquire the irrevocable property 'finished.' Here is how Trodgdon and Livingston re-read the Géricault case in terms of dispositions rather than decisions:

Suppose that Géricault made his initial completion judgment about his work at t1. Shortly thereafter he hired people to move his canvas out of his studio. After making this judgment, he went on to change the painting—suppose he completed these changes at t2. We think that, while Géricault judged that the painting was complete at t1, he lacked a refrainment disposition (let alone a completion disposition) with respect to his work at that time; that this is so is supported by the fact he went on to change the work shortly after t1. So our view is that, while Géricault made artistically significant changes to his work after t1, the changes he made were not post-completion changes. It is of course possible that Géricault did have a completion disposition with respect to his work at t1 only to lose it shortly thereafter—our claim is just that the way he acted in this case provides defeasible evidence that he lacked such a disposition at t1. This take on the case comports with *the natural idea that the painting was not actually complete* when Géricault made his initial completion judgment.[50]

Contrary to Trogdon and Livingston's interpretation, it does not seem "natural" to me to say that the work was not finished during the liminal period between Géricault's decision to send it to the Salon and his decision to work on it some more. It is important to them that we not read this case as a situation in which Géricault's alterations effectively destroyed a finished work and made a new one, but it would be much simpler to say that the artist finished the painting, and then he changed his mind and made some changes to the work when the chance availed itself. I agree with Livingston that Géricault's last-minute changes did not destroy the work, but not because it was not truly finished when it left his studio, but because artwork completion does not lock in the formal properties of the work. This, it seems to me, is a much more 'natural' way of understanding the scenario in question. Indeed, the Géricault story comports with the nineteenth-century tradition of 'Varnishing Day,' or *vernissage*, in which painters put the finishing coat of varnish on their paintings, or even made small alterations, the day before an exhibition's official opening. ('*Vernissage*' today means 'preview' because invited guests were also permitted to attend.)

Livingston et al. want a theory that can fix the moment at which a work acquires the property 'finished.' But one strange consequence of their theories is that they only enable us to discern retroactively when the work was finished, as we must wait and see whether the artist refrains from changing the work, under what circumstances it was changed, and how much was changed in order to say whether a completion decision or disposition had been in place. If Géricault had not made any changes to the *Raft* after it left the studio, it would seem 'natural' to assume that the artist had finished it there. Then we would say that the initial completion

---

[50] Trogdon and Livingston, "The Complete Work," 231. Emphasis added.

decision or disposition—I think these are actually the same thing, because the disposition requires effective practical decisions that manifest in behavior—had been successful.[51] But their theory is unable to give an adequate account of success here. They assert that the completion disposition is irrevocable once the transfer of the property 'complete' to the work itself has taken place: "In our view, once an artist acquires a completion disposition, the artwork is complete, and if the artist later loses this disposition, the artwork is still complete assuming that the artwork still exists."[52] This is the moment in their theory when the transfer of properties from artist to artwork occurs: being finished ceases to be simply a property of the artist, and now becomes fixed in the work. But the problem is that the existence of the artist's completion disposition, which is necessary for work completion, can only be retrospectively inferred from the artist's subsequent behavior and decisions. Their theory does not tell us what, besides the artist's refrainment behavior and "psychological equilibrium" toward the work, would cause it to shift from unfinished to finished.[53] Since that behavior can change, and dispositions, as they acknowledge, can be gained and lost, we have failed to find a mechanism based simply in the artist's beliefs and behaviors which fixes the work itself as 'done.'

Consider again the hard case of the unpublished work. What will enable us to determine that the artist has acquired a successful completion disposition with respect to her work? Livingston and Trogdon understandably do not stipulate a length of time an artwork must remain untouched in order for us to say that the artist's completion disposition has successfully shifted the work from being complete to incomplete. It seems that the only way we can determine whether the shift has happened is if some other socially acknowledged external indication, such as public declaration by the artist that it is done, allows us to regard the work is finished. The completion disposition is supposed to be what *makes* the work fixed and finished, and yet we never know whether there was one until we have some other, empirically verifiable reason to believe

---

[51] See K. E. Gover, "Ambivalent Agency: A Response to Trogdon and Livingston on Artwork Completion," *Journal of Aesthetics and Art Criticism* 73, no. 4 (2015).

[52] Trogdon and Livingston, "The Complete Work," 231.

[53] Kelly Trogdon and Paisely Livingston, "Artwork Completion: A Response to Gover," *Journal of Aesthetics and Art Criticism* 73, no. 4 (2015): 460.

that the work is complete. This threatens to be viciously circular: If there is an effective completion decision, then the work is finished, but the completion decision is only deemed effective if we regard the work as finished, which means we will have to appeal to other reason, such as its uncoerced publication, or to some arbitrarily stipulated amount of time that the artist refrains from making further changes.

This accounts for the reasoning about the Géricault case: Livingston wants to say that it must not have been finished, and therefore there was no effective completion decision when it left the studio, because he changed it again before publication. But a better response is to acknowledge there is no moment in which the work crosses the Rubicon of completion, that works are always only provisionally finished, and that there are borderline situations, such as the unpublished work left in the studio, in which it is impossible to say whether it is finished or not. Because artworks, unlike turkey legs, do not irrevocably acquire the property 'done' under certain predetermined conditions, it is a mistake to look for some behavior or mechanism that will permanently bestow this property to the work.

However, we can ask when a work was published. And that is why publication, as an empirically verifiable fact about the work, is the default method of determining a work's completion status. Hick has argued that it is akin to making a move in a chess game: once you have released the piece, you have made your move, and it is irrevocable, even if the player (or artist) regrets it later.[54] For this reason, Hick argues that, provided there is no explicit statement by the artist to the contrary, publication of the work with the artist's consent is possibly the only sufficient condition—and there are no necessary ones—for artwork completion. Hick is right to point out the crucial role that publication plays in establishing a work's status as finished and 'fixed.'[55] But publication is not what finishes the work. Normally we imagine that the artist first finishes the work, and then puts it into the world. Uncoerced publication is simply the most readily available, externally verifiable sign that the

---

[54] Hick, "A Reply to Paisley Livingston."

[55] While Livingston has challenged Hick on this point, his remarks in other works suggest that he agrees that publication effectively fixes the work: Paisley Livingston, "Pentimento," in *The Creation of Art*, ed. Berys Gaut and Paisley Livingston (Cambridge: Cambridge University Press, 2003), 94; Livingston and Archer, "Artistic Collaboration and the Completion of Works of Art," 446.

artist authorizes the work to be viewed as complete, as the 'work itself.' Publication also makes it much more difficult for the artist to make changes to the work once it has begun to circulate *as* a certain work with certain formal properties.

And yet. Not even publication can guarantee that the work is finished, if we are looking for some definitive sign that the work has crossed the threshold from incomplete to complete. Hick's analogy of artwork publication to the release of a chess piece during play is flawed because the 'rules' of artwork completion are not as codified as they are in a chess game. As we will see, artists do sometimes make changes to their artworks after having exhibited or published them. On the other hand, artists sometimes devise their own completion rituals and routines that indicate when their works are finished. When sorting through the works left behind in the studio of a sculptor who died unexpectedly, the executors were able to identify the finished from the unfinished because the artist always put a coat of wax on the ones that were done.[56] An artist might signal to herself and others that a work is finished by putting a photograph of the work on her website, or sending a photo to her gallerist. But, unlike the rules of chess, these self-determined rules and routines for completion can always be renegotiated.

While it is indeed true that there are customs and practical concerns that discourage artists from making post-publication changes, it can and does happen. Malcolm Lowry famously used to pull copies of his novel *Under the Volcano* down from the shelf in bookstores and correct the text in pencil. We would regard that as a failed attempt at post-publication changes to a work. But Walt Whitman continued to make changes to *Leaves of Grass* after its initial publication in 1855, publishing several new versions over the course of thirty-three years until his 'deathbed edition' of 1892.[57] At that point the poem had grown from twelve poems to over four hundred. Hick would likely reply that each published edition of the poem is, ontologically speaking, a new work, even if very similar to the previous one. But we adhere to the 'locking-in'

---

[56] Personal conversation with Jon Isherwood about the studio of Andrew Dunhill, February 2015.

[57] I thank my colleague Ben Anastas for bringing these examples to my attention.

principle upon pain of rejecting the poet's own view of what he did, as he announced in the New York *Herald* two months before his death:

Walt Whitman wishes respectfully to notify the public that the book *Leaves of Grass*, which he has been working on at great intervals and partially issued for the past thirty-five or forty years, is now completed, so to call it, and he would like this new 1892 edition to absolutely supersede all previous ones. Faulty as it is, he decides it as by far his special and entire self-chosen poetic utterance.[58]

If we reject the locking-in principle, we can say that Whitman kept making changes to *Leaves of Grass*, rather than adopting the view that he kept destroying and remaking new, similar works with the same name. Of course, one of the features of the *Leaves of Grass* example and other literary cases like it is that the nature of the literary work enables us to consult the previous published iterations of the work after the author has made changes. This is not the case if we are considering object-based visual art such as paintings or sculpture. In those cases, it is more tempting to tell the ontological story that the alteration effectively destroyed the work and remade a new one in its place.

So let us consider in detail just such a case, in which a visual artist changed his work multiple times post-publication. Sir Anthony Caro (1924–2013) was an English sculptor who made his reputation in the 1960s by creating works out of scrap metal welded into abstract forms. He was profoundly influenced by David Smith, who was a close friend. Like Smith, Caro was one of the post-war Abstract Expressionists championed by Clement Greenberg. To Greenberg's chagrin, Caro, like Smith, also had a tendency to paint his sculptures.[59] Caro's own particular completion ritual was as follows: when he decided that a sculpture was finished, he would make what was called the 'sheet': on specially prepared pieces of paper, he drew a picture of the work, gave it a title, date, recorded the dimensions, and described the paint colors he used, in case it one day needed to be restored (as steel sculptures left outside in the elements inevitably will). The 'sheet' was also the place where the

---

[58] Justin Kaplan, *Walt Whitman: A Life* (New York: Simon and Schuster, 1979), 51.

[59] About the paint on Caro's sculptures, Greenberg wrote, "I know of no piece of his, not even an unsuccessful one, that does not transcend its color, or whose *specific* color or combination of colors does not detract from the quality of the whole (especially when there is more than one color)." Clement Greenberg, "Contemporary Sculpture: Anthony Caro" (1965), in *Clement Greenberg: Collected Essays and Criticism*, vol. 4, p. 207, quoted in Hammill, "Polychrome in the Sixties: David Smith and Anthony Caro at Bennington," 95.

post-completion details of the work's history were recorded: who bought it; for what price; where it was exhibited; which catalog essays and works of criticism mentioned it; where the work resided.

When we examine a typical instance of a Caro 'sheet,' such as the one for *Bennington* (1964), we can find all of these details (Figures 3.1 and 3.2). However, a closer look tells a more complicated story. The 'sheet' serves as the artist's official record of the piece from the moment it was finished and at key moments of its circulation in the art world; however, it is also a record of changes that were made to the work after its ostensible completion and even publication. Reading from top to bottom, we see the title, year, the artist's sketch of the sculpture, and the size. Then we notice that the "Medium" is listed as "Steel painted orange." The typed word "orange" has been crossed out and rewritten in Caro's handwriting. Under "Paint" we see that it was originally painted in "Kem Bulletin Sherwin Williams medium orange," though the artist notes that he would prefer a different brand of orange paint. Next to the typed description of the paint, however, we find a note in the artist's handwriting which states: "(now painted blue—mixture of Brilliant blue and Dark Blue [and underneath] as Titan)." *Titan* (1964) is a sculpture from the same exploratory series made at Bennington College, in which Caro worked with tilted I-beams and rejected the pedestal in favor of placing

Figure 3.1. Anthony Caro, *Bennington* (1964) Steel, painted blue 40 × 166 × 133.5"/102 × 422 × 339cm. © Courtesy of Barford Sculptures Ltd. Photo: John Goldblatt.

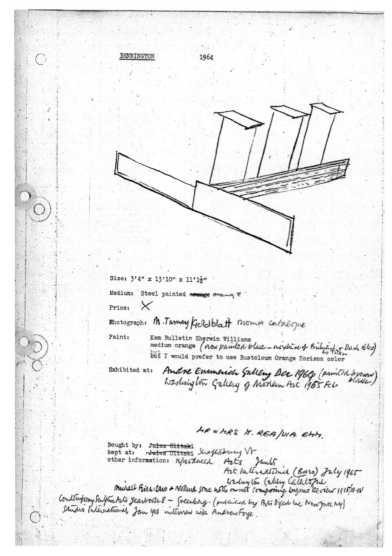

Figure 3.2. Anthony Caro's 'sheet' for the sculpture *Bennington*. © Courtesy of Barford Sculptures Ltd.

the sculptures directly on the ground.[60] The note "as Titan" tells us that *Bennington* is now painted the same color blue as *Titan*. But the question

---

[60] Ian Barker, *Anthony Caro: Quest for the New Sculpture* (Hampshire: Lund Humphries, 2004), 123ff.

is, when did *Bennington* go from orange to blue? When we look at the next note, things become more complicated. It says that the sculpture was first exhibited at the André Emmerich Gallery in December 1964, in yet a different color: "(painted brown black)." Beneath that, we see it was shown at the Washington Gallery of Modern Art in February 1965. Some sleuthing reveals a catalog listing from that 1965 show describing *Bennington* as "orange."[61] A story begins to suggest itself: when Caro made the 'sheet' in 1964, the sculpture was orange. But he changed his mind and painted the sculpture brown/black for the December 1964 show at the Emmerich Gallery. Within a couple of months, however, he changed his mind again and repainted the sculpture orange for the February 1965 Washington Gallery show—hence the strange detail that the original typed word "orange" was crossed out and written in again. Sometime after that, however, Caro evidently changed his mind once more, and painted *Bennington* the same mixture of brilliant and dark blue that *Titan* had. This is the final color for the sculpture, and the one that his estate would authorize any future restoration of the sculpture to be painted.[62]

Hence we can see that publication of an artwork—in this case, exhibiting it in two different galleries, in two different cities—did not prevent the artist from making changes to the work.[63] Again, any theorist who insists on the locking-in principle will have to read this story in one of three ways, all of which clash with both common sense and the artist's own understanding of his behavior. First, they could argue that *Bennington* was not really finished until its final color was chosen. But what makes the color final is the contingent fact that its color was never changed again, not because some sort of transformation that occurred to the work once it was painted blue. Livingston and Trogdon might insist that their disposition account can make sense of this case, by showing that Caro failed to have a successful completion disposition toward the work until he painted it blue

<hr />

[61]   Anthony Caro and Toby Glanville, *Caro by Anthony Caro* (London: Phaidon, 2014), 115.

[62]   If one wonders how Caro was able to get away with changing the paint on a sculpture that, according to the sheet, was owned by someone else, the answer is simple: Jules Olitski, abstract expressionist painter, was Caro's close friend and colleague, and part of the same stable of artists that Clement Greenberg brought to Bennington College in the 1960s to live and make work. Caro was at Bennington when Smith died there in May 1965.

[63]   It is admittedly a convenient advantage that the photographs in that time were black and white, obscuring the actual color of the work at any given moment.

and stopped fiddling with the color. But such an account is unhelpfully post hoc; we are only able to say that the artist was disposed to treat the work as complete because, looking back, we can see that he never changed its color again. However, this may have been because the opportunity to change the color never presented itself again, not because the artist was not disposed to do so. Second, those committed to a locking-in principle could claim that each color change effectively destroyed the original work and made a new, similar work. But what do we gain from this strange stretching of what it means to destroy a work, other than a badge of ontological rigor? The artist did not see the color changes as destroying *Bennington*. He saw them as changes to the work. Apparently, Caro often struggled to arrive at the right color that would unify the form to his satisfaction, and we see in the record of this work's changes (as with the sheets of many of his other sculptures) that it took several attempts before he settled on blue.[64] This shows that completion is provisional, but it does not mean that his previous completion decisions were inadequate or somehow less real than the final one. Third, one might try to account for this case by saying that color was not essential to the work, and so changing the color did not destroy the fixed and finished work. But Caro certainly did not think that the color of his sculptures was inessential—note the care with which each change in color is noted on the sheet. When he was alive, he personally authorized every restoration of his sculptures and signed off on their color in accordance with the 'sheet.' So, again, if we want to insist that color is inessential, we do this on pain of contradicting the view of the artist, his estate, his dealers, collectors, and assistants, all of whom are committed to maintaining his sculptures in their correct hue.

Perhaps, one might say, this example only shows that the 'sheet' is not in fact a certificate of completion. Maybe there is some other completion ritual that fixes the work more definitively than the 'sheet.' Indeed, if we probe more deeply into Caro's working methods, we learn that beginning in 1981 he began compiling a catalogue raisonné of his work, overseen by a German man named Dieter Blume. Whereas catalogues raisonnés are typically created after the death of an artist, Caro decided to begin compiling and publishing one at the midpoint of his career. Typically,

---

[64] Personal conversation with Jon Isherwood, one of Caro's former studio assistants, December 2016.

this meant that when Caro completed an artwork, it was photographed and the photo along with a copy of the 'sheet' was sent to Dieter, who would give it a "Blume number," and publish the works in volumes organized by medium and year. We might look to the moment when the work was cataloged as the point where it was 'locked in' as final. And yet, when we consult the Blume book for *Bennington*'s listing, we find the following: "BENNINGTON 1964 steel painted primer red."[65] Hence we cannot even treat the work as it appears in the catalogue raisonné as the definitive record of its finished form.

What can this example add to the philosophical discussion of artwork completion? In Caro's case, neither public exhibition nor publication in the catalogue raissoné could guarantee that the work was immune from alteration. If the artist thought it could be improved, and he had access to it, he changed the work. While the changes recorded on the 'sheet' show that Caro's completion decisions were provisional, it does not show that Caro was cavalier about the alterations he made or that completion had no meaning for him; quite the contrary. The fact that each color change was documented by the artist shows that he took seriously his authority to make alterations, as well as his responsibility to record the changes so that future collectors and museums would know his intentions.

One might object that the Caro and Whitman cases of post-publication changes to a work are exceptions and that we should not base our theory of artwork completion on outliers. First, I would hazard a guess that such changes probably happen more often than the public is aware. When admiring an artwork in a museum we are not privy to the potentially quite complicated details of its history before it arrived at its final resting place. Second, I think that artists generally do respect the custom that discourages against making changes to a published work. But we ought not to make an ontological principle out of a practice that is largely circumstantial: once a work is in the hands of another, or once it is off to the printer, it is very difficult to pull it out of circulation and make changes, even if the artist would like to. And once the work is out of the artist's hands, she may have moved on to other projects and is content to regard the work as done because she is effectively done with it.

---

[65] Dieter Blume, ed. *Anthony Caro. A Catalogue Raisonné. Steel Sculptures 1960–1980*, 14 vols., vol. 3 (Cologne, Germany: Galerie Wentzel), 188.

Because the completion status of the work, as with its endorsement, is so closely tied to the intentions of the artist, the border between finished and unfinished is at times vague, indiscernible, or indeterminate. And yet *something* happens that enables us to speak meaningfully about completed works, as if the works themselves had that property. Philosophers Hick and Livingston have productively wrestled with this question by showing the many complexities that underlie such a fundamental distinction when regarding works of art. Some of the questions and puzzles they have raised dissolve, however, when we recognize that artwork completion is not like a chemical reaction in which the artist's conferral of this status mystically transforms the work into a different kind of thing. The norms and conventions surrounding the finished work are real, and have consequence, but they are not as codified and institutionalized as, say, changes in marital status or elections to political office. "Married" and "mayor" are also intentional properties, but the rules governing their acquisition and loss are more stringent than the ones that allow us to infer whether a work is finished. Most of the time, artists stop making changes to their artworks once they are released into circulation as finished. But not always.

As we draw this discussion to a close, I want to address the question of what I call 'theoretical completion skepticism.' Livingston's disposition theory, which focuses on behavior and not on judgments, attempts to take into account the possible ambivalence of the artist regarding the completion of his work, while still according him full authority over its status.[66] He points out that some artists may claim never to have the belief that a work is finished. Such a line of thinking is different from the sociological principle of artwork indeterminacy discussed at the beginning of this chapter. Sociologists agree that the distinction between finished and unfinished is an important, non-arbitrary, functional distinction, even as they insist on its contingency and provisionality. Livingston recognizes that this difference is widely treated in the art world as fundamental, for reasons we have discussed earlier in this chapter.[67] The sociologists' point is not to deny that finished works exist, but only to show that

---

[66] Trogdon and Livingston, "Artwork Completion: A Response to Gover."
[67] Livingston and Archer, "Artistic Collaboration and the Completion of Works of Art," 440–1.

completion is not 'natural' or inherent to the work, but a status that is negotiated between artist and audience, both of which are operating in a larger context of established social conventions. As one observer puts it, "the indeterminacy of the artwork in this sociological sense is an empirical and historical fact rather than a primarily ontological and philosophical one."[68] Moreover, these two spheres do not impinge upon each other in any practical sense. One can be a theoretical completion skeptic and still produce finished works. I take this to be Livingston's underlying insight as well, and the reason why he has articulated a theory of work completion that accommodates the theoretical completion skeptic. But one does not need to go so far as that to explain how such an artist can make finished works.

In the case of an artist who makes the principled claim that his works are only ever "abandoned," never complete, or for example Picasso's provocative suggestions that two of his best-loved works were unfinished, I follow Livingston in holding that what counts are the artist's practical decisions and behaviors regarding the work. The artist can still decide whether it should be indexed as finished for pragmatic purposes even if the artist claims to hold the philosophical view that all works are inherently incomplete. The fact that this means that the theoretical completion skeptic seems to hold contradictory beliefs about artwork completion is not the problem that it might seem to be. People do it all the time: atheists willingly go to church and send Christmas cards. Epistemological skeptics still claim, in everyday life, that they know where they live, how to drive a car, and the name of their spouse. Postmodern theorists proclaiming the death of the author sign their essays and collect their royalties. The artist who believes, on some deep level, that works are never finished may still behave towards some of his works as if they were, and that means he holds certain beliefs about which works he wants to index as such. He can distinguish the ones that are 'in progress' from the ones he sends to his gallerist for sale or display. He may never have the occurrent thought "this work is finished," and yet he can still make the pragmatic decisions that result in finished works.

The Picasso examples illustrate the problem posed for theories of artwork completion by the potential gap between an artist's stated beliefs

---

[68] Eduardo de la Fuente, "The 'New Sociology of Art': Putting Art Back into Social Science Approaches to the Arts," *Cultural Sociology* 1, no. 3 (2007): 422.

about the completion status of his own work and his effective behaviors toward it. We give full authority to the artist to make the determination that his work is complete, and yet sometimes the message is contradictory: in the case of the *Demoiselles* and *Guernica* above, Picasso's assertions about their (potential) incompletion contravene his effective decisions to treat these masterpieces as finished. In those cases, as with the completion status of artworks generally, behavior is more authoritative than belief.

V. Two or Three Moments?

In the case of valued artists, their sketches, models, and unfinished pieces can be objects of fascination and study, perhaps because their works' incomplete state offers a clearer view into the creative process—a peek into the kitchen, as it were. In the David Smith case, the estate may have decided that the potential costs of circulating his unfinished sculptures outweighed the loss that would be incurred by destroying them or permanently withdrawing them from view. On the other hand, an incomplete work precludes us from knowing to what extent it actually represents its author's final intentions because it has never been declared—either through words or deeds—'done.' It occupies an unstable, liminal state as having issued from the artist, and in that sense, being authored by him. But because it is not yet a complete work, it is impossible to say what, exactly, has been authored, and whether it is something that the artist would have wanted to recognize as his own.

Put in terms of the dual-intention theory, unfinished works reveal what is important to us about artworks and authorship. To some extent they fulfill the generative moment of authorship—they have issued from the artist, and are in that sense his—but because they are unfinished they also lack the final ratification that the second moment of intention represents: the moment when the artist approves of the work, and claims it as his own. But a difficulty arises because logically, ratification and completion are not the same thing, even if in practice we collapse them. The conceptual and epistemic problems that surround artwork completion, such as determining when and how the property 'finished' is effectively transferred from the attitudes and behaviors of the artist to the work itself, apply equally to ratification. An artist may deem a work acceptable at one moment only to change his mind later. If the work is in his studio, we may not know whether he endorses the work or not. And, as with completion, our best indication, even if ultimately provisional, that an artist endorses her work in this second sense of authorship is its uncoerced publication.

Hence it turns out that authorship, in the fullest sense of the term, entails three intentional moments on the part of the artist: the intention to make a work of art; the intention to index the work as complete; and the intention to endorse it as the artist's own. When we encounter works of art in parks, museums, galleries, or on the walls of collectors' homes, we take these elements for granted as essential to the concept of artistic authorship. It is only when one or more of these elements are missing or contested that we can see that authorship, in the fullest sense, is not just a matter of making something, but of fixing it as the work itself, and choosing to accept it as one's work: as good, or good enough, to bear its author's name.

So must we revise the dual-intention theory to accommodate three separate moments of intention: generation, completion, and ratification? We do not. Completion is the endpoint of the first, generative moment. While in practice completion is often tantamount to endorsement, because the work continues until the artist deems it 'good enough' to ratify as hers, they are logically separate moments. In the cases where a work is made in public, the artist gives up his prerogative to disavow authorship of something he has made, though of course he is free to say that he does not like it.

The artwork at the center of the Mass MoCA controversy discussed in the following chapter was caught in the indeterminate space between these standard scenarios. The museum understood itself to be an open platform in which artists were invited to create their installations in public. It wanted the court's permission to put Büchel's abandoned, unfinished work on display. The artist, on the other hand, understood himself to be creating his work privately, and sued the museum for violating his right of divulgation. He did not want his reputation as an artist to be harmed by what he regarded as an inadequate representation of his artistic intentions—inadequate not only because it was unfinished, but because he did not like how the creation of the work unfolded. For its part, the court had to decide whether moral rights protections even applied to unfinished works: since the materials in the museum's largest gallery were not recognized as comprising an individuated work of art, it was unclear what they were. The artist insisted on his freedom to decide when the work was complete and whether he found it satisfactory, but that freedom was compromised by the highly collaborative and semi-public conditions under which the work was generated.[69]

[69] I want to thank my anonymous reviewers for spurring me to make significant changes and improvements to my argument in this chapter.

4

The Artist and the Institution

Elliott (lawyer): We respectfully submit, and we have submitted expert testimony on this, that to show a work in its unfinished state against the protest of the living artist is a distortion, which is the word that VARA uses, is a distortion of the highest order.

Judge Ponsor: What are you distorting here? How can you distort something that hasn't been created yet? I think of distortion as the lunatic who went after the Pietà with a hammer. You have a work of art which is completed and then it is distorted.[1]

I. Büchel v. Mass MoCA

In spring 2007 the Massachusetts Museum of Contemporary Art (Mass MoCA) sought permission in federal court to show an unfinished artwork in its football-field sized Gallery 5 to the public. The installation, which had originally been scheduled to open in December 2006, would have been Christoph Büchel's first major US museum show, and his largest to date. Büchel is a Swiss artist who creates meticulously, obsessively assembled environments made mostly out of used everyday objects and junk. The piece was to be called "Training Ground for Democracy," and it was about the war in Iraq.

Büchel's initial concept for the gallery was relatively sparse. There was to be a giant meteor at the opening that visitors would squeeze around, which would open up to an abandoned cityscape. The meteor was eventually replaced by a closed local movie theater, which was removed and reassembled in Mass MoCA's gallery, including the original ceiling tiles and the worn red seats. While the details changed and grew, the concept for the work remained the same. It was meant to evoke the

---

[1] *Christoph Buchel v. Mass Museum of Contemporary Art*, No. 07-30089-MAP, p. 23, line 17.

simulated environments that the US military used to train its soldiers for the war in Iraq. It was a simulation of a simulation, but using real objects and structures. The initial budget for the project, based on Büchel's sketches and the gallery mock-up that he made during a visit to North Adams in late August, was $160,000, though Büchel contends that the museum was never clear with him about the bottom line. Director Joe Thompson tackled the project with a mixture of can-do optimism and grave concern about whether they would have the time and money necessary to complete the project. Mass MoCA's total annual operating budget was $800,000, and they knew that it would be impossible to get corporate sponsorship for such a politically incendiary show as "Training Ground" promised to be. They would have to rely on private donors and to apply for grants from the Swiss government. As Thompson explained in an email to Büchel in September 2006, three months before the show was to open, "I'm terrified about the costs, by the way. So far, we have zero in sponsorships, nada."[2] Büchel promised to return in mid-October with his three Swiss assistants to begin the creation of the work once the museum had spent several months gathering materials and preparing them for the artist's arrival.

The six-week collaboration in fall 2006 did not go well. Büchel had explained that his working methods were extremely hands-on and fluid, which is why he had given the museum relatively little instruction about his intentions for the installation before his arrival. Rather than planning things out in advance on paper, the artist preferred to work out his design in situ, adding, deleting, and adjusting elements as he went. While the museum was used to the vagaries of the creative process, and in fact expected it, the sheer scale of the project combined with Büchel's extreme sensitivity to minute detail proved to be overwhelming. Among the items installed, in addition to the movie theater, were an oil tanker which had to be cut open and decontaminated, a smashed police car, a truck, a used mobile home, deactivated bomb shells, a replica of Saddam Hussein's 'spider hole,' nine shipping containers, and a 1400 sq ft two-story Cape Cod-style house that was lifted out of the ground, sliced into four pieces, and reassembled. The museum ran out of money before they could obtain the 727 fuselage Büchel had asked for, and continued to insist on.

[2] *Mass MoCA v. Büchel*, No. 08–2199, R at A634.

Büchel left North Adams on December 17, five days before they installed the house. At that point, the museum had spent over $300,000 on the show, it was still unfinished, and they were out of money. Büchel complained bitterly that the museum was not following his instructions, and he blamed Mass MoCA for going over budget by not finding cheaper versions of the items he requested. The museum began looking for more donors, including asking Büchel's London gallery, Hauser & Wirth, to help realize the show, even though Büchel had told the museum not to ask his galleries for money. While Dante Birch, MoCA's preparator, continued to send frequent updates to Büchel about the work they were doing in his absence, Büchel was becoming increasingly angry. He was furious that the museum was allowing unofficial tours of the installation to selected guests, which he got wind of through the accounts which began to appear in blogs and in the press. Eventually he stopped communicating with the museum, and instead published in the *Boston Globe* a seven-page letter listing his conditions for returning, which included being given an unspecified amount of money in a bank account in his name.

On March 28, 2007, Mass MoCA sent Büchel a letter setting forth two alternatives: the first, that Büchel return to North Adams and complete the exhibit; and the second, that he remove the materials in Building 5 and reimburse Mass MoCA for the costs it incurred in connection with the exhibit. Mass MoCA strongly indicated its preference that Büchel complete the exhibit and offered to make additional funding available for this purpose. The artist refused to comply with either request, so the museum covered the exhibit in tarps and allowed the public to walk through the covered gallery. It then sued the artist in federal court, asking permission to show the work to the public, which Joe Thompson regarded as "the best unfinished work of art of the century."[3] The artist countersued, arguing that the museum had violated his moral rights, which are protected by the Visual Artists' Rights Act (VARA). He argued that the museum violated his right of disclosure by allowing the public to walk past the exhibit whose tarps only partially hid it from view, and he complained that the museum did not follow his instructions in constructing the work.

In his summary judgment, Judge Michael Ponsor ruled that Mass MoCA did have the right to show the work, and that VARA did not

---

[3] *Massachusetts Museum of Contemporary Art Foundation, Inc. v. Christoph Büchel*, No. 08–2199, R at A1108 and A1244.

apply in this case because the work of art in question was unfinished. He also took heavily into account the fact that Mass MoCA had paid for the majority of the cost of making the work, and was actively involved in its realization. So long as Mass MoCA put up a disclaimer stating clearly that Büchel had disavowed the piece, it had the right to show the objects assembled in Building 5. Despite winning the lawsuit, Mass MoCA never displayed the unfinished "Training Ground for Democracy" to the public. Instead, it removed the materials in Gallery 5 at its own expense and dumped most of it into a landfill. Büchel appealed Ponsor's decision, and in January 2010 the court partially overturned the first circuit's ruling. It determined that the question of whether Büchel's VARA rights were in fact violated must be decided in a jury trial. Before a trial date could be set, however, the artist decided in early December 2010 to withdraw the suit.

II. Authorship and Institutions

The Mass MoCA case dramatically reveals the potential difficulty of disentangling the ownership rights and responsibilities of two parties over one artwork. Here a two-story Cape Cod house, a movie theater, a trailer home, a smashed police car, a decontaminated oil tanker, and tons of junk taken from a small economically depressed town in the Northern Berkshires become caught in a suspended state of artistic purgatory, in which the same objects were simultaneously the spiritual property of the artist and the physical property of the art museum. The museum's attempt to show the installation over Büchel's protests provoked the impassioned opposition of many in the art world, who saw this as a clear transgression of Büchel's moral rights over the work, and as yet another case in which an artist is victimized by a large, powerful institution. The lawsuit between Büchel and Mass MoCA gained attention in the international press. Influential art critics such as Roberta Smith at the *New York Times* and Ken Johnson at the *Boston Globe* published editorials about the case in which they blamed Mass MoCA for its mistreatment of the artist. They expressed outrage at the museum's usurpation of his authority over his work.[4] Their opinions,

---

[4] See Roberta Smith, "Is It Art Yet? And Who Decides?" *New York Times,* September 16, 2007 and Ken Johnson, 'No Admittance,' *Boston Globe,* 1 July 2007. *Massachusetts Museum of Contemporary Art Foundation, Inc. v. Christoph Büchel,* No. 08–2199, R at A1273.

along with those of curator Robert Storr, were admitted to the court as expert testimony on behalf of Büchel's defense. They all blamed the museum and said it was unacceptable to show an artist's work unfinished against his wishes, no matter how much money and labor it had cost the museum to produce it.

This is not to say that the artist went unscathed in the press coverage. On the other side were the populist wags who wrote opinion pieces for the local paper with titles like "Crap Under Wrap," referring to the tarps behind which the museum shrouded the unfinished artwork while it waited for the court's decision. Their position was that Büchel was yet another fraudulent contemporary artist. He was not only wasteful, difficult, and ungrateful, but was trying to pawn off a sow's ear as a silk purse by literally making art out of garbage. Smith and Johnson anticipated just this kind of reaction in their equally ardent defense of Büchel, painting him as a victim of both the art institution that commissioned his work in the first place, as well as the populist philistines who would look to the dispute as confirmation of their bias against contemporary art generally.

The tendency for both sides to turn the controversy into a debate about the merits of contemporary art in general was unfortunate if not surprising, since there was never any question that the museum was dedicated to cutting-edge art. Founded in the late 1980s, Mass MoCA is essentially postmodernism's answer to the traditional art museum. Rather than attempting to present a comprehensive collection of rare and important artifacts, it produces large-scale, temporary installations, often with an overtly social or political content. At Mass MoCA, established and emerging artists such as Gregory Crewdson, Jenny Holzer, and Cai Gao-Qiang are invited to the museum to create works that are on display for most of a year and then removed or destroyed. The museum does not collect works, but emphasizes process over product, intentionally showing both visual and performing art works in progress. It sees itself as an 'open platform' rather than a curio cabinet or closed box. The windows of the galleries are left uncovered so that viewers can see the gritty town outside while touring the galleries: a small detail, but jarring in comparison to the windowless nowhere of the conventional 'white cube' to which museum visitors are accustomed.

In her 1990 essay "The Cultural Logic of the Late Capitalist Museum," Rosalind Krauss talks specifically about the then newly founded Mass MoCA as an art institution uniquely suited to postmodern art.

She describes it as an innovative institution, one that would reject the diachronic, encyclopedic approach to art that museums usually have, and would instead be more suited to the transformed understanding of art represented by contemporary movements such as Minimalism. And she specifically highlights the implications that this would have for artistic authority:

To make the work happen, then, on this very perceptual knife edge—the interface between the work and its beholder—is on the one hand to withdraw privilege from the formal wholeness of the object prior to this encounter and from the artist as a kind of authorial absolute who has set the terms for the nature of this encounter, in advance.[5]

Krauss anticipated that such an institution could have a profound impact on our understanding of the artist and the artwork. It would demystify both object and author, because viewers would not encounter the artworks as complete objects presented for our admiration and contemplation; their existence would be much more contingent and specific to the artist's engagement with the museum where it was conceived and made. However, as the Büchel controversy unfolded, it became clear that the supposed withdrawal of privilege from the artist as the "absolute" authority over his creation occurred only at the theoretical or rhetorical level. It did not in fact lead to a transformed understanding of the responsibility and authority that characterizes the relation between the artist and his work.

Both the artist and the museum agreed officially for legal purposes that Büchel was the sole author. In reality, however, the development of the work was a highly collaborative process in which the museum not only paid for almost all of the expenses in realizing the installation, but also collaborated creatively as well. In an internal email, Mass MoCA curator Susan Cross pointed out the conflict between the practical realities of the work's production and the supposedly obsolete but persistent ideology of authorship in play: "The single author/artist idea is such an outdated notion, really. Artmaking is much more collaborative these days—but it is still very muddy."[6] Don Zaretsky, Büchel's lawyer, admitted that the court case "put Christoph in the position of having to explicitly argue

---

[5] Rosalind Krauss, "The Cultural Logic of the Late Capitalist Museum," *October* 54 (1990): 8.

[6] Email from Susan Cross to Joe Thompson, January 31, 2007. MASS MoCA 07843.

that he was the sole author of the work—in effect forcing him into staking out a position for legal purposes (the author as lone genius) that I know he was not entirely comfortable with from the point of view of his artistic practice."[7]

Even as museums like Mass MoCA become more and more involved in the production of artworks rather than their mere exhibition, they tend to be regarded as artistic midwives or patrons than co-creators. While there is nothing wrong in principle with this practice, it deliberately disrupts the usual relation between artist and institution. As a result, such unconventional arrangements can leave both parties in a peculiarly vulnerable position for which there is little legal or theoretical precedent. Judge Ponsor prefaced his summary judgment by commenting: "This controversy doesn't belong here. This is a passionate disagreement about aesthetic ideology and the rights of an artist and the process of creation that is extremely ill-suited to the courtroom." On the other hand, he also relished the opportunity to preside over a case in which important humanistic principles were at stake. Noting that VARA is an undeveloped area of the law, he remarked that

it is a judge's dream [. . .] to have a chance to work on a case that doesn't involve sorting out discovery in a dispute between two behemoth corporations, but really has to do with what it means to be human and what it is to create works of art and to attempt to display them.[8]

In the Büchel controversy, the museum's difficulties arose from the fact that it functioned simultaneously in several, usually separate roles: as the artist's assistant, carrying out his orders to fabricate and install the work; his benefactor, as it provided all of the resources to create the work; and as public institution, lending its prestige and institutional approval to his art because they deemed it worthy of public regard. While such a blending of traditional roles and responsibilities was amply justified from a postmodern theoretical standpoint, the conflict between Mass MoCA and Büchel revealed the limits of theory in the face of a messy real-world conflict in which authority, responsibility, reputation, and money were all palpably at stake.

---

[7] Don Zaretsky, email to author, December 17, 2007.

[8] *Christoph Büchel v. Massachusetts Museum of Contemporary Art Foundation, Inc.*, No. 07-30089-MAP Motion Hearing, US District Court, District of Massachusetts Western Section, September 21, 2007, (Springfield MA).

Indeed, when examining the editorials in support of Büchel, the principled appeals to artistic authority, autonomy, and freedom are not simply about an artist's right to determine when his work is finished, nor are they about the unique ability of certain artists to transform everyday objects into artworks. Rather, the conflict became a symbol of the power that art institutions generally have over artists in giving them recognition, prestige, and cachet within the art world. For example, *Brooklyn Rail* art reporter Thomas Micchelli unfavorably compared Mass MoCA to the Bush administration for what he saw as its abuse of power, despite the fact that the museum had risked its budget and reputation in order to realize Büchel's politically edgy artwork, which in fact was directly critical of US foreign policy.[9] Ruba Katrib, a curator at the Museum of Contemporary Art in North Miami, criticized Judge Ponsor for ultimately siding with the museum, once again invoking the principle of an artist's absolute creative freedom. As she put it:

Ponsor continually concedes that Büchel acted irresponsibly, didn't show up, overcharged, etc., rather like a hired hand not performing his duties as expected. While this jobbing analogy is partly accurate, artists have no obligation to pursue anything other than their own interests or live up to anyone else's expectations— though that of course is the issue. Why did Mass MoCA allow this now well-rehearsed relationship, the commissioning and execution of a major new work, to reach a stalemate over pragmatism?[10]

Katrib's rhetorical question here smuggles in the assumption that the failure of the collaboration was the institution's fault. In assigning all the blame for the installation's failure to the institution, and wondering why it allowed the pragmatic concern over a few hundred thousand dollars to get in the way of Büchel's art, Katrib articulates the ideology of the absolute freedom of the artist that divests him of any professional or financial obligation. The artist simply cannot be held responsible for the failure of the collaboration because by definition artists hew only to the call of art itself. By assigning all of the responsibility to the museum— Mass MoCA "allowed" this failure to happen—Katrib both denies the agency of the artist and grants him full autonomy.

[9] Thomas Micchelli, "Purgatory Lost: Mass Moca Trashes *Democracy*," *Brooklyn Rail*, October 3, 2007.

[10] Ruba Katrib, "Institutional Anxieties: MASS MoCA v. Christoph Büchel," *ArtUS* 22 (Spring 2008): 24.

The critics' defenses of Büchel revealed their shared assumption that it was *in principle* impossible for a museum to be mistreated by an artist. Drawing upon a nineteenth-century cultural trope of the artist's antagonistic relation to society, they cast him as the maligned sufferer and rebel struggling against the oppressive institution.[11] In that sense, the case recalls the 1980s *Tilted Arc* controversy, in which Richard Serra fought with the government to keep his large steel sculpture in New York's Federal Plaza. Both insisted on their right of disclosure. While Serra insisted on his right for the work to *remain* on public display, Büchel argued that he had the right to prevent Mass MoCA from disclosing his work to the public. In both cases, moreover, the artists were seen to be flag-bearers on behalf of contemporary art against a suspicious and hostile public. Büchel's supporters voiced concern that the conflict might confirm the popular suspicion that contemporary artists are frauds and charlatans. 'Artistic freedom' became a catchall concept for all of these issues.

III. Authorship and Autonomy

Although the art experts did not exactly define what artistic freedom entails, it is clear from their commentaries on the controversy that it includes an artist's right to determine when an artwork is finished and suitable for viewing—no matter the circumstances of the work's production. Roberta Smith articulated this principle in the *Times*: "In the end it doesn't matter how many people toil on a work of art, or how much money is spent on it. The artist's freedom includes the right to say, 'This is not a work of art unless I say so.'"[12] In order to make her case for the absolute freedom of the artist to determine when the work is finished, Smith tells a story about Robert Rauschenberg. In 1961, he was asked to contribute to a show of portraits of the dealer Iris Clert. He sent a telegram that read, "This is a portrait of Iris Clert if I say so." But it is not clear that Rauschenberg did in fact succeed in turning the telegram into a portrait. We might disagree with Rauschenberg that he can make a

---

[11] For a historical overview of this cultural trope, see Alexander Sturgis et al., *Rebels and Martyrs: The Image of the Artist in the Nineteenth Century*, ed. National Gallery (London: Yale University Press, 2006).

[12] Roberta Smith, 'Is It Art Yet?'

portrait—not just a work of art, but also a portrait—from a telegram bearing no resemblance to the person in question.[13] The 'Rauschenberg Principle' that Smith appeals to here does not in fact support the conclusion for which she argues—that the museum violated Büchel's artistic freedom by trying to show his work against his wishes. If anything, the telegram story merely illustrates the basic principle of the readymade: an artwork can be made of anything and take any form.

As both the title of her editorial ("Is It Art Yet?"), and her use of the Rauschenberg story show, Smith assumes that one of the central issues in the Mass MoCA case is the question of when and how the assembled materials in Gallery 5 become a work of art. She seems to assume that the installation only becomes transfigured into a work of art once the artist has declared it finished. But this is surely mistaken. If artworks only become art at the moment they are finished, then there is no such thing as an unfinished artwork, which is absurd: artists' studios are full of them. While in the case of some readymades and 'found' artworks, such as those made from telegrams, the transformation from everyday object to artwork renders the period in which it is an unfinished artwork vanishingly small so as to be nonexistent, in the case of the Büchel installation—which by the time the artist walked away from it had taken nine months and thousands of hours of labor to assemble, build, and install—there was no question that it was an unfinished artwork. Nor was there any dispute over the fact that, *qua* art, it was Büchel's.[14] What was at issue was not whether it was art yet, but whether the museum could present Büchel's unfinished work in its Gallery 5 over his protests. Smith conflates an ontological question about artworks with an ethical question concerning the museum's right to display an unfinished artwork that was generated by Büchel but lacked completion or ratification.

And yet Smith was not alone in her confusion over this point. As the epigram to this chapter shows, Judge Ponsor was unsure whether it was possible to distort a work of art that had not yet been fixed as finished,

---

[13] Cynthia Freeland, for example, argues that portraits must necessarily bear a resemblance to their subjects. See Cynthia Freeland, *Portraits and Persons* (New York: Oxford University Press, 2010). I thank Sherri Irvin for this observation.

[14] Initially the museum did argue that the installation was co-authored by Mass MoCA and hence they were equally owners of the copyright. But they ultimately dropped this line of argument and conceded that Büchel was the sole author.

as the 'work itself,' in Becker's phrase. Büchel's lawyers also pressed this issue by asking Mass MoCA director Joe Thompson during his deposition whether he was an artist. The implication was that Thompson usurped the artist's role in two ways. First, it was claimed that he violated the artist's rights by making decisions about the arrangement of some of the materials in Büchel's installation without his approval, which the artist regarded as "sabotage."[15] Second, it seemed to Büchel and his supporters that Thompson was taking over the artist's prerogative by attempting to reveal the unfinished work to the public—thereby, in a sense, declaring it finished. And yet it is hard to see why such a self-identification by Thompson as 'artist' would matter in either case. Let us suppose that Thompson in fact likes to paint watercolors of lobster boats during his vacations to the Maine shore; that would not give him any more right as an 'artist' to declare another artist's work to be finished. The tacit assumption behind the lawyers' question is that an artist is not just someone who makes art, but who has a special kind of authority to make art that non-artists do not.

Thompson's reply to the lawyers reveals a conflation similar to Smith's confusion concerning three different issues—when an artwork is finished, the artist's ratification of the work, and the authority to confer art status. In his deposition, Thompson explained:

The rule of thumb in our business, since Marcel Duchamp declared it and it became an accepted fact, is that art exists when an artist says it's so. They're the ultimate makers, the ultimate arbiter of whether or not their work is art . . . it's almost a rule of law in our business that art is what an artist says it is.[16]

Here we see that Thompson shifts from the question of "when" something becomes art to "what" counts as art. In his remarks, Thompson, like Smith, seems to assume that the moment when an artist declares

---

[15] The difficulty here is that Thompson and the rest of Mass MoCA's staff were constantly making decisions about the arrangement of the materials in the installation, both in response to and in anticipation of Büchel's instructions. Büchel was only present for a total of six weeks out of the nine months in which the museum constructed the work. The museum emailed him photos of the work in progress for approval and further instruction. Sometimes, however, the artist changed his mind about how he wanted certain elements of the exhibition arranged, or misunderstood the reports, and then blamed the museum for not following his instructions. He also reacted with anger and disbelief to the museum's reminders that the installation had to conform to local fire and building codes.

[16] *Massachusetts Museum of Contemporary Art Foundation, Inc. v. Christoph Büchel*, No. 08–2199, R at A494.

something to be finished is also the moment when it becomes a work of art. In fact, in its arguments before the court, the museum argued that the assembled objects and structures in Gallery 5 were just "Materials," like paints next to a canvas, waiting for the artist's brush.[17] And yet this argument by the museum was highly disingenuous and unconvincing. By the time Büchel abandoned it, the installation in Mass MoCA's largest gallery stood in various stages of completion, but it was not simply a random collection of stuff. Furthermore, the items in the gallery—many of them highly idiosyncratic—were procured and assembled at Büchel's direction.[18] In that sense even the so-called "Materials" reflected his artistic vision and creative contribution.

Curator Robert Storr's argument in support of Büchel was less polemic than Smith's, though he articulated many of the same ideas and concerns. He maintained that the museum's financial and logistical support was a form of patronage, which meant that the artist retained the authority to determine when and whether the work is disclosed to the public. His statement to the court reads, in part:

In my view, under no circumstances should a work of art be shown to the public until the artist has determined that it is finished. Speaking as someone who has commissioned or sponsored many comparable artistic projects, I strongly maintain that public institutions that act as sponsors for art projects should only do so with the full knowledge that those projects may not meet their expectations, and, in the end, may even prove unfeasible. No matter how much money may be spent on the creation of a work by an institution on behalf of their public, such sponsorship belongs to the category of patronage and does not buy that institution or its public any degree of ownership of or any proprietary rights over the project much less any decision making authority with respect its readiness for public presentation.[19]

---

[17] *Massachusetts Museum of Contemporary Art Foundation, Inc. v. Christoph Büchel,* No. 3:07-cv-30089-MAP. Roberta Smith claimed that the stalled installation in Gallery 5 did not look like a real "Büchel," but appeared to be just a collection of stuff.

[18] I should add that Büchel claims that the museum did not assemble all of the items in the way he requested or to his liking, and this charge of intentional distortion of his work is one of the issues that the appellate court determined must be decided by a jury trial. While I am not in a position of legal authority on this issue, having read all of the evidence submitted to the court, I find it abundantly clear that the museum understood itself to be acting on behalf of the artist and on his behest as well as they could under the circumstances, and within the limits imposed by the budget, building codes, and the circumstances of the collaboration.

[19] *Massachusetts Museum of Contemporary Art Foundation, Inc. v. Christoph Büchel,* No. 08–2199, R at A1273.

Storr does not display the same confusion as Smith concerning the art-status of an unfinished work of art. Nevertheless, he does assume—incorrectly—that a necessary condition for public display is that the artist regard the work as finished. Empirically, of course, this is not the case: museums display the preliminary sketches and unfinished works of artists all the time. Usually, however, those artists are dead.[20] Moreover, this principle is particularly difficult to apply in Mass MoCA's case, since the institution includes as part of its mission statement a commitment to showing artworks at all stages of production. Hence it is strange for Storr to assert that an art institution should only show finished artworks to the public, since curators in general regularly show unfinished works to the public, and Mass MoCA in particular makes a virtue of this practice.

Presumably he means to make a narrower claim, which is that institutions should not show unfinished works to the public over the living artist's protests. But why? In the case of finished works of art, we do not recognize this principle if the art object is owned by someone else. After all, artists regularly sell works that they later feel embarrassed by and wish they either had not made or could revise (just as philosophers publish essays that they later regret). But this does not give the artist the right to take the work back or to change it once it has passed into someone else's hands.[21] Once the artwork has been acquired by another, the artist relinquishes control over the work, even while retaining authorial ownership. The artist is not free simply to destroy or alter another's property, even if the work is 'his' insofar as he is its author. In other words, we must recognize that the artist's 'ownership' rights to a work of art that he or she has sold or given away are in fact much more limited than the rhetoric of artistic freedom would imply: it means that the artist has the right to be acknowledged as the author of the work and that it is a work that he at least at one time endorsed as good enough to attach his name and reputation to. Of course, in the Büchel case, the installation was

---

[20] Mass MoCA's lawyers pointed out that Storr did not behave in accordance with his own stated principles. In the 2007 Venice Bienalle that he curated, Storr presented a work by Felix Gonzalez-Torres that was found in the artist's studio after he died, and which had never been officially deemed "finished" by the artist. *Massachusetts Museum of Contemporary Art Foundation, Inc. v. Christoph Büchel* No. 08–2199, R at A1338.

[21] German and Italian moral rights law actually does permit this 'right of withdrawal' under certain circumstances. See Cyrill Rigamonti, "Deconstructing Moral Rights," *Harvard International Law Journal* 47, no. 2 (2006): 363.

unfinished and unendorsed, two key aspects of the work that only the artist can determine. It might seem that Mass MoCA had indeed violated his freedom by attempting to put it on display. The difference, however, is that Büchel undertook the generation of his work in a public, or semi-public setting, and at the financial and logistical expense of another. And that relationship, I argue, limits his freedom to withhold endorsement of the work he promised to produce.[22]

IV. Cakes and Control

We can begin to sort out the confusion between authorship and ontology if we consider the example of an unfinished cake. If Jones is in the process of making a cake and someone takes the cake and serves it to the waiting guests before he has finished frosting it, it is still a cake—an unfinished cake, but a cake nonetheless. Jones might protest that the prematurely served cake is not *his* cake, and by that he means that it is not the cake he had intended to serve; it does not reflect his final intentions for the cake. Notice, again, the close relation of completion and ratification: we expect and assume that the moment of ratification requires a complete work, and we also treat finished works as ipso facto ratified. And yet to say that the prematurely served cake is, indeed, cake, but not *Jones'* cake is misleading, because even the unfinished cake is the product of his cake-making decisions, intentions, and actions (chocolate and not carrot, three-tiered instead of two, and so on).[23] And so even the unfinished cake is 'his'; the

---

[22] One might argue that Storr is right: the museum's financial support should be thought of as an act of charity or patronage, and they should simply write off as a loss any unrealized works of art whose creation their grant was intended to enable. But several factors in this case weigh against seeing Mass MoCA's financial and logistical support as patronage plain and simple: they invested over one-third of their annual operating budget and nine months of labor on its realization, largely through the remote direction of the artist. This level of commitment indicates that the museum was expecting and even depending on Büchel to deliver an artwork that they could display at the end of the collaboration. Furthermore, the fact that Büchel walked away from the unfinished installation and demanded that Mass MoCA dispose of it at its own expense indicates that at least to some extent he did regard the assembled materials as their property, or at least their problem. The notion that the artist should have total freedom to use the museum's material resources in this way without any corresponding responsibilities either to deliver a finished and ratified work, to reimburse the museum's costs, or even to take responsibility for the disposal of the failed work's remains stretches the spirit and usual sense of what patronage entails. I thank an anonymous reviewer for raising this question.

[23] Let us leave aside for now the question of who bought the ingredients, cracked the eggs, etc.

problem is that it is not the cake he wanted to present to the world as 'Jones's cake,' and he might be unhappy that others will draw conclusions about his cake-making based on the unfinished cake they were served.[24] As the cake analogy shows, the issue in the Mass MoCA case is not the ontological status of the abandoned installation in Gallery 5, for it was clearly an unfinished work of art. Nor is Büchel's authority to transform objects into a work of art in question. Hence Smith's use of the Rauschenberg telegram to support her argument is misleading and inappropriate.

Of course, one might object that cakes and contemporary artworks are very different kinds of things and cannot be usefully compared. In some ways, they are indeed very different. Whereas no one, not even Rauschenberg, can turn a telegram into a cake, he might very well be able to turn it into a work of art. This is why Smith and Thompson mistakenly conflate the moment that the work of art is finished with the moment that it becomes art in the first place: when art can be made of anything and take almost any form, we understand the work to be whatever the artist has indexed as such. The art-status of some contemporary artworks, unlike cakes, is tied much more tightly to the artist's intentions regarding the disposition of the work. When visible inspection is insufficient to tell us whether something is a work of art at all, much less whether it is a finished work of art, we require the artist to provide an indication that he or she intends it to be seen as a work of art, as well as to tell us what, exactly, the work consists in. Timothy Binkley makes a great deal out of the moment of declaring a readymade work of art 'done' for this reason: it is the external indication that an object has undergone the shift in status from everyday object to artwork.[25]

The indexing conditions are different for more traditional kinds of art: if I attempt to paint a picture of my dog Salty, no such declaration is necessary for it to count as a work of (likely bad) art. But with readymades it is different, and Büchel's work makes extensive use of found objects. Thus it may seem as though Büchel's refusal to finish the installation at

---

[24] Büchel was very concerned about how the unfinished installation might affect his artistic reputation, not to mention the negative press coverage about the controversy. It seems to have been unfounded, however: in 2008 he was a finalist for the $100,000 Hugo Boss Prize for contemporary art.

[25] Timothy Binkley, "Piece: Contra Aesthetics," *Journal of Aesthetics and Art Criticism* 35, no. 3 (1977).

Mass MoCA meant that he was also withholding art-status from it, in a way that cannot be done with unfinished cakes. The fact that he expected the museum to deinstall and discard the unfinished work at its own expense as if it were simply a collection of junk would seem to support that interpretation. However, what is important about Büchel's refusal to declare it 'done' was not that its status as art depended on such a declaration but rather that he did not want to present a work to the public under his name that did not reflect his artistic intentions.

What makes the situation of dual ownership in the Mass MoCA case so much more complicated than the usual transaction between artists and their collectors is that the work was unfinished and unratified; hence, Büchel both did and did not claim authorship of the unfinished installation in Gallery 5. On the one hand, he was unhappy with the project and had no faith that it could be realized according to his wishes. He accused the museum of not following his instructions. Hence he did not want the work to be shown to the public as a 'Büchel' because he was not, and had never been, satisfied with it. In that sense, he disavowed authorship of the installation. On the other hand, he was unwilling to allow it to be shown under any circumstances—he would not permit it to be shown anonymously or with a disclaimer explaining its unfinished state, because he regarded the work as his artistic property even though it was the museum's physical property. So in a sense he did regard himself as the author of the unfinished piece.

It might seem wrong to allow Büchel to have it both ways, but we can make sense of this as case of interrupted authorship caught between the two moments identified in the dual-intention theory: he recognizes that he is to a large extent responsible for the generation of the work, and in that sense it is 'his', but he does not want to be associated with it as a work he endorses.[26] Smith toes this delicate line of both wanting to

---

[26] A similarly paradoxical claim was made by Henri Rousseau's heirs, in their 1971 lawsuit against Galeries Lafayette, the Paris department store. The store had used altered versions of Rousseau's paintings to decorate their store windows. The plaintiff complained both that Rousseau's moral rights were infringed by the misrepresentation of his work *and* that Rousseau was not credited because the displays were unsigned. John Henry Merryman, "The Refrigerator of Bernard Buffet," in *Thinking About the Elgin Marbles: Critical Essays on Cultural Property, Art, and Law* (Alphen aan den Rijn: Kluwer Law International, 2009), 413, fn 22. The logic here is similar to the Woody Allen joke about the old ladies at the Catskill resort who complained that not only was the food terrible, but the portions were too small.

acknowledge Büchel's ownership of the abandoned installation while at the same time sharing in his disavowal of it as 'his' when she says,

My first thought while walking along the tarps [covering the installation during the lawsuit] is that no one working at the museum had ever seen a finished Büchel . . . there may be parts of the installation proper that Mr. Büchel considers finished, but what is visible above and below the tarps is barely the skeleton of a Büchel. It's just a lot of stuff.[27]

Since Büchel's work is often designed to look precisely like a chaotic pile of "stuff," Smith is asserting her own authority as connoisseur when she claims to be able to discern the difference between a true 'Büchel' and the mere ingredients of one. Of course, if the installation, or certain parts of it, truly were just a collection of materials, then presumably the artist and his supporters should not have any grounds on which to refuse the museum the right to show it to the public. What is important here is not whether Smith really does know a real 'Büchel' when she sees one.[28] Rather, her position tacitly reflects what I have been calling the dual-intention theory of artistic authorship: she wants the artist to be able to claim ownership, and thereby control, over the materials in Gallery 5 without thereby having to recognize those materials as having been endorsed by the artist as a work he has authored. As is often the case, the designation of being 'finished' is conflated with the artist's second-order intention to endorse the work as his, since in practice published works are usually both finished and authorized.

As I argued in Chapter Three, what covaries in practice can easily come apart logically: finished works can be unauthorized, just as authorized works can be unfinished, and any combination can be made public. Smith's argument reflects the conventional assumption that an artist's baptism of the work as finished both guarantees its status as an artwork and is also a sign that the artist authorizes its display in public. But it is a mistake to focus on the unfinished state of Büchel's work in the Mass MoCA case, when in fact its status as finished or unfinished is not decisive. For presumably Büchel could have finished the artwork, been

---

[27] Roberta Smith, "Is It Art Yet? And Who Decides?," *The New York Times*, September 16, 2007.

[28] Such a claim also assumes that his work has a consistent, recognizable look that will be manifest in any of his future work, a corollary to the notion that artworks are tied to the innermost self of the maker.

unhappy with it, and still have insisted that he had the right not to allow the museum to display it. The question is thus whether Büchel has the moral right to prevent the display of an artwork—finished or not—with which he was never artistically satisfied, but which in an important sense he did not own.

Thinking back to the cake analogy, let us imagine that a talented pastry chef is invited to make a cake that is larger and more intricate than anything she could ever produce with her own resources. The chef agrees to produce a cake, and to serve it on a certain date. Imagine that you provide the eggs, the sugar, all the ingredients, the equipment, and the sous-chefs to help realize the cake. You even skip meals and cut back on your monthly food budget just to provide the resources the pastry chef requests to make this special cake. But the production of the cake does not go well. The chef is dissatisfied with it and pushes back the date of completion so as to have more time to get it right. She blames you for providing shoddy and inadequate ingredients, and for not providing adequate support. Eventually she is so fed up that she walks away and refuses to finish it, and refuses to serve what is there, even though next door there is a room full of hungry people waiting expectantly for the cake. The cake is edible, but it has not been frosted to the pastry chef's liking. At this point, you suggest that the unfinished cake will have to be served anyway, even though it is not 'her' cake—the cake she thinks would adequately represent her abilities and vision. But she demands that the cake be thrown away instead, because it is still 'her' cake, and she has the right to determine whether it is served. Robert Storr might suggest that the offer to provide financial and logistical support to the pastry chef should be understood as a no-strings-attached gift in support of the pastry chef-artist's freedom to make whatever she fancies, in the hope that we might benefit from the results. But it seems clear from the context, even in the absence of a signed contract, that your offer to pay for the making of the cake is not simply a grant: a considerable investment was made with the expectation that an edible cake would be the end result.

In the Mass MoCA case, we have a similar overlap of ownership, but with an unfinished and abandoned art installation: the institution paid for, procured, installed, and constructed the objects that made up Büchel's unfinished artwork. They owned and were responsible for the material that made up the work; he owned and was responsible for its immaterial aspect—the form or disposition of the work. The museum's attempt to show the installation to the public that Büchel refused to complete was not a usurpation of his authorship, but a reflection of the fact that they owned the artwork. Because Büchel attempted to make a work of art with someone else's resources, the attempted installation was never simply his property as it would be if he had made it in his own studio, with his own money, and his own labor.[29] In a way, my point is quite simple: the common, everyday distinction that we make between the owner of an artwork and the artist who made it can sensibly be applied to the Mass MoCA case: the museum did not claim that it was the author of the installation in Gallery 5. But it did own the artwork, and it therefore had the right to display it, in the same way that David Rockefeller can own a Rothko painting and have the right to display it, sell it, or give it away without thereby implying that he, Rockefeller, is its author.[30]

Before we turn to that question in the following section, one final consideration remains: what if Mass MoCA director Joe Thompson had treated the abandoned installation as "found art" and declared it to be a "Thompson" once Büchel had walked away? This possibility might also have motivated the lawyers' query whether Thompson considered himself to be an artist, under the assumption that only artists can turn everyday objects into art. (How one becomes such an artist in the first place is another question). While it is logically possible that Thompson or Mass MoCA could have treated Büchel's abandoned, unfinished artwork as one, big collective readymade and declared it a finished work of art, it would have been neither practical nor ethical to do so. Museums, after all, are in the business of showing artworks, not authoring them. Although Büchel had abandoned the work, it nevertheless reflected—albeit imperfectly—his vision and creative contribution. For another putative artist simply to claim the contents of Gallery 5 as his own work of art is not the same as Duchamp's appropriation of the urinal for *Fountain*, or even Sherrie Levine's appropriation of a Walker

---

[29] Readers might wonder why the contract between the artist and the institution did not prevent this dispute. In fact, there was no signed contract, which may be surprising but is in fact quite common in the art world.

[30] But does he have the right to use his Rothko painting as a bath mat? We will return to this question in section V.

Evans photograph. In the latter two cases, the objects appropriated were ontologically stable, and the act of appropriation became part of the meaning of the new artworks created. To claim authorship of Büchel's artwork simply because he no longer approved of it or cared to complete it is not a meaningful form of artistic appropriation; it is scavenging. While the readymade makes a hypothetical act of artistic scavenging logically possible, in this case there is no reason to think that Mass MoCA's proposal to show the contents of Gallery 5 amounted to an implied claim of appropriative authorship.

To assert one's right to present to the public the abandoned, unfinished project—be it cake or art—does not impinge on artistic freedom or authority; rather, it reflects the fact that one and the same object is owned by two parties at once, and in different respects: to display the unfinished and abandoned work against the artist's wishes is not to step in as author of the work, but is simply a reflection of the fact that in agreeing to allow Mass MoCA to sponsor the creation of his artwork the artist effectively sold the work before it was created.[31] This does not mean that the institution has the right to call the unfinished installation in their gallery a 'Büchel.' As I have argued with the dual-intention theory, the artist has the right to decide whether to disavow authorship of the unfinished— and even the finished—works that issue from his hand. The court made clear that Büchel could write and post an invective-free renunciation next to Gallery 5 publicly disavowing his authorship of its contents. Büchel argued that such a disclaimer would be ineffective because his role in the work's generation was already public knowledge. But the risk of making a work in the public sphere and at the institution's expense rather than in the privacy of the artist's own studio, as Büchel did with Mass MoCA, is that the artist risks being associated reputationally as the author of something she or he deems a failure because of the history of its generation.

One might argue that the cake analogy fails because a salient difference between cakes and works of art is that cakes are not a reflection of the chef's personhood in the same way that artworks are an extension of the artists who make them. This presumed intimate bond, after all, is

---

[31] This is not to deny that in some cases artists are granted no-strings-attached awards to realize their work. My point is only that the Mass MoCA situation was clearly not such a case.

behind the moral rights legislation that protects visual artists but not pastry chefs. My point in developing the cake analogy is to reject some of the idealization and mystification surrounding artists and their artworks. I have attempted to show, first, that unfinished works of art are nevertheless art just as an unfinished cake is still a cake. In neither case is it always clear at what moment in the process it ceases to be a collection of raw materials and begins to be an unfinished work or cake, but that does not mean that unfinished artworks do not exist and do not have authors. My second point was to show that we should not confuse the freedom of an artist (or cake maker) to refuse to finish the work with the freedom to refuse publication. In some situations, as when the work is owned by another, the artist abrogates that right just as he or she does when selling an already finished work.

V. The Destruction of Artworks

Christoph Büchel's demand that Mass MoCA discard his unfinished and abandoned art installation resulted in the destruction of an artwork that was reportedly very impressive and emotionally moving. Mass MoCA director Joe Thompson called it "the best unfinished artwork of the century" and "the *Guernica* of our time."[32] In his ruling, Judge Ponsor described at some length how impressive he found the exhibit:

I have to say, as I said before, I will not soon forget the opportunity to view Mr. Büchel's work, and regardless of whether I've done the right thing from the point of view of aesthetic ideology or from the point of the law, I do believe that this is an exhibition that deserves to be seen.[33]

When we talk about the destruction of Büchel's unfinished work, we must of course keep in mind that the installation was by nature temporary. It was made with the understanding that it would be dismantled and at least partially destroyed once the planned exhibition period was over.

---

[32] *Massachusetts Museum of Contemporary Art Foundation, Inc. v. Christoph Büchel,* No. 08–2199, R at A1108 and A1113. Because of his role as Mass MoCA's fundraiser and cheerleader, Thompson's remarks may sound more like good advertising than a serious aesthetic evaluation. In private conversation, however, he did confirm to me that one of the reasons why he persisted in trying to realize "Training Ground" was that he believed it to be the best work of art that Mass MoCA had ever produced.

[33] *Massachusetts Museum of Contemporary Art Foundation, Inc. v. Christoph Büchel,* No. 08–2199, R at A1701–1702.

Nevertheless, the fact that he refused to allow the museum to exhibit the work before its deinstallation and disposal amounted to its premature destruction. The judge's lament that the work would go unseen by the general public raises the question of whether the public should be able to prevent artists from destroying their own artworks.

The orthodox view of moral rights holds that artworks are an extension of the artist's personhood in a way that other sorts of objects are not. If this were so, then it would also seem that an artist could legitimately destroy his or her own work of art. And they do. Artists' studios are littered with discarded works that they have rejected, painted over, torn apart, or recycled for one reason or another. To say that it is wrong for any artist to ever destroy his or her creations is absurd. If I paint a portrait of my dog Salty and I am unhappy with the results, it seems obvious that I should be able to destroy the offending portrait with impunity. Indeed, we may actively encourage the destruction of bad art. (I will leave aside the vexed question of whether we can tell the difference between good art and bad art.)

On the other hand, when we imagine a culturally important artist such as Picasso or Frankenthaler destroying his or her own works, we recoil. Artists do not always know when their own works are finished, or whether they have aesthetic value. Kafka and Virgil, whose instructions to destroy their manuscripts after their deaths were ignored, are classic examples of this.[34] But are there any plausible arguments to support the intuition that aesthetically valuable works of art should not be destroyed, even by their own creators? In his article, "Destroying Works of Art," James Young makes this claim. He argues that Georges Rouault ought not to have destroyed 315 of his own paintings because, in a sense, good artists do not author their works:

> it is plain that an individual is never the sole cause, or creator, of an artwork. It is much more accurate to say that artworks, especially the best artworks, are the product of an artistic tradition. The individual artist is simply the last stage in a causal chain which has included many other artists. To suggest otherwise is to adopt an implausible Romantic conception of the artist as lonely hero . . . Since works are products of traditions, if artworks are owned, they are owned by

---

[34] Those cases are not strictly analogous because Virgil and Kafka did not destroy their own manuscripts, which they surely could have done if they had wanted to, but instead entrusted the deed to others.

traditions, by communities of artists. This being the case, it is absurd to suppose that individual members of traditions are free to dispose, as they see fit, of the products of that tradition.[35]

Young's reasoning here is akin to the argument that one ought not take one's own life because no one is the cause of her own existence, and hence does not have the right to destroy that existence. But we can agree with Young that artworks, like people, belong to a lineage, without at the same time going so far as to deny artists any agency or responsibility for the creation of their works, which is the implication of Young's argument here. His argument suggests that the best artists are just passive vehicles for a tradition that guides them in their creations and hence the tradition, not the artist, is the real author. Such a view is far more 'Romantic' than the notion that artists are more than just the efficient cause of their works, even when they do belong to an artistic tradition. Furthermore, Young's argument also implies that bad artists, such as amateur dog-portraitists, have more ownership of their works than good artists, such as Georges Rouault or Picasso, do. If this is so, it is not because good artists' works are actually owned or authored by the community of (dead) artists that came before them, as Young asserts. It is rather that their art has been embraced and claimed by the culture—the living community of non-artists—that values the work as significant.[36]

This is not to claim that the community is thereby an author or co-author of the work. However, we sometimes speak as though works of art are a form of communal property, even when privately owned by a collector or museum. In such cases only the cherished artists and artworks are meant, which is reflected in the law: VARA only protects the destruction of artworks of "recognized stature." We might expect that this applies to good or important works of art that are still in the possession of their makers. Should we be able to rush into Jasper Johns' studio and stop him from torching his own canvases? As much as we may want to, we cannot. So long as we recognize and value artworks

<hr />

[35] James Young, "Destroying Works of Art," *Journal of Aesthetics and Art Criticism* 47, no. 4 (1989): 372–3.

[36] Alan Tormey goes so far as to suggest that works of art themselves have rights: Alan Tormey, "Aesthetic Rights," *Journal of Aesthetics and Art Criticism* 32, no. 2 (1973). See also Francis Sparshott, "Why Works of Art Have No Right to Have Rights," *Journal of Aesthetics and Art Criticism* 42, no. 1 (1983).

because they are the result of an intentional process of an artist's creative activity, then we also have to permit artists to destroy their own works, so long as the artwork is not owned by anyone else. Only once it has passed into the public sphere can the culture at large claim an interest in the works' continued existence. In some cases, however, as with Christoph Büchel and Mass MoCA, a work of art has passed into the public sphere and out of the artist's hands before he has even begun to make it.

5

Boundary Issues
Reconsidering the Artist's Sanction

The normalization of the abnormal is an *a priori* principle of
excellence that applies to every artist. Henceforth, normality in art
consists of being outside of the norms.[1]

I. Sweets and Sanctions

The 1991 Felix Gonzalez-Torres work *"Untitled" (Portrait of Ross in L.A.)*
consists of a pile of small, multicolored, wrapped candies, weighing 175
pounds, in the corner of an art gallery. Viewers are invited to consume
the candies, thereby slowly diminishing the pile, which is to be continually replenished by the gallery. Since one does not usually touch (much
less consume) artworks on display in galleries and museums, it is not
clear when first encountering the work that one is invited to take a candy
from the pile. This kind of uncertainty is not uncommon in encounters
with contemporary art. The minimalist sculptor Carl Andre makes
artworks that one is tacitly permitted to walk on, for example, though
few visitors do.

Once it becomes clear that viewers are intended to take a candy from
the pile of *"Untitled,"* other questions arise. A text on the wall explains
that the "Ross" referred to in the title was Gonzalez-Torres' partner who
died of AIDS. The ideal weight of the candies corresponds to Ross's
weight when he was healthy. The slowly dwindling pile represents the
loss of his weight and vitality during the illness. The fact that the pile is

---

[1] Natalie Heinich, "The Van Gogh Effect," in *The Sociology of Art: A Reader*, ed. Jeremy
Tanner (London: Routledge, 2003), 125.

constantly replenished represents perpetual life.[2] While the wall text has given us some important keys to appreciating the symbolic function of the candies surely the information provided does not exhaust the possibilities for interpreting the work. As we search for further clues to our interpretation, we might wonder whether the specific kind of candy is essential to the work. We might ask further whether not only the flavor, but also the brand of candy is essential.

While this information is relevant to the interpretation of the work, it also has a practical significance for those who seek to purchase or exhibit it. What happens to the work if the candy factory goes out of business, or the wrapper design changes?[3] If the artist has indicated that the candy brand is a constitutive feature of the work, then the owner of such a work stands in danger of losing the work forever should the brand be discontinued. Since such works operate, often deliberately, outside of or against cultural and institutional norms, we cannot rely on our own assumptions and expectations to guide us in apprehending these works. We become unusually dependent upon the artist to tell us what is and is not essential so that we can see what properly constitutes the work of art.

This extra information from the artist might be necessary, for example, when dealing with new artistic media for which there is not yet a robust set of norms and conventions, such as the relatively recent genre of internet art. As a result, artists are sometimes called upon to be more explicit about their intentions for what, exactly, the work consists in and under what conditions it can be preserved.[4] In other cases, the artists themselves declare a work of theirs to have been ruined, not because the object itself has been irreparably harmed but because a condition of its display or appreciation has been altered. For example, in 2013 the artist James Turrell declared that one of his works at the Nasher Sculpture Center in Dallas, Texas, was destroyed because a forty-story

---

[2] A description of the work including these details can be found on the Art Institute of Chicago's website: http://www.artic.edu/aic/collections/artwork/152961?search_id=1. Accessed October 10, 2017.

[3] According to Ann Temkin, once the candies originally used to realize Gonzalez-Torres' work become unavailable, "[t]he museum might stop allowing people to take the candies (explaining in a label that they would once have been allowed to do so)." Ann Temkin, "Strange Fruit," in *Mortality/Immortality? The Legacy of 20th Century Art*, ed. Miguel Corzo (Los Angeles: Getty Conservation Institute, 1999), 48. I owe this reference to Sherri Irvin.

[4] See Amie Thomasson, "Ontological Innovation in Art," *Journal of Aesthetics and Art Criticism* 68, no. 2 (2010): 124.

high-rise was built in its sight line. Turrell's work, *Tending, (Blue)*, was part of his *Skyscape* series in which viewers are invited to enter a space and contemplate the sky through an opening in the ceiling. When a tower of luxury condominiums called *Museum Tower* was built in such a way that it intruded into the visitor's field of vision through the opening, Turrell objected, and the museum agreed to stop allowing visitors into the space. Apparently an unobstructed view of the sky is essential for *Tending, (Blue)* to be what the artist intended.[5]

II. Authorship and Sanctions

In Chapter Four, we examined the case of an artist who walked away from his unfinished art installation because he lost confidence in the ability and good will of the sponsoring museum to facilitate its realization to his satisfaction. This put him in the curious position of both asserting and disavowing authorship of the incomplete artwork that he abandoned in the museum's gallery: he did not want the work disclosed to the public because he did not like it, did not approve of it, and therefore did not want his name and reputation to be associated with it; on the other hand, he was unwilling to let the museum show the unfinished installation alongside a disclaimer in which he renounced his authorship. The artist saw the work as his intellectual property even as he withheld his full endorsement from it.

The dual-intention theory of authorship, presented in Chapter Two, can make sense of this puzzling stance. The artist recognized his authorship of the work in the genetic sense while still withholding his ultimate endorsement of it as fully authored by him. The artist and his supporters saw this as a principled stand for his freedom as an artist to be the sole authority in charge of the disposition of the work, its completion, ratification, and publication. While I agree that artists have the freedom to decide whether or not to accept a work as theirs, I argued in the previous chapter that the artist's control is curtailed when the work is undertaken at the significant material and logistical expense of an institution that was expecting—and to some extent depending on—the installation's successful

---

[5] Turrell did not just declare the work a ruin, however. He is working with the museum to create a new version with the clear sight-line restored. See http://hyperallergic.com/73609/how-to-destroy-a-james-turrell/. Accessed October 10, 2017.

completion. There are certainly cases of pure patronage for artists, but this was not such a case. Büchel had the right to disavow the work as his, but not to tell the museum what to do with the unfinished installation he abandoned in its gallery.

In the present chapter I examine another conflict between an artist and a museum, this time involving a finished work of art, called *Time and Mrs. Tiber*, which began to rot prematurely (and toxically). The principle at stake here is what philosopher Sherri Irvin has called the "artist's sanction," and the case study was used by Irvin to illustrate her theory. It concerns the artist's authority to determine the disposition of her artwork in cases where ordinary conventions and assumptions about what the work consists in will either be insufficient or incorrect. Normally the artist's sanction remains unstated and unquestioned as an implicit condition of artistic authorship. As with the norm of the finished work, we take it for granted that the artist has authority over the appearance of his artworks. It is just this responsibility for having made certain decisions and choices among a set field of options that we understand artistic authorship to consist in. The artist's sanction becomes necessarily explicit, however, in cases where the proper boundaries of the work or its constitutive features are ambiguous. As a theory it is particularly relevant to avant-garde works that contravene established norms for the disposition and treatment of artworks.[6] Irvin accurately points out that "mature critical practice with respect to contemporary art accords artists a significant degree of stipulative authority regarding the features and boundaries of their works."[7] As galleries and museums embrace artworks that defy or challenge audience expectations regarding not only appearance or material constitution but even the ontological status of the work, they have become particularly reliant on artists to make explicit the persistence conditions of the work.[8] In some cases, the stipulative authority granted to artists by art world institutions extends

---

[6] While some may assert that the term 'avant-garde' is no longer applicable to Western art made after the 1950s, I use it here in its generic sense to mean artworks that push, challenge, or violate established conventions, either in their message or in their very nature.

[7] Sherri Irvin, "The Ontological Diversity of Visual Artworks," in *New Waves in Aesthetics*, ed. K. Stock and K. Thomson-Jones (Basingstoke, UK: Palgrave Macmillan, 2008), 1.

[8] See Martha Buskirk, *The Contingent Object of Contemporary Art* (Cambridge, MA: MIT Press, 2005); Ben Lerner, "The Custodians: How the Whitney Is Transforming the Art of Museum Conservation," *The New Yorker*, January 11, 2016.

beyond that which the law recognizes. It is unlikely that James Turrell would have been able to convince a court that *Museum Tower* violated his moral right of integrity simply because it obstructed the view through *Tending, (Blue)*. Presumably the law would protect against unauthorized alterations to the viewing room that he designed, but would not recognize the work as plausibly staking claim on a column of airspace extending up from it for several thousand feet.

When successful, the artist's sanction names the artist's special authority to fix some features of an artwork through her actions and communications, in addition to those she gives to the art object itself. In her theory, Irvin's focus is on the explicit use of the sanction in contemporary artworks. As she recognizes, however, the artist's sanction is relevant to all artworks. In light of our analyses in previous chapters, we can see that completion and ratification are two essential moments in the authorship of a work that the artist sanctions in just the way that Irvin describes: not by making the work look a certain way, and not simply because she intends it to be so, but through her effective, practical decisions and communication.

The principle of the artist's sanction is different from the dual-intention theory of authorship, but they are closely related. Both concern the nature and limits of an artist's authority over her work. The principle of the artist's sanction articulates the artist's freedom to determine the features of her work even (and indeed especially) when it violates institutional and cultural norms for the display and treatment of art. It is thereby related to both the generative and evaluative moments of the dual-intention theory without residing simply within one or the other. An artist's decision, for example, to make an artwork out of perishable materials could be seen as part of the creation of the work, and hence belongs to the first, generative moment. This is logically separate from her evaluation of the work as good enough to count as having been authored by her. Irvin connects the artist's sanction to the generative moment when she says, "if we wish to be true to the nature of many contemporary artworks, we must appeal to information related to the artist's intention at relevant points during the work's production."[9] Irvin's point is that these sanctioned features of the work are just as

[9] Sherri Irvin, "The Artist's Sanction in Contemporary Art," *Journal of Aesthetics and Art Criticism* 63, no. 4 (2005): 315.

constitutive of it as the physical features of the object in which it inheres. Hence they are part of the work's generation.

On both a theoretical and practical level, the institutional acceptance of artworks with contra-standard features puts a great deal of pressure on the artist to specify what the artwork consists in, since the usual conventions do not hold. As Martha Buskirk explains,

> the freedom to draw from multiple sources can also be seen as a form of pressure, however, since under these circumstances no artist can escape the obligation of having to make a series of self-conscious decisions about issues that include format, medium, context, content, appearance, duration, and relationship to precedents, with each read as a conscious choice and no decision that can be taken as assumed or given.[10]

The decision to defy artistic convention may seem on the surface like a form of liberation, a sign of the artist's expressive freedom and liberation from ideological constraints. But it can also be a burden for artists and collectors alike, since nothing about the nature of the art object can be taken for granted. The notion that sanctions belong to the work's creation is complicated by the fact that in practice they are not always made explicit until after the work has been finished, endorsed, and sold to a museum or collector. The ex post facto nature of some artist's sanctions is an aspect of the theory that Irvin's own case study exemplifies, but which she does not fully explore the implications of. In the case of *Tending, (Blue)*, for example, does it matter *when* Turrell stipulated that the existence of his work depended on its offering a clear blue sky? If he had made this explicit when the Nasher Sculpture Center first acquired the piece, would such a stipulation have more weight than one that came years after the fact, when done in reaction to the new development? Would he have also objected if a tree had grown tall enough to obtrude into the space, or is it specifically the presence of the high-rise that he objects to? We do not know. On the one hand, Irvin regards the artist's sanction as belonging conceptually to the work's generation, and as having as much legitimacy as the features given by the artist's physical manipulation of the art object; on the other hand, her theory does not draw any distinctions between sanctions that the artist communicates when the work first leaves her possession and those that

---

[10] *The Contingent Object of Contemporary Art*, 12.

the artist makes in response to or in protest against some problem. As we will see, however, artists sometimes attempt to use their sanctioning authority as a defensive strategy to take a stand, for example, to protest the removal of a work (or the erection of a luxury high-rise).

In the world of contemporary visual art, where the contravention of institutional norms is not only commonplace but even (somewhat paradoxically) expected, the principle of the artist's sanction is an important means for artists to assert their authority over the disposition of their works. However, there are two main questions regarding artistic authority that Irvin's theory exposes but does not fully resolve: what are the limits of an artist's authority to sanction features of her artwork? And can we in fact maintain a clear distinction between the artist's declarations about the work's features and its proper interpretation? Irvin's theory hinges on the difference between the artist's declarations about the work's features, and his declarations about the proper meaning and interpretation of the work itself. She grants the artist authority over the former, but not the latter. "When artists make statements about messages purportedly conveyed by their works," she explains, "these statements typically have no more force than those of ordinary interpreters."[11] Irvin rejects the theory of actual intentionalism, which holds that artists' statements about the meaning of their works are determinative. We ought to consult the artist when questions arise about the conditions and parameters under which the work itself is to persist, but not about matters of meaning. As Irvin puts it, "although the artist's sanction plays a crucial role in fixing certain features of the work, the artist's intention, effectively expressed or not, does not fix the proper interpretation of the work."[12] In other words, the artist's sanction determines *what* is offered up for interpretation, but not *how* we interpret it. The artist's sanction is part of the creative act of making the work what it is, and serves as a discursive frame to delineate its boundaries. Ideally, interpretation presupposes and follows from an already existing artwork that the interpretation attempts to elucidate. Whereas the artwork features delineated by the artist's sanction are a product of the artist's effective intentions, the force of these intentions stop, as it were, at the boundaries of the artwork.

[11] "The Ontological Diversity of Visual Artworks," 5.
[12] "The Artist's Sanction in Contemporary Art," 325.

According to Irvin, there is no such thing as a failed sanction: they "are either successfully established or nonexistent."[13] By this I take her to mean that sanctions function like speech acts such as christening a ship or getting married: the declaration effectively changes the artwork by bestowing it with a feature that must be taken into account when apprehending and interpreting the work. But there are both practical and theoretical problems with an infallibilist stance toward artists' sanctions.[14] Museums, collectors, and the public at large may have an interest in preserving certain artworks as historical artifacts even when the artist has designed it to self-destruct over time. Or, as we will see in the case of artworks declared to be site-specific, the legitimate interest of owners and other stakeholders in removing an artwork from a certain location may clash with the artist's insistence that such a removal from the site is tantamount to the work's destruction. On a philosophical level, it raises the question of when we might reasonably reject an artist's declarations that his work has certain constitutive features, or that certain display conditions must be met in order for the work to be itself. The Nasher Sculpture Center accepted Turrell's assertion that *Tending, (Blue)* was ruined by the presence of the condominium high-rise. But it is not clear that they had to just because he said so.

In section III, I return to the case study that was the centerpiece of Irvin's initial exposition of her theory of the artist's sanction. I argue that the relation between sanction, intention, and interpretation is more complex and ambiguous than Irvin's theory allows. In section IV, I turn to a common use of the artist's sanction: site-specificity. I use Richard Serra's *Tilted Arc* controversy as well as the lawsuit *Phillips v. Pembroke* to show that the normative nature of artists' sanctions makes them weaker than other, more objective means of fixing work features. Both of these cases reveal instances of failed attempts by Serra and Phillips to index their sculptures as site-specific. Finally, in section V, I summarize my argument about the artist's sanction. Because it is not

---

[13] Ibid., 322.

[14] In a subsequent discussion of her theory, Irvin points out that there can be cases of sanctioning failure "if the artist makes contradictory statements, or expresses preferences that would be dangerous or impossible to carry out within the framework of the institution." I take this to mean that the attempt to sanction failed, not the sanction itself. See "The Ontological Diversity of Visual Artworks," 5–6. I thank my anonymous reviewers for calling this reference and point of clarification to my attention.

always possible to separate artists' declarations about the disposition of their works from statements about their meaning, there are limits to an artist's freedom to determine the constitutive features of her own work, particularly when those features are not physical properties of the object itself but normative claims about what features the work ought to be understood as having.

III. *Time and Mrs. Tiber* Reconsidered

A central feature of Irvin's presentation of her theory is a case study of an artwork by Canadian artist Liz Magor called *Time and Mrs. Tiber* (1976). I want to discuss it in some detail here because a careful reconsideration of Irvin's analysis will reveal some of the problems with the theory of the artist's sanction. *Time and Mrs. Tiber* consisted primarily of a wooden cupboard, stocked with jars of homemade preserves, some of which were found by the artist in an abandoned house, and some of which were prepared by the artist herself. As Irvin explains, National Gallery of Canada acquired the work in 1977 for its collection, but the contents of the jars soon began to degenerate. The jars that Magor had prepared developed botulism and were discarded because of the health hazard they posed to museum employees. The contents of others rapidly degenerated into an unsightly brown mush.[15]

Upon learning of the problem with the work, Magor's initial response to National Gallery conservators was that the work should be discarded once it could no longer be exhibited. Essentially, she instructed them to destroy the work. However, the institution did not want to de-accession a work from its collection, and encouraged the artist to find another solution that would enable it to preserve the jars of preserves. (One wonders why an institution unwilling to de-accession works from its collection would acquire a perishable work of art in the first place. We will return to this point below.) In the end, after further negotiation with the museum, Magor sanctioned some changes to the jars of preserves that would enable the museum to keep *Time* (or so they thought) rather than just discard it. She agreed to the addition of chemical preservatives to the remaining jars, she prepared some new ones using proper canning

---

[15] "The Artist's Sanction in Contemporary Art."

techniques to replace the toxic ones, and she permitted the work to be archived in the institution's "Study Collection" once it was no longer suitable for public view.

These measures were taken so that the National Gallery could keep *Time* in its collection. According to Irvin's analysis, however, these decisions and interventions, because the artist sanctioned them, "clearly changed the work," and therefore must be taken into account in subsequent interpretations of it.[16] Irvin offers this case study as an example of how the artist's instructions to the museum about the contents and location of *Time's* constitutive objects actually changed the artwork itself because it would no longer decay in the same way and at the same rate that the work originally would have. This makes sense in light of our observation in Chapter Three that an artwork's status as 'finished' serves an important function as an indication that the work has become ontically sealed off as 'the work itself,' to use Becker's phrase. Philosophers tend to assume that artwork completion is a transformative moment in the generation of an artwork. According to this view, if an artist sanctions changes to her work after it has already been completed, then the work itself has been altered. On the other hand, if the museum had made these changes without consulting the artist, the work itself would not have changed, but our access to it would, in the same way that a damaged painting makes it difficult to encounter the work as the artist intended it to be but does not alter the work itself.

In her analysis, Irvin implies that Magor's initial response to the museum—to throw the jars away—was the only response that was consistent with the original meaning and intent of the work. She says, "with regard to the decision that the work should not be discarded but transferred, I take the view that the artwork was altered in a way that alters, in turn, the range of appropriate interpretations of the work."[17] This leads to the surprising and ironic result that the National Gallery's attempts to maintain *Time* in their collection failed, even though, and indeed *precisely because*, they secured the artist's sanction and cooperation in their interventions to try to preserve the jars of preserves. While the National Gallery's board of trustees might have rested easy once the artist permitted the preservation of her work and they no longer had to

---

[16] Ibid., 324.   [17] Ibid.

face the first-ever de-accessioning of an item from their collection, if Irvin is correct, they are mistaken—they no longer have the work they originally acquired, but some altered version of it or a new work completely.[18]

This is because Irvin regards the original *Time* as an artwork whose meaning is contingent on both its future projected rate of active decay and its location. Originally *Time* was perishable; now, with the artist's permission and cooperation, it is to be preserved indefinitely. As she puts it, "initially, the work had the feature that its associated object would one day deteriorate and be discarded; now it has the feature that the object will be preserved indefinitely."[19] Irvin understandably views this as a significant change to the work itself that results in a different range of interpretations. As I see it, however, the changes to the art object enabled the museum to have the objects that both parties thought it had when *Time* was first acquired: jars of preserves that would last decades, not months. While the work was made of perishable materials, it was not meant to decay so rapidly and in such a toxic fashion as it did. We can just as plausibly see the sanctioned interventions as a repair to the work rather than an alteration of its essential features. As Irvin points out, when she sold it, Magor believed that the jars of preserves would last at least fifty years. Thus it seems safe to say that when the National Gallery acquired *Time*, both the museum and the artist assumed that the preserves would last for a reasonably long time after the Gallery's acquisition of the work. The museum probably also assumed, rightly in my view, that archiving the work in its Study Collection once the jars became unsightly was not only within their rights as owners of the work, and hence did not require the artist's permission, but that its location would not affect its meaning. This explains why the National Gallery was willing to acquire the work in the first place, despite their policy against de-accessioning pieces of their collection. Another way to understand the case is that the work was underspecified when the National Gallery first acquired it.

---

[18]   In both the Mass MoCA and the National Gallery of Canada cases the problem of the artist's sanction arose in part because the institutions took on more than the traditional role of simply exhibiting a work. In Mass MoCA's case, they also acted as patron, producer, and collaborator. In the National Gallery's case, as Irvin sees it, they are a kind of conceptual collaborator, whereby a constitutive feature of the work is that it violates institutional norms even as it belongs to and is exhibited by the institution.

[19]   Irvin, "The Artist's Sanction in Contemporary Art," 322.

When the jars of preserves became toxic and unsightly, Magor was asked to further specify what the work consisted in, and, upon the Gallery's urging, she sanctioned some interventions that would permit the museum to keep rather than discard the work, even going so far as to 'remake' some of its preserves.

The question at stake in the Magor case, and in the theory of the artist's sanction generally, is the extent to which artists have the authority to determine the constitutive features of their artworks, particularly when those works deliberately violate institutional defaults. Normally, for example, the location of an artwork is irrelevant to its meaning: I can hang my Monet painting anywhere I like and its nature is unaffected. The question, then, is what an artist would have to do to effectively make an artwork whose location is an essential feature. Irvin claims that artists are able to provide their artworks with certain features through success-ful acts of sanctioning. These declarations are normative: they prescribe how the artwork should be understood (as site-specific, for example), or how the art object should be treated (e.g., whether it is to be eaten, walked on, discarded after a certain period, replenished, and so forth). These sanctions also have illocutionary force: they do not just describe how the artist intends for the artwork to be treated or understood; rather, they actually cause the artwork to have the essential feature in question. In other words, the sanctions are constitutive, not just regulative.[20] In the Turrell case, he claimed that *Tending, (Blue)* was dependent on the surrounding location not being developed to include tall buildings, and the museum agreed.

How do we decide whether to regard the sanctioned interventions to *Time and Mrs. Tiber* as a repair to the work, an increase in specificity, or as a fundamental alteration to the work itself? Irvin asserts that Magor's cooperation with the museum to preserve *Time* resulted in an alteration not only of its constitutive objects, but also of the work itself that must be taken into account in subsequent interpretations. While it seems fair to infer this based on the perishable materials used in *Time and Mrs. Tiber*, the situation is more complicated than Irvin's statement makes it seem. After all, it bears noting that those perishable objects were jars of *preserves*. Irvin points to the title of the work, the jars of preserves, and

---

[20] I owe this clarification to an anonymous reviewer.

the artist's own statements as support for her claim that "any adequate reading of the work must identify decay as one of its central themes."[21] In her analysis, Irvin relies on the artist's testimony about her intended meaning, as well as Magor's initial instruction to the museum—*after* the jars developed botulism—to simply discard the jars and hence the work, as warrants for her claim that Magor's subsequent sanctions changed the work irrevocably.

Although Irvin denies that her theory commits her to actual intentionalism, it is worth noting that she appeals to statements by the artist in order to support her interpretation.[22] She says, "from the beginning, Magor said that this work is about decay and about our attempts, always doomed, to preserve ourselves and other things against the injurious effects of time."[23] Since Irvin argues that her theory of the artist's sanction does not commit her to AI, strictly speaking she should not use this kind of evidence to draw her inference that decay is a central theme of *Time*. I point out this inconsistency not in order to make an ad hominem attack, but because Irvin appeals the artist's declaration about the meaning of her work in order to support her claim about its nature, its essential features. And yet this contradicts Irvin's claim that artists' sanctions are qualitatively different from declarations about the intended meaning of the work. The former determine the nature of the work itself; the latter, for adherents of AI, determine correct interpretation of the work. The appeal to Magor's declaration about her intended meaning for *Time* lends authority to Irvin's focus on the decay of the work as central to its meaning, but it also shows that artists' attempts to sanction features of their artworks are subject to interpretive scrutiny, something that Irvin wants to deny. It also requires her to downplay the significance of Magor's acknowledgment that she had expected the work to last about

---

[21] Irvin, "The Artist's Sanction in Contemporary Art," 324.

[22] There are many different versions of actual intentionalism (AI), too numerous to cite and explain here. Suffice it to say that it is often contrasted with hypothetical intentionalism (HI). One of the main differences between the two positions, and the one most relevant to Irvin's argument, is that AI holds that artists' pronouncements about the meaning of their work can be determinative, whereas HI holds that artists' statements about the meaning of their own artworks should not be consulted and that they are not determinative of meaning. Irvin wants to insist that artist's sanctions, while they take the form of public declarations, are able to determine what constitutes the work itself, but that this is altogether different from a comment on what they intended the work to mean.

[23] Irvin, "The Artist's Sanction in Contemporary Art," 317.

fifty years. Notice that this latter statement by the artist is *not* an interpretive claim, but rather a statement about her beliefs and intentions concerning the object's physical state. Why does Irvin, who rejects AI,[24] lean so heavily on Magor's assertion that the work is about "decay," even when the artist herself admits that she did not mean for the jars to decay as fast as they did?

Furthermore, a silent assumption of Irvin's analysis seems to be that *Time and Mrs. Tiber* is only "about" decay if its constitutive objects are actively decaying, and that it is only "about" the violation of institutional norms if it is actively violating them. And yet works of art do not need to be actively decaying in order to be "about" decay, mortality, or the passage of time: vanitas paintings are proof of this.[25] Furthermore, the claim that the work is "about" decay still leaves undetermined just what rate and degree of decay are essential to the work, if any. Indeed, because the work consists of preserved vegetables and fruit, we might reasonably infer that the work is as much "about" the preservation of perishable objects as it is about "decay."[26] The point here is that our understanding of the relation between the object's actual decay, its intended rate of decay, and the significance of both the real and projected rates of decay for the meaning of the work will then inform how we understand Magor's decision to permit the museum to rescue *Time and Mrs. Tiber* from an untimely demise. I suspect that Irvin's theory is designed to articulate precisely that insight.[27] But there is a considerable amount of play here in how we understand the relative weight of these factors in determining the correct interpretation of the work, especially in the absence of a contract between the artist and the museum at the time of *Time's* acquisition. This calls into question the theory's assumption that

---

[24] See Sherri Irvin, "Authors, Intentions, and Literary Meaning," *Philosophy Compass* 1, no. 2 (2006).

[25] The notion that the work is about decay because some of its constitutive objects are decaying, and because it violates Western cultural norms to make perishable sculptures has been referred to as "exemplification" and "contextual implicature" by Carroll. See Noël Carroll, "Cage and Philosophy," *Journal of Aesthetics and Art Criticism* 52, no. 1 (1994).

[26] We should also pause to notice here the vagueness of the preposition "about" when speaking of artwork meaning. This trope is particularly prevalent in the context of contemporary visual art, and this is due, I think, to the inherent difficulty of translating visual meaning into language.

[27] See, for example, her useful comparative analysis of different hypothetical versions of *Untitled (Ross in L.A.)* in Irvin, "The Ontological Diversity of Visual Artworks."

interpretations follow from a stable, unambiguous set of features bestowed upon the work—either in speech or in deed—by the artist. In this case, her interpretation of the projected original work is what drives Irvin's assertion that Magor's sanctions fundamentally altered the work, and thereby its meaning.

Furthermore, Irvin's analysis of the Magor case hinges on her premise that this violation is an essential feature of *Time*—a feature that is then altered once Magor sanctions the museum's preservation of the artwork, thereby cooperating with institutional norms rather than flaunting them. Irvin regards the National Gallery of Canada as in principle incapable of determining the proper way to manage this particular work in its collection. As Irvin explains it:

> to regard the work's features as being fixed by institutional policies will result in a serious misapprehension. Those policies will not settle which rate of deterioration is relevant to the interpretation of the work. In fact, they will get it exactly wrong. An important feature of the work, especially before Magor changed her view, is its violation of institutional defaults. Magor's work is in specific tension with the institutional will to immortalize (or at least mummify) the art object, and so simply to apprehend the work in accordance with the institution's default practices, without considering the artist's sanction in relation to those practices, would be a mistake. It is the artist's sanction, not the default policy or practice, that fixes the features of the work that must be apprehended and then considered for purposes of interpretation.[28]

As I have pointed out, the Magor piece was not *simply* in violation of or in tension with the institutional will to mummify artworks. Had it been made of fresh fruits and vegetables, that would be a more plausible interpretation. Because it was originally intended to be made of successfully sealed jars of preserves, it seems better to see the work as a commentary on or satire of that institutional practice. The behavior of the museum once the jars began to decay at an unexpectedly rapid rate shows that they, too, respect the artist's authority to sanction repairs or changes to the work rather than simply consulting institutional norms for conserving works. After all, once the work is their property, one might argue that they should be able to care for it and store it however they see fit.[29] It is also important

---

[28] "The Artist's Sanction in Contemporary Art."

[29] Curator and art historian Ivan Gaskell argues along these lines. He insists that institutional interests must take the artist's intentions into account, but they are not bound to them: "In the present, at any given time, an artwork is subject to the interests

to note that the most salient institutional norm governing this case is not the National Gallery's default policy for handling perishable artworks, but the fact that its default policy was to consult the artist and negotiate with her until they received her sanction.

Irvin's theory assumes that artist's sanctions will be relevant to, and will in fact determine, plausible interpretations of the work, but not the other way around. And yet her analysis of the *Time* case shows what her theory wants to deny: the line of influence between artist's sanctions and interpretations is more of a hermeneutic circle than a unidirectional vector. The features of the work that are deemed essential to it and which are fungible will depend in part on what the work is seen in advance to be "about."[30]

Irvin presents this case as an illustration of the ability of artists to create at least some features of an artwork through effective forms of communication and behavior. Yet one of the difficulties here is that this is a situation where the artist has intervened after the work was ostensibly finished because of flaws in its construction. In this respect the *Time and Mrs. Tiber* case is similar to another, more notorious case of art that was initially made of improperly preserved biological material. Damien Hirst's *The Physical Impossibility of Death in the Mind of Someone Living* (1999) consists of a shark suspended in a tank of formaldehyde. It had already begun to decompose when he sold it to Steve Cohen for eight million dollars in 2004. As the tank became filled with decaying organic matter, the question arose whether it would be acceptable to replace the shark and liquid with a new, and properly preserved shark. Because it is relatively unusual for artworks to consist of embalmed animals, it was

of a community, and the curator's responsibility is to that community rather than to the artist alone. The good use of artworks cannot be confined to the elucidation of artists' intentions in either making or disposing of them . . . artworks are not so much expressions of ideas as objects of visual interest. As such, and as objects that change over time in unpredictable ways that can enhance as well as detract from their aesthetic and other interesting qualities, a curator's practice should be governed by putting those objects to good use." Ivan Gaskell, "Being True to Artists," *Journal of Aesthetics and Art Criticism* 61, no. 1 (2003): 53.

[30] As Lamarque points out, this does not commit us to what Robert Stecker calls the constructivist's dilemma, because it does not claim that interpretations can determine the properties of objects, but rather they pick out the salient features of works. Peter Lamarque, "Object, Work, and Interpretation," *Philosophy in the Contemporary World* 12, no. 1 (2005): 6.

unclear, on the face of it, whether the artwork essentially consisted of the original shark, or whether the shark could be changed out, like a light bulb, as needed. As with the Magor case, the artist's sanction was sought by the owner once the work was in a state of crisis. In both cases, their decisions to permit the replacement of the befouled art object were compared against their presumed original intent for the work. Whereas Irvin judges the interventions into *Time's* constitutive objects to be incompatible with the original intention of the work, at least one scholar has argued that in Hirst's case the original shark was not essential to the work, and that, even though the work is about death and decay, its ongoing replacement in fact enhances its meaning.[31] Others complained, however, that the replacement shark was not as scary-looking as the original.

Both of these cases illustrate the limits of the artist's sanction: on the one hand, owners of artworks seek the ratification of repairs to art objects by the artists whenever possible; the artists have special authority over the works as their creative property, and hence are the only ones allowed to intervene in and possibly alter the work.[32] At the same time, however, in both the Magor and the Hirst cases, their decisions to allow the replacement of rapidly decaying art objects were not simply accepted, but judged against other contextual and interpretive cues in order to determine whether their respective decisions were true to the original work. Despite the artist's special authority as the creator of the work, it becomes a question for interpretation whether the artist has in fact violated his or her own original intention for the work.

---

[31] Lange-Berndt evaluates Hirst's decision to permit the replacement of the shark and concludes that, even though the work is in a sense about death and decay, it is not inconsistent with the concept of the piece: "The substitution of the shark does not contradict the concept of this group of works [the *Natural History* series] at all—on the contrary, it strengthens the desired effect of mass production. The substitution of the animal should thus not be rated as a surrogate of an original but as a remake . . . a continuity of performance." Petra Lange-Berndt, "Replication and Decay in Damien Hirst's *Natural History*," Short Discussion Document, *Tate Papers*, no. 8 (2007), http://www.tate.org.uk/research/publications/tate-papers/08. Accessed September 10, 2017.

[32] The widespread practice of consulting the artist, whenever possible, before restoring an artwork helps to ensure its provenance and ensures against moral rights violations, but it also has some practical downsides. It is not surprising, for example, that an elderly British sculptor may not recall accurately, in 2012, what precise paint shade a given piece made in the 1960s, with the help of assistants, was. He may not remember that decades earlier he authorized the addition of hidden feet welded to the base of the sculpture so that it could sit in the landscape properly. See https://www.thenational.ae/arts-culture/art/artist-anthony-caro-disowns-his-own-sculpture-1.414843. Accessed October 10, 2017.

This brings us to two points. First, as Buskirk's quote in section II suggests, artists cannot be expected to anticipate ahead of time all of the parameters of the work that need to be stipulated. In both the Hirst and Magor cases, the artists were unaware at the time of the sale of the work that the biological material in their art objects had been inadequately preserved. To ask what the sanctioned replacement of the object means with respect to the original intended features of the work is to overlook the fact that artists may not give any consideration to the preservation conditions of their works at the time that they send them out into the world. Indeed, they may not have any definite answers (or care) whether it violates their original intentions, because there may not in fact have been any intentions regarding certain features of the work one way or the other at the time of its creation or publication.[33] Second, while sanctioned features are supposed to logically precede interpretations, in cases where they occur after the work has been finished, the artist may have the authority to sanction interventions with respect to the art object, but it can be a matter of interpretation and debate whether the artwork has been altered or not by the sanctions.

Irvin's infallibilist account of the artist's sanction overlooks the fact that artists' sanctions are susceptible to interpretation, debate, and even rejection, just as artist's statements about the meaning of their work are. But this indeterminacy seems to be exactly what Irvin attempts to avoid by making her distinction between sanctions and interpretations in the first place. In section IV, I will consider two more controversial cases in which artists have tried and failed to determine artwork features through verbal declarations.

IV. Site-Specificity

Although there are purportedly different kinds of site-specificity, in general it means that the location or environment of the art object is an essential element in the work.[34] The existence of the artwork is then dependent on its intended location in a way that contravenes the usual

---

[33] Cf. Carol Vogel, "When Modern Art Shows Its Age, Conservators Struggle to Reconstruct the Fragile and Ephemeral," *New York Times*, April 5, 2001.

[34] See Jason Gaiger, "Dismantling the Frame: Site-Specific Art and Aesthetic Autonomy," *British Journal of Aesthetics* 49, no. 1 (2009).

expectation that the object is self-contained and that its meaning is unaffected by its site. Since this contra-standard feature is not always evident through visual inspection of the object, it is up to the artist to inform the public that this is the nature of the work.[35] Advocates of site-specific public art often contrast it with so-called 'plop art,' a derogatory term used for public artworks that can presumably be placed anywhere without any essential change to their meaning.

In this section I will discuss two cases of the artist's sanction involving claims to site-specificity: Richard Serra's *Tilted Arc,* and the case of *Phillips v. Pembroke Real Estate.* I argue that both of these cases reveal failed attempts to sanction the art object's location as an essential feature of the work. This is for two reasons: first, as we will see, the artists themselves do not provide consistent public declarations about the nature of their artworks as site-specific. More importantly, however, because they are not properties of a material object, but in a feature given to the work through a verbal declaration, these features are weaker than other, more objective features of the work. In fact, even though these statements are claims about the nature of the artwork rather than its meaning, a distinction that is crucial for Irvin, I argue that they incur many of the same liabilities of the view that artists' pronouncements about work meaning are determinative. In fact, some declarations that would fall under the category of artists' sanctions are logically indistinguishable from declarations about artwork meaning. Second, the inherent weakness of the artist's sanctions regarding these features is reinforced by the fact that critics, viewers, and judges rejected Serra and Phillips' respective claims to site-specificity. This, too, shows that artists can, in fact, fail to give their artworks the feature of site-specificity simply by insisting that it be seen and treated that way.

Perhaps the most notorious case of an artist insisting on his authority to sanction the art object's site as an essential feature of his artwork is Richard Serra's *Tilted Arc.* In 1979 American sculptor Richard Serra was commissioned to design a sculpture for New York City's Federal Plaza. His design, which was approved by the commissioning body, was to place a ten-foot high, one-hundred-and-twenty foot long piece of rusted

---

[35] Irvin mentions site-specificity in the introduction of her essay in such a way that suggests she regards it as an instance of the artist's sanction. Irvin, "The Artist's Sanction in Contemporary Art," 315.

Cor-Ten steel through the space. Immediately upon its installation in 1981, the work was controversial. The *Arc's* detractors claimed that it was not only aggressively unattractive, but that it rendered the plaza unusable by the employees who work in the surrounding buildings. Rejecting the offer by nearby Storm King Art Center to transfer the piece to its grounds, Serra argued that *Tilted Arc* was site-specific. Because the arc's placement in the plaza was an intrinsic feature of the work, he insisted that the relocation of the object would result in the artwork's destruction. After years of petitions, debates, editorials, and hearings, Serra's sculpture was eventually removed from the plaza, over the artist's (and his supporters') vehement protests, in 1989.[36]

I mention this case not to reopen the discussion about the nature of public art, which is the context in which it is usually raised, but simply to offer two observations, both related to the artist's sanction. First, there is some evidence that Serra contradicted himself by declaring the work to be site-specific. The contract that he signed with the commissioning body (the Arts-in-Architecture program of the US Government Services Agency) gave them permission to move the sculpture and put it in the Smithsonian.[37] While commentators on the controversy have focused on the GSA's violation of Serra's contract, insofar as they approved his sculpture and then later removed it, Serra seems to have violated his own prior approval to allow the work's relocation, because he later forbade the removal of the work from the Plaza. This suggests that Serra had initially viewed the location of *Tilted Arc* as an extrinsic or inessential property of the work, but then later changed his mind once the controversy erupted. While there is nothing wrong with a sculptor changing his mind about the importance of a sculpture's site to its meaning, it does pose problems for the artist's sanction if we are to regard such declarations as determinative (and not merely suggestive) of artwork properties. Surely a signed contract is more binding than a post-hoc declaration.

The claim that a site-specific artwork will be destroyed if its constitutive object is relocated was also used in the 2006 lawsuit between the sculptor David Phillips against Pembroke Real Estate, Inc. In 1999,

---

[36] The literature on this controversy is substantial, so I will not rehearse the details at length here.

[37] Buskirk, *The Contingent Object of Contemporary Art*, 49.

David Phillips, along with three other artists, was commissioned by Pembroke Real Estate to create a public sculpture park with a nautical theme in the South Boston Waterfront District. The sculptures and stone walkways that made up the design of Eastport Park were installed in 2000, but in 2001 Pembroke decided to redesign the park because of design and maintenance problems. They hired a landscape artist to redesign the park, who suggested that they remove Phillips' sculptures. Phillips filed suit in federal court, citing the 1990 Visual Artists' Rights Act, which prevents the mutilation or destruction of artworks of recognized stature.[38] This was one of the first cases in which an artist sued on the basis of VARA, which had not yet been passed by Congress during the period in which the removal of *Tilted Arc* was being considered.

Despite Pembroke's offer to relocate the artworks, Phillips claimed that the free-standing sculptures and decorative stone walkways "are meaningful only if they remain in Eastport Park, the location for which they were created."[39] He argued that not only was each piece of work in the park site-specific, but all of the elements in the park made up one large gestalt, one integrated site-specific work: "if [keeping all of my work in the Park] means that Eastport Park must be declared to be an inviolate work of art [as a whole], then so be it."[40] In other words, Phillips argued that, if necessary, he would assert that the park as a whole, including the work of the other artists, was a single work of integrated, site-specific art. In this case, we see that Phillips overestimates the extent of his artistic authority.

Firstly, it is unlikely that Phillips has the authority to declare the work of other artists as part of a single, integrated, site-specific work. Furthermore, we see the instrumental nature of Phillips' attempt to declare the objects in the park to be site-specific: like Serra, he wields his artist's sanction after the work has been created and installed, once the work was threatened with removal. Just as artists may be asked to sanction the replacement or repair of art objects in order to please collectors, in other cases they may use their authority to sanction work features as an act of defiance against the object's owners. In the Turrell, Magor, Serra, and Phillips cases we see that the artists were willing to change or invent sanctions in response to a given set circumstances. The phrasing of

---

[38] *Phillips I*, 288 F.Supp.2d.   [39] Ibid., 43.   [40] Ibid., 47.

Phillips' statement, in which he suggests that he will declare the objects in the park to be site-specific if doing so will prevent their removal, is revealing. It treats the declaration of site-specificity as a kind of trump card to be exercised at will in the artist's dispute with the park's owners, rather than as a feature of the work just as fixed and objective as the bronze crabs and spiraling stone designs that made up Phillips' material contributions to the park landscape.

I am not suggesting that artists lack integrity, are mendacious, or act to abuse their authority. Rather, what is in question is the nature of the artist's sanction as a binding illocutionary act, as something that has the power to determine artwork features as strongly as the art objects themselves: as we can see in both the Serra and the Phillips cases, their assertions that the works were site-specific arose only once the removal of the work was threatened. In the Serra case, it seems to have contradicted his earlier contractual agreement to allow the relocation of the object. In the Phillips case, his sanction is contingent on the circumstances surrounding the location of the work; it seems to have arisen in response to his frustration that Pembroke is no longer pleased with his designs for Eastport Park, and wielded as a threat to prevent its alteration. The feature of site-specificity is sometimes spoken of in high-minded conceptual terms, as a way in which the artwork has been "liberated" from the "modernist constraints" of earlier art practices that prized the self-contained, self-sufficient work of art.[41] In both the Serra and Phillips cases, however, the motivation for claiming that the work is site-specific is not so much conceptual as it is defensive: they want to prevent the relocation of their art objects, and claiming that the site is equally part of the work is a way to stake a kind of spiritual ownership over a piece of land that the artist does not have any material claim to.

One might object that it makes absolutely no difference what motivates the artist's assertion that his work is site-specific; the point is only that the artist has the authority to declare it so. The fact that artists' sanctions may be motivated by factors other than an artist's single-minded concern for the realization of his artistic vision is not in and of itself a problem. However, the notion that we ought to accept these declarations as just as powerful in determining features of the work as

---

[41] Gaiger, "Dismantling the Frame: Site-Specific Art and Aesthetic Autonomy," 46.

the art objects themselves stretches credibility. Irvin explicitly compares the features fixed by artists' sanctions to the physical features of an artwork, asserting that they have an equivalent status: "the artist's sanction, even when it is established through means other than presenting an object with particular features, plays an ontological role in fixing features of the artwork. For this reason, information about the sanction is often critical to the apprehension of a contemporary work."[42] Serra and Phillips both invoked the same analogy of a sculpture's relation to its site being akin to the paint on a canvas when arguing that their sculptures' location was an intrinsic feature of the work. Serra reportedly claimed that *Tilted Arc* had "a proprietary claim upon the plaza just as real as that of a painting to its canvas."[43] In the Pembroke lawsuit, sculptor David Phillips argued that "taking the sculpture from [Eastport Park] and locating it on a private campus in Rhode Island not near the ocean . . . would be like painting over the background landscape in the Mona Lisa."[44] Both of these analogies make use of the paradigm example of an artwork as an easel painting in order to advance their case that the site is an essential feature of the artwork. In the first example, Serra suggests that *Titled Arc* is the paint to Federal Plaza's canvas. In the second one, Phillips does not mention the canvas but focuses just on the painted features of an iconic painting: his sculptures are the figure (the portrait) and the park in which they are located is the painted background. While their analogies use different points of comparison, both of them attempt to draw upon our intuitions about paintings in order to advance the case that the site is inextricable from the object in their respective works of art. (And by invoking the Mona Lisa, Phillips is perhaps suggesting that the destruction of *his* artwork would be a similar case of iconoclasm.)

And yet neither analogy succeeds. In Serra's case, he compares Federal Plaza to the canvas in which a painting is made, presumably because they are physically inextricable once the painting is finished. But because the canvas itself is blank, featureless, and interchangeable, the analogy does

---

[42] Irvin, "The Artist's Sanction in Contemporary Art," 320.

[43] Quoted by Rep. Ted Weiss during the hearings to decide whether *Tilted Arc* would be removed. Alex Neill and Aaron Ridley, eds., *Arguing About Art: Contemporary Philosophical Debates* (New York: Routledge, 2007), 399.

[44] *Phillips I*, 288 F.Supp.2d at 68.

not really advance the point that, *qua* art object, *Tilted Arc* is not just the 110-foot steel arc, but also the site on which it rests. In Phillips' case, he suggests that the landscape of Eastport Park is akin to the painted landscape behind the figure of the Mona Lisa. This overlooks the important difference that Phillips did not create the Park as he did the sculptures in the Park. It seems that the more accurate analogy would be to compare the Park to the wall on which the Mona Lisa is hung: just as she can be moved to a different spot in the Louvre without altering the artwork in any essential way, why can't the sculptures themselves (even though they have a nautical theme) be removed from their seaside location without alteration?

Moreover, the problem with claiming that artists' sanctions fix artwork features is that these verbal declarations can be pronounced after the artwork has been finished, and they can be given or revoked at the artist's will, whereas fixed features of a material object cannot be. In this sense, they are subject to the same hermeneutics of suspicion as artists' declarations about correct interpretation. Of course, it is impossible to have perfect epistemic access to artists' intentions and motivations regarding the statements that they make about their artworks, even when those assertions are made in the name of artwork integrity and meaning.[45] The assertion that a work is site-specific, like the assertion that a work is 'about' this or that, must be judged against a constellation of factors surrounding the work and its constitutive object.

In both the Serra and Phillips cases, their attempts to sanction features of their works were rejected on hermeneutic grounds. In the Serra case, philosopher and art critic Michael Kelly argued that *Tilted Arc* was neither public art nor site-specific. Obviously, by denying that it was public art, he meant 'public' in a normative rather than descriptive sense: the outcry erupted precisely because the sculpture was prominently positioned in a public plaza. By arguing that it was not in fact public

---

[45] The French painter Balthus supposedly had a habit of repudiating works owned by former lovers or art dealers against whom he had a grudge, for example. "Ruling on Artistic Authenticity: The Market vs. The Law", Patricia Cohen, *New York Times*, August 5, 2012. The difference between Balthus's situation and that of Serra and Phillips is that Balthus was making a factual claim about the work: he was asserting that he had not, in fact, made it. (The court found that he was lying). But when it comes to features of the work such as site-specificity, it is not an empirical question whether the work has that feature, but is instead a normative one: the artist is insisting that we understand the work in that way, taking its location into account as an essential feature of the work.

art, he was claiming that it did not fulfill the requirements of public art, which is that it be responsive to the needs of the public, rather than antagonistic to them. But he also claimed that *Tilted Arc* was not site-specific because it closely resembled other sculptures that Serra had made in other contexts and which were not deemed site-specific.[46] Kelly's challenge to Serra's authority to make the work site-specific by declaring it so once again underscores the provisional, suggestive nature of such statements by artists.

This happened as well in the *Phillips v. Pembroke* real estate case. The court looked at the art objects in order to judge whether or not Phillips was correct in asserting, first, that his sculptures in the Park made one integrated whole and, second, that they were site-specific. While both of these declarations fall under the purview of the artist's sanction, the district court partially rejected both of Phillips' claims. First, rather than simply taking the artist's word for it that his own sculptures in Eastport Park made one integrated whole, the court determined what was and was not a part of the integrated work by looking at the formal features of the arranged objects on the site. The court found that

the sculptures along the northwest to southeast axis of the Park, including "Chords" and the medallion sculpture, as well as the Stone Elements, are one integrated "work of visual art." It begins with a spiral in the northwest corner along Seaport Boulevard, includes Plaintiff's "Chords" sculpture, and continues along a spiral path of mosaic paving stone, culminating in the bronze medallion. In determining that the sculptures along this axis, as well as the related Stone Elements, are one work of visual art, the Court relies on the integrated marine theme and recurring spirals, as well as the use of marine granite boulders and pavers. However, the remainder of the sculptures . . . that do not lie along the axis are not part of the same work of visual art. While these sculptures share the marine theme, the Court finds these pieces are individual free-standing pieces of sculpture, which are not integrated into the other pieces by spirals or granite.[47]

The court also rejected Phillips' assertion that the entire Park was one integrated work of art, reasoning that

many elements in the Park were not created by Phillips. . . . Substantial areas of the Park are unrelated to Phillips' sculpture and not integrated with it. . . . While

[46] Michael Kelly, "Public Art Controversy: The Serra and Lin Cases," *Journal of Aesthetics and Art Criticism* 54, no. 1 (1996).

[47] *Phillips I*, 288 F.Supp.2d at 93, 98. Quoted in http://openjurist.org/459/f3d/128/phillips-v-pembroke-real-estate-inc. Accessed October 10, 2017.

Phillips certainly assisted in designing the stone elements in the paths and walls and in placing his own sculptures, the Park as a whole is not an integrated work of art.[48]

In both of these excerpts from the district court's ruling we find that Phillips' attempts to sanction the objects in Eastport Park as a single, integrated artwork failed. Rather than simply accept his word for it, the court made a decision based, in part, on the formal features of the works and their location. The arrangement of the objects along a certain axis, the shape that they made, and their themic unity—that is, the aesthetic properties of the objects themselves—weighed more heavily in their interpretation than the artist's own declarations.

Perhaps a defender of the legitimacy of the artist's sanction would argue that the court's decision does not show the flimsiness of artist's sanctions but simply shows how little respect the court has for artists' moral rights. Given the highly contingent nature of those declarations, however, and the relative ease with which they can be given or revoked by the artist, it is a mistake to treat them as functionally equivalent to the properties of the art objects themselves. The court's reasoning reflects the fact that the art objects themselves are more authoritative than the artist's verbal sanctions because the objects, unlike the sanctions, are fixed and public. Like artists' declarations about their works' meaning, their sanctions are more suggestive than determinative. They are subject to the same critical evaluation as interpretive claims, and in fact the same kinds of evidence that count as valid in judging interpretations are also deployed when judging the plausibility and validity of artists' sanctions.

Richard Serra's claim that *Tilted Arc* is site-specific was not simply an instruction to viewers about how he would like them to consider and interpret the work; rather, it was an attempt to assert his moral right as an artist to enjoin the owners of Federal Plaza from removing an art object on their property. Similarly, in the case of *Phillips v. Pembroke*, the court saw that Phillips' attempt to proclaim the Park as a site-specific artwork would, if successful, not only violate the rights of the owners of the Park but also the owners of the land surrounding the Park. They did not disagree with Phillips that the work, at least some of it, was site-specific; however, they did reject his right to assert that the rights of his

---

[48] *Phillips I*, 288 F.Supp.2d at 93, 98.

artwork to exist on that site outweighed the rights and interests of the property owners of and around that site. It would put the landowners at the mercy of the artist's will, and of an artwork that might exist indefinitely on the site. If the Visual Artists' Rights Act, which protects the moral rights of artists, applied to site-specific works, the Court ruled,

> not only would Pembroke's ability to move [Phillips'] work or alter Eastport Park be subject to Phillips approval, but also the owners of nearby property who had nothing to do with the purchase or installation of Phillips' works would be subject to claims that what they do with their property has somehow affected the site and has, as a result, altered or destroyed Phillips' works.[49]

The Court took heavily into consideration the material and practical consequences of protecting works of art that include their location as an essential and constitutive feature of the work. The claim that an artwork will be destroyed if the object is removed from its location is not merely an idle theoretical possibility or a suggestion for interpretation. While the artist's verbal declarations about the boundaries of the work can be made or revoked in an instant, can be made earnestly, or out of resentment and malice, the potential consequences of such declarations extend far beyond the conceptual realm. Essentially, these artists are asserting a moral and spiritual ownership over a site that happens also to be the material property of another. Both Serra and Phillips cast themselves as victims of the commissioning institutions that wanted to move and hence 'destroy' their artworks. The Court, on the other hand, considered the potential victimization of the property owners that such declarations, if legally protected under VARA, could lead to. The artistic freedom to declare a work of art to be site-specific does not necessarily entail any practical responsibilities on the part of the artist who makes such an assertion.

V. Sanctions and Interpretation

Irvin argues that there is a clear distinction between artists' sanctions, which determine the nature of the artwork, and artists' declarations about artwork meaning, which determine neither its nature nor its meaning. In this chapter I have argued that artists' sanctions overlap

---

[49] *Phillips I,* 288 F.Supp.2d at 89.

considerably with declarations about meaning and are subject to the same liabilities of the view held by actual intentionalism, though with potentially much greater stakes. Artists' sanctions are supposed to affect the meaning of a work, but not vice versa. I have tried to show that the relation between the meaning of a work and the interventions that an artist sanctions to that work is more accurately described as a hermeneutic circle, in which sanctions are interpreted according to the artist's projected original intention. This casts doubt on the claim that artists' sanctions necessarily belong to a different category than interpretive claims, and that they have as much ontological force as the fixed features of the art object itself. Furthermore, I have pointed out that artists' attempted sanctions can and do fail. The observation that artist's sanctions are particularly important for ill-defined artworks that violate institutional norms needs to be balanced by the recognition that the success of a sanction depends on institutional uptake and assent.

As the cases discussed in this chapter show, the very existence of the artwork itself is at stake when artists attempt to verbally sanction properties of their artworks rather than merely comment on their meaning. This is because their assertions about the nature, boundaries, and persistence conditions of the artwork itself impinge on the object that can be bought, sold, moved, altered, destroyed, and interpreted by others. However, as we have seen in the Serra and Phillips cases, artists' claims about the boundaries of their artworks can be rejected not only because they conflict with the property rights of others, but because their assertions can be unconvincing in light of the other properties of the work.

The insistence on an artist's right to determine through public declarations the boundaries of an artwork might seem to be a vote in favor of artistic innovation. This is particularly so when we notice how often the discourse surrounding contra-standard artworks participates in a narrative of liberation from the 'oppressive constraints' of prior art world norms.[50]

---

[50] As the testimony surrounding *Tilted Arc* shows, those who called for the removal of the sculpture from Federal Plaza were quickly cast as enemies of avant-garde art generally. Similarly, the widespread condemnation of Mass MoCA for trampling on Büchel's rights by prominent critics such as Roberta Smith, Ken Johnson, Robert Storr, and others seemed like an attempt on the part of the commentators to align themselves publicly with the beleaguered artist and on the 'side' of avant-garde art and against the museum. This was so even though the museum has a long and successful history of championing contemporary art and artists.

6

Taking Pictures

Appropriation Art, Copyright, and Intentionalism

DANIEL BROOKS [lawyer]: Okay. So your view is if you create a work of art—do you consider this a work of art?

RICHARD PRINCE [artist]: Yes, I do.

BROOKS: If you create a work of art anyone else who wants to is free to copy it and sell it?

PRINCE: That's the optional or the operative word you just said. Free.

BROOKS: Right.

PRINCE: And art is about freedom. It's not about being restricted. If I was restricted then I couldn't transform these images.[1]

I. Genius Steals

In 2008, French photographer Patrick Cariou sued artist Richard Prince for copyright infringement over his use of the images in Cariou's book, *Yes, Rasta*. The book is a collection of classical portraits that Cariou made of Rastafarians living in the Jamaican jungles. Prince reproduced Cariou's photographs in a series of thirty collages called *Canal Zone*, in which he pasted images of guitars in the hands of the Rastafarians, placed ovoid shapes over their eyes and mouths, and incorporated images of naked women in provocative poses (See Figure 6.1. This side-by-side comparison is slightly misleading because it distorts the change in scale that Prince also made, as he often does with his appropriations. Prince's

---

[1] Prince Dep. 120–1. Reproduced in Greg Allen, ed. *Canal Zone Richard Prince Yes Rasta: Selected Court Documents from Cariou v. Prince Et Al* (greg.org, 2011).

Figure 6.1. Patrick Cariou's photograph of a Rastafarian living in the Jamaican jungles, from his book *Yes, Rasta* (left) and Richard Prince's appropriation of it, from his work *Canal Zone* (right). Used with permission by both artists.

version was much bigger than the original photo that he copied from Cariou's book. It also added color.) As we can see in the exchange that opens this chapter, taken from the transcript of his seven-hour-long deposition, Prince also appeals to the principle of artistic freedom to justify his use of Cariou's images. Without directly answering the lawyer's question about what others are free to do with his work, Prince seizes on the word 'free' in the exchange. He pivots from the lawyer's question about others and shifts the focus to his own freedom: it is what allows him to take others' photographs and 'transform' them into his own authored artworks. Prince also draws on the conception of artistic freedom as essentially negative in character, insofar as it is defined by an absence of restrictions on the artist.

The controversies we have examined in the previous chapters involve artists doing battle with institutions or owners over the fate of their work. The case of *Cariou v. Prince* is different from these because it involves a conflict between two artists. It raises the question of how to adjudicate between the right of one artist to protect his intellectual property and the right of the other to use that property as the raw material for his own work, which he then claims as his own creation. *Cariou v. Prince* is also significant because it involves a form of contemporary visual art that poses a particular challenge to copyright law: appropriation art.

In this chapter I begin by laying out the ways in which appropriation art occupies a paradoxical position with respect to authorship: it depends on the very ideals surrounding artistic authorship that it ostensibly undermines. I argue that the dual-intention theory of authorship can make sense of this apparent contradiction. It enables us to distinguish between the generative moment of authorship, which the appropriation artist seemingly negates but does not fully eliminate, and the second moment of endorsement, which the act of appropriation throws into high relief as the key moment in which authorship occurs. I then turn to the case of *Cariou v. Prince*, in order to ask whether philosophical reflection might help clarify some of the key questions at issue in cases where appropriation artists are accused of copyright violation. My answer is both yes and no: on the one hand, the long-running debate in philosophy of art over the proper role and function of artists' intentions in the interpretation of their work proves to be highly relevant to *Cariou*. On the other hand, art theorists and philosophers are not uniquely equipped, as some have argued, to adjudicate whether a given instance of appropriation art constitutes fair use. Finally, I argue that appropriation art should be considered derivative and hence presumptively *unfair*. This is actually more in accord with appropriation art's theoretical purpose to undermine originality as an ideal of authorship.

'Appropriation art' refers to the strategy of taking already-existing objects, images, or artworks and openly using them in whole or in part as one's artwork.[2] It has been an important trope in leading-edge art in the past century, beginning with Duchamp's readymades and continuing with the wildly successful, if critically polarizing, work of Jeff Koons. What distinguishes appropriation as an artistic strategy from other instances of copying, imitating, or influence in art is that the taking itself is central to the meaning of the work. In other words, appropriation art has an inherently self-referential structure, whereas in cases of plagiarism

---

[2] I will not attempt here to recapitulate a detailed account of appropriation's etiology, significance, and key moments, since excellent descriptions are already readily available in the literature. Arthur Danto's philosophy of art theorized the difference between visually indistinguishable artworks—works that are visually indistinguishable from everyday objects, or from one another; his *Transfiguration of the Commonplace* is the *locus classicus* here. But for a thorough overview of the cultural and legal significance of appropriation art in the twentieth century, see John Carlin, "Culture Vultures: Artistic Appropriation and Intellectual Property Law," *Columbia VLA Journal of Law and the Arts* 13 (1988).

or forgery the appropriation is concealed.[3] Because in its purest, most absolute form, appropriation art can look exactly like its source, the difference between the source and the appropriation is based on concept and context rather than perceptible features. This gives interpretive claims about the meaning of an appropriation a great deal of importance, because on its face the work may appear to be a mere copy of the original and nothing more.

Appropriation, broadly defined, is a quintessential trope of postmodern art, and it can take a variety of forms. While Duchamp and Koons have used the appropriation of everyday objects to exemplify theoretical questions about what kind of objects can be classified as art, artists such as Elaine Sturtevant and Sherrie Levine have appropriated iconic artworks by Roy Lichtenstein and Walker Evans in order to raise questions about the nature of artistic authorship. (As it turns out, Sturtevant and Levine have also made Warhol and Duchamp, respectively, targets of appropriation, perhaps to show that appropriators can be subjected to their own treatment). Richard Prince, on the other hand, takes a third path, often choosing as the target of his appropriations neither everyday objects nor artworks, but mass-produced images in popular culture. Prince made a name for himself as an appropriation artist by re-photographing advertisements, (most famously the Marlboro cigarette ads featuring cowboys), which he considers to be essentially authorless and therefore not a violation of the photographer's rights as an artist.[4]

---

[3] "In many ways, appropriation art is <u>about</u> appropriation: the viewer is meant to know that the objects and images presented <u>are</u> appropriated, and this is meant to say something about the objects and the authorship of the original and new works." Darren Hudson Hick, "Appropriation and Transformation," *Fordham Intellectual Property Media & Entertainment Law Journal* 23 (2013): 124. I am indebted to Hick's very thorough overview of the legal context for this case throughout this chapter.

[4] As Prince explained: "Advertisements have no authors. They're art directed thought, and I believe—I believe that sincerely. I believe they're psychologically hopped-up images that are too good to be true. They look like they have a life of their own, and they look like a film still. I don't believe I've ever seen an author or an artist's signature on an advertisement. What I believe—they're associated with products. And I believe I started taking them, rephotographing them because of those qualities." Prince Dep. 75–6. The question of whether Prince is right to claim that advertisements have no authors is beyond the scope of the current discussion, and nothing I argue here depends on my taking a position one way or the other on the question. Prince is certainly right that advertisements and other kinds of work-for-hire imagery in popular culture are not associated with their authors in the way that artworks are; their works are often unsigned and their creators are generally anonymous to the public at large. Legally, the copyright of the images belongs to the

The orthodox account of appropriation art sees it as a significant challenge to the ideology of artistic authorship associated with modernism. One might say that it is a visual-art analogue to the "death of the author" theses that proliferated in literary circles. Its advocates claim that the form addresses the central preoccupations of post-World War II avant-garde art: "Defined broadly, Appropriation is a, if not the, definitive aspect of post-modernism. The lack of traditional originality is precisely what challenges the Romantic myth of the artist that persisted through the Modern era, up to and including Abstract Expressionism."[5] The usual conceptual justification for appropriation art is that it boldly exemplifies the notion that *all* artists borrow from existing images, works, and ideas.[6] The appropriation artist merely makes this hidden truth of authorship—that there is nothing new under the sun—explicit. By taking a readymade object or image and indexing it as one's own, different work of art, the appropriation artist is seen to be refuting the notion that authored works are original, and in both senses of the term: it denies that authors are the source of their works (this is the less-grandiose sense of 'original' that US copyright law employs), and it thereby attacks the notion that artworks can be original in the absolute sense, of being a new and innovative contribution to the culture at large. According to the orthodox theory of appropriation art, the appropriating artist is making a broader claim about the nature of authorship: that *all* artists essentially do what she does: take, borrow, or steal from the realm of already existing works and index it as her own. Since nothing is truly new or original, it suggests that authors have no natural proprietary claim over their creations.[7]

commissioning corporation and not the author or team of authors that designed it. But this is not to deny that advertisements are not on some more basic level authored. Insofar as someone (or several) will have been responsible for their creation, they certainly are.

[5] Carlin, "Culture Vultures: Artistic Appropriation and Intellectual Property Law," 136.

[6] See also Willajeane McLean, "All's Not Fair in Art and War: A Look at the Fair Use Defense after Rogers V. Koons," *Brooklyn Law Review* 59 (1993): 389–90. "Entrenched in the modernist aesthetic tradition . . . is the idea that one can look at a particular painting of water lilies and know that it is a 'Monet.' This artistic concept of authorship—the attribution of a painting to its creator as its sole source of origin—is challenged by Appropriation. An appropriated image, particularly one that exactly copies the original work, defies the notion of a masterpiece or a master. In addition, the techniques employed by postmodern artists to create—that is, multiple editions often fabricated by others—also strain the idea of authorship and originality."

[7] This common interpretation of appropriation art, which aligns it with Barthes' and Foucault's 'death of the author' theses, does not commit one to the suggestion that the

On the face of it, the orthodox doctrine represented by appropriation art would challenge both the emotivist and the responsibility accounts of authorship discussed in Chapter Two. Insofar as the appropriated artwork consists of an image made by another, it cannot have issued from the appropriator's innermost feelings or expressive needs, as the emotivist account would have it. Nor can the appropriator claim responsibility for the work if, as the theory behind appropriation art has it, authors do not really create the works that bear their names. However, appropriation art's relationship to authorial responsibility is more complicated than it first appears. As Irvin puts it, "the work of appropriation artists affirms and exposes, rather than undermines, the artist's ultimate authorial status."[8] Even if the appropriation artist intends to undermine her own status as author by refusing to generate her own material, she not only fails at this aim, but she in fact underscores her own status as the one singularly responsible for selecting and re-presenting the work as her own.[9]

Put in terms of the dual-intention theory, it might seem that appropriation art involves just the second moment—authorization—without the necessary act of generation that must logically precede it. But appropriation art does not entirely do away with the generative moment; it simply whittles it down to the act of selection from existing source materials. It subverts the expectation that artistic authorship entails the artist's creation of 'new' images (either new to the artist, or new in a stronger sense, to the world at large), and simultaneously suggests that there is ultimately no such thing. While minimizing the generative moment, appropriation art reinforces the second intentional moment of authorship, the endorsement or authorization step. Because there is literally nothing new to see in a work of pure appropriation art, and yet it is a new and differently authored work, appropriation art highlights the

---

appropriation artists themselves hold this attitude about authorship. The theoretical 'work' that appropriation art is seen to be doing with respect to the concept of authorship is kept separate from claims about appropriators' actual beliefs regarding themselves as authors or the authorship status of their sources.

[8] Sherri Irvin, "Appropriation and Authorship in Contemporary Art," *British Journal of Aesthetics* 45, no. 2 (2005): 24.

[9] The fact that the 'death of the author' theses are *inevitably* and yet without any apparent sense of irony associated with their authors—Barthes and Foucault—illustrates this dynamic in another way, but just as well.

act of authorization as the essential moment in which authorship properly resides. The provocative act of taking another's artwork, duplicating it, and signing that duplication as one's own artistic expression serves as a bold assertion of artistic authority, rather than simply a renunciation of it. The appropriation artist seems to abjure the standard of originality for artworks but is in fact unable to escape being so: she is original by refusing to be original in the usually expected sense.[10] This is why appropriation art actually utilizes and further mystifies the Romantic ideal of artistic authorship that it supposedly rejects. For which is more mysterious and god-like: authorship that results from eighteen months of labor on an oversized canvas, or authorship that consists of selecting an already-existing work so as to claim it as one's own new and different work of art?

II. Appropriation Art and the Law

The paradoxical character of appropriation art's relation to authorship has proven to be especially problematic when considering its legal status in relation to copyright and moral rights. On the one hand, unauthorized appropriation art could be seen as an act of civil disobedience, challenging the very nature and legitimacy of copyright and the concepts of authorship on which it stands. On the other hand, however, appropriation artists claim authorship for themselves and the legal entitlements that follow from it, even as they seem to deny it in an abstract, theoretical sense.

There is, of course, a legal middle ground between the all-or-nothing approach to copyright. The doctrine of fair use in the United States is designed to loosen the monopoly that copyright grants artists over their creations so that others may, under certain conditions, use the work of others in the creation of their own works. At first glance, it might seem that the fair use doctrine is highly congruent with the foundational ideology of appropriation art, since both serve to recognize that influence, reference, and repetition are inevitable in the creation of newly authored works. And yet appropriation art, through its use of readymade

---

[10] Nor is this line of argument original to me, except insofar as I am relating it to my dual-intention theory of authorship. Sherry Irvin articulates this in Irvin, "Appropriation and Authorship in Contemporary Art."

creative material, is often understood to be making philosophical gestures in visual form that challenge our traditional expectations about
artworks. The fair use doctrine, on the other hand, is much more
pragmatic in nature. The statute was designed to facilitate uses such as
(but not limited to) "criticism, comment, news reporting, teaching...
scholarship, or research" so as to serve the public interest in advancing
knowledge. It designates four factors to be considered when judging fair
use: 1) the purpose and character of the use; 2) the nature of the
copyrighted work; 3) the amount used; 4) the effect of the use on the
market for or value of the copyrighted work.[11]

Both US copyright and the fair use doctrine that limits it are designed
with the same instrumental aim of promoting cultural progress.[12] Fair
use limits the monopoly that unrestricted copyright would grant to
authors, which would thereby inhibit the circulation of ideas and the
development of new works. And yet the fair use exemption is notoriously
difficult to adjudicate because there are no clear standards of application,
nor guidance over how to weigh the four factors against one another.[13]
The evaluation of a secondary use for fairness is an "open-ended and
context-sensitive inquiry."[14] The lack of a clear standard has meant that
often the only way appropriation artists can know whether their works
count as instances of fair use or not is to get sued. Authors must take
what Judge Pierre Leval has called a "guess and pray" approach when
using unlicensed material, especially because the existing litigation surrounding fair use has been so inconsistent.[15]

In the absence of a clear legal standard by which to assess fair use,
'transformation' has become the key concept for determining the legitimacy of a secondary use.[16] The idea is that transformative works
contribute to the purpose of copyright, which is to spur the creation of

---

[11] 17 U.S.C. § 107.

[12] The instrumental motivation for granting copyright protection to authors and inventors is enshrined in Article 1, Section 8 of the US Constitution: "to Promote the progress of
Science and useful Arts."

[13] A 2014 report by the College Art Association argues that the doctrine of fair use has had a
stifling effect on its presumed beneficiaries because of the lack of clear standards of application.
See http://www.collegeart.org/pdf/FairUseIssuesReport.pdf. Accessed October 10, 2017.

[14] *Cariou v. Prince*, No. 11-1197-cv, 10 (2d Cir. 2013).

[15] Pierre N. Leval, "Toward a Fair Use Standard," *Harvard Law Review* 103 (1990): 1107.

[16] The standard of 'transformation' in fair use cases was established by the Supreme
Court's decision in the landmark case *Campbell v. Acuff-Rose Music, Inc.*, 510 U.S. 569.

new works.[17] And yet it is not clear what counts as transformative, or how to ensure that it is used consistently.[18] When we look at the ways in which this standard has been articulated, it seems to encompass two seemingly contradictory ideas: on the one hand, the appropriating work must transform the original by offering a "new expression, meaning, or message."[19] And yet this requirement that the work present a new meaning is mitigated by the court's expectation that the work also "in some way comment on, relate to the historical context of, or critically refer back to the original works."[20] This latter requirement presents a significant limitation on the notion that the appropriating work must 'transform' the source material. The reason seems to be that if one simply had to claim that a given piece of appropriation art offered a new expression or meaning in order to be deemed fair, then it would open the door to what has been called "copyright anarchy": a slippery slope that would legitimize almost any instance of secondary use.[21]

The inconsistent decisions in the lawsuits against artist Jeff Koons are a useful illustration of the confusion surrounding the 'transformation' standard in fair use cases involving appropriation. In the 1992 suit *Rogers v. Koons*, he was found to have violated photographer Art Rogers' copyright by using it as the basis for his sculpture *String of Puppies*. Koons commissioned the sculpture to be made based on Rogers' photograph that he found on a card in a museum gift shop. He argued, unsuccessfully, that the work was a "satirical critique of our materialistic society," and hence was protected by the fair use provision.[22] The court found that the sculpture was not a parody of Rogers' (relatively unknown)

---

[17] "Such works thus lie at the heart of the fair use doctrine's guarantee of breathing space within the confines of copyright, and the more transformative the new work, the less will be the significance of other factors, like commercialism, that may weigh against a finding of fair use." *Campbell v. Acuff- Rose*, 510 U.S. 569, 579, qtd in *Cariou v. Prince*, 11-1197-cv, 15 (2d Cir. 2013).

[18] See Hick, "Appropriation and Transformation," 126–36.

[19] *Cariou v. Prince*, 11-1197-cv, 15 (2d Cir. 2013), quoting *Campbell*, 510 U.S. at 579.

[20] *Cariou*, 784 F. Supp. 2d 337 at 348–9.

[21] "If an infringement of copyrightable expression could be justified as fair use solely on the basis of the infringer's claim to a higher or different artistic use . . . there would be no practicable boundary to the fair use defense." *Rogers v. Koons*, 960 F. 2d at 310, qtd in *Cariou*, 11-1197-cv, 17 (2d Cir. 2013).

[22] *Rogers v. Koons*, 960 F.2d 301, 310 (2d Cir.1992), *cert. denied*, 506 U.S. 934, 113 S.Ct. 365, 121 L.Ed.2d 278 (1992), cited in *Cariou v. Prince*, 784 F. Supp. 2d 337, 348 (S.D.N.Y. 2011).

photograph specifically; hence it was not a form of commentary and did not count as fair use.

A decade later, however, Koons prevailed in a copyright lawsuit using much the same strategy, this time over his use of an advertisement for Gucci sandals. The original image featured a pair of scantily clad woman's feet, crossed at the ankles and resting on a man's lap in an airplane cabin. He used part of the advertisement in a painting called *Niagara*, which depicts four pairs of women's feet dangling over pastries with the Niagara Falls in the background. In *Blanch v. Koons*, the court agreed that his use of the ad was sufficiently transformative because his work was a commentary on consumer culture and its attendant imagery.[23] What was significant about the ruling is that Koons did not have to show that his artwork was specifically targeting the photograph for parody or commentary; rather, it satisfied the court that his painting was a critical commentary on the banality of consumer culture in general, with the Gucci ad as an exemplar of that phenomenon.

The decision in *Blanch v. Koons* is surprising because it permitted Koons to appropriate a copyrighted image as raw material for his own artwork, without requiring that the secondary use be a comment on that image in particular. Presumably Koons could just as easily have used a different mass-produced advertisement for luxury products featuring female feet to make the same point in *Niagara*.[24] Koons' victory in the *Niagara* case seemed to open the door again to appropriation artists who wanted to produce a critique of mass culture generally without being a targeted parody of the specific work appropriated. Nevertheless, the unpredictability of the rulings in fair use cases such as these suggests that, as one commentator puts it, "the line between inspiration and unlawful copying is remarkably thin."[25] If we look to the theoretical justifications of appropriation art, it would seem that its aim is precisely to do away with (or at least cast into serious doubt) the notion that such a line between inspiration and replication necessarily exists. But this does

---

[23] *Blanch v. Koons*, 467 F.3d 244 (2d Cir. 2006).

[24] It probably helped that the appropriated image was an advertisement and not a work of art, for the reason that Richard Prince articulates in fn 4, above: we tend to treat advertisements as authorless, as opposed to artworks, whose authorship we regard as essential to its status, value, and meaning.

[25] Liz McKenzie, "Drawing Lines: Addressing Cognitive Bias in Art Appropriation Cases," *UCLA Entertainment Law Review* (2013).

not help the would-be appropriator who wants to stay on the right side of the law when making her artworks.

This disagreement about what constitutes a transformative and hence fair use came dramatically into play in *Cariou v. Prince*. Initially, the district court imposed the stricter version of the standard, yielding a rule it referred to as "transformative comment" when determining whether Prince had infringed Cariou's copyright. It declared that "Prince's paintings are transformative only to the extent that they comment on [Cariou's] photos."[26] In order to count as fair use, Prince's paintings could not simply say something different from Cariou while using his artwork, but they had to say something new that was at the same time *about* the original photos.

District Court Judge Deborah Batts ruled that Prince's paintings failed the test in both respects. The court found that the core message of Cariou's photographs was retained in Prince's paintings, and that Prince's aim, like Cariou's, was "a desire to communicate to the viewer core truths about Rastafarians and their culture."[27] Even more importantly, however, the court found that "Prince did not intend to comment on Cariou, on Cariou's Photos, or on aspects of popular culture closely associated with Cariou or the Photos when he appropriated the Photos," and so it concluded that Prince had violated Cariou's copyright.[28] And it took heavily into account Prince's defiant and potentially self-sabotaging testimony that his work "doesn't really have a message" and that he was "not trying to create anything with a new meaning or a new message."[29]

We might wonder about the seeming contradiction between these two judgments: on the one hand, the court found that in his *Canal Zone* paintings, Prince was attempting to "communicate core truths about Rastafarians" and at the same time it took him at his word when he claimed that they did not really have a message. It would seem that, strictly speaking, a work of art could not simultaneously have no message *and* be about core truths concerning Rastafarians. However, the court took this to mean that without a new message of his own, either about Rastafarians or about Cariou's photos of them, Prince was simply copying Cariou's images *and* their message, and therefore violating his copyright. Batts granted Cariou's motion for summary judgment and

[26] *Cariou*, 11-1197-cv, 16 (2d Cir. 2013).
[27] *Cariou*, 784 F. Supp. 2d 337, 349.   [28] Ibid.   [29] Prince Dep. 360.

ordered Prince to deliver the over-$10 million-worth of illegal paintings and their publicity material to Cariou to dispose of as he wished.

For a while it seemed that the tide had turned against appropriation art. Two years later, however, the appellate court mostly reversed the district court's decision in *Cariou v. Prince*. It ruled that twenty-five of the thirty *Canal Zone* paintings were in fact instances of fair use. It remanded the other five paintings back to the district court for judgment using a corrected standard. The appellate court not only rejected the district's decision, but it pointedly rejected its use of the artist's testimony as evidence, instead giving primacy to the viewer's aesthetic judgment. The district court relied heavily on Prince's statements about the meaning of his paintings and his reasons for using Cariou's photographs, and it used those statements against him. The appellate court, on the other hand, accorded interpretive authority to the "reasonable observer," not the artist: "What is critical is how the work in question appears to the reasonable observer, not simply what an artist might say about a particular piece or body of work."[30] It found that there were obvious aesthetic differences between the *Canal Zone* paintings and the *Yes, Rasta* photographs which did make Prince's use transformative. Whereas Cariou's photos were "serene and deliberately composed," Prince's paintings were "crude and jarring," which showed (at least in twenty-five of them) that the paintings "manifest an entirely different aesthetic" from the borrowed material.[31] The court found that these aesthetic differences were not merely cosmetic, but that they signified a transformation of Cariou's images into new works with new meanings. Moreover, it rejected the district court's requirement that the appropriation be a commentary aimed either at the source or at popular culture in general. The most decisive factor in its determination of fair use was whether the public good was served by the introduction of a new and different artwork, even if that artwork uses the authored work of another as its source material.[32] Such

---

[30] *Cariou v. Prince*, 714 F. 3d 694—Court of Appeals, 2nd Circuit 2013, 707. In response to this, Judge Wallace of the appellate court issued his partial dissent: "Unlike the majority, I would allow the district court to consider Prince's statements in reviewing fair use.... I see no reason to discount Prince's statements as the majority does."

[31] *Cariou v. Prince*, 714 F. 3d 694—Court of Appeals, 2nd Circuit 2013, 708.

[32] "The 'ultimate test of fair use . . . is whether the copyright law's goal of 'promoting the Progress of Science and useful Arts' . . . would be better served by allowing the use than by preventing it.'" *Cariou v. Prince* appeal, p. 11, quoting Castle Rock, 150 F.3d at 141.

a ruling would seem to open the legal door to appropriation art even wider than had Koons' victory with *Niagara* in *Blanch v. Koons*. Whereas the ruling in *Blanch* was based on the notion that parody is a presumptive instance of fair use, the appellate court in *Carou v. Prince* did not even require that the secondary use be a parody or satire; it simply had to be different enough in look and attitude, as twenty-five of the thirty *Canal Zone* paintings were found to be.[33]

III. Appropriation Art and the Intentionalism Debate

To the observer versed in academic philosophy of art, a remarkable feature of the two decisions in *Cariou v. Prince* is that they unwittingly recapitulate the decades-long intentionalism debate in aesthetics. The district court and the appellate court pointedly disagreed on the proper role that the artist's testimony should play in determining the status of his works. This reflects two sides of an apparently intractable philosophical disagreement about whether, and to what extent, artists' pronouncements about the meaning of their artworks should be determinative for the interpretation of those artworks. While there have been some exceptions, the discussion has focused to a great extent on literary artworks.[34] Anti-intentionalists and extreme actual intentionalists represent the two poles of the debate. The former divorce the meaning of the work entirely from reference to the historical author's intentions, whereas the latter collapse them. Neither pole has many remaining adherents.

For the past twenty-five years, the argument has largely coalesced around versions of two intermediate positions, often called hypothetical intentionalism (HI), and moderate actual intentionalism (AI). While there are many variations among the proponents of these positions, two representative voices in this debate are Jerrold Levinson, a proponent of HI, and Robert Stecker, who has given nuanced defenses of AI over the years. Generally speaking, hypothetical intentionalism stops short of permitting artists' statements about work meaning to be determinative,

---

[33] The foundation for this ruling is *Campbell v. Acuff-Rose*, in which the rap group 2 Live Crew's parody of Roy Orbison's song "Oh, Pretty Woman" was found to be fair.

[34] For an overview see Sherri Irvin, "Authors, Intentions, and Literary Meaning," *Philosophy Compass* 1, no. 2 (2006).

even as it acknowledges the necessity of referring to the intentions of the artist in determining what category the artwork belongs to. Moderate actual intentionalism, on the other hand, "preserves the idea that the author of a work does have a special degree of authority with respect to its meaning," while recognizing—this is why it is 'moderate'—that one must approach such statements skeptically.[35]

Hans Maes points out that the debate between proponents of HI and AI has proven surprisingly durable, even though it seemed to be drawing to a close over twenty years ago.[36] (Levinson published "Intention and Interpretation: A Last Look" in 1992, and yet the debate soldiers on.)[37] This is so despite the fact that there are very few, if any, test cases that effectively divide supporters of AI and HI.[38] The question of the proper role of authorial pronouncements about work meaning has a zombie-like persistence in clawing itself back into the arena long after it has been pronounced dead. Even Dennis Dutton, who in 1987 penned "Why Intentionalism Won't Go Away," probably thought it would have by now.[39] As I see it, the debate is symptomatic of an ineluctable tension in our experience of artworks: we understand artworks to be the expressions of their authors, and so they are naturally attached to the author's expressive intentions. At the same time, however, artworks are not simply reducible to the meaning that their authors intended to give them. They are cultural artifacts. They have lives of their own.

The disagreement between the adherents of HI and AI was uncannily recapitulated by the differing rulings in *Cariou v. Prince*. The appellate court pointedly rejected the use of Prince's statements about his own works as determinative when judging whether they were sufficiently transformative of Cariou's images. Instead, they appealed to a hypothetical 'reasonable observer' in assessing the differences between Prince's paintings and Cariou's photographs. One of the surprising aspects of this case is that Prince's testimony was used against him in the initial ruling.

---

[35] Ibid., 119.

[36] Hans Maes, "Intention, Interpretation, and Contemporary Visual Art," *British Journal of Aesthetics* 50, no. 2 (2010).

[37] Jerrold Levinson, "Intention and Interpretation: A Last Look," in *Intention and Interpretation*, ed. Gary Iseminger (Philadelphia: Temple University Press, 1992).

[38] See K.E. Gover, "What Is Humpty Dumptyism in Contemporary Visual Art? A Reply to Maes," *British Journal of Aesthetics* 52, no. 2 (2012).

[39] Dennis Dutton, "Why Intentionalism Won't Go Away," in *Literature and the Question of Philosophy*, ed. Anthony J. Cascardi (Baltimore: Johns Hopkins University Press, 1987).

Of course, the district court's motivation for its reliance on Prince's testimony about the meaning of his own work may have been opportunistic rather than a principled stand in favor of AI: by playing the role of a self-abnegating Cordelia to the court's King Lear, Prince made it easier for a judge who may have been already unsympathetic to appropriation art to find that his paintings were not transformative.

While the appellate court's ruling is a legal victory for Richard Prince, it is premature to label this as a win for appropriation art in general, as some commentators have.[40] The appellate court's decision was based on the degree to which Prince's paintings were visibly different from Cariou's original images. Thus, it did little to set a guideline for how appropriation art per se might be protected by the fair use provision, since in its purest or most extreme instances, works of appropriation art are visually indistinguishable from their source material. Indeed, one might say that the most radical premise of appropriation art is that the meaning of a work is *not* borne on its face, but is determined by that which, as Arthur Danto so famously declared when discussing Warhol's facsimile *Brillo Boxes*, "the eye cannot descry": its context.[41]

The problem with appealing to a 'reasonable observer' to make decisions about the legality of appropriation art, is that it is not clear who that observer would be and what context they will be viewing the work from. Hick argues that in such cases, the appeal to evidence about artistic intention—and the attendant problems of using such testimony—is inevitable:

when the court reduces the question of transformation to how the work would appear to a "reasonable observer," it fails to ask whether this observer is a

---

[40] NYU law professor Amy Adler approved not only the decision of the appellate court but their rejection of actual intentionalism: "This is a major win for Prince on at least two counts . . . The court decided that artwork does not need to comment on previous work to qualify as fair use, and that Prince's testimony is not the dispositive question in determining whether a work is transformative. Rather the issue is how the work may reasonably be perceived. This is the right standard because it takes into account the underlying public purpose of copyright law, which should not be beholden to statements of individual intent but instead consider the value that all of us gain from the creation of new work." But Adler here assumes that the secondary use in question *is* a new work, which begs the question of how to determine the difference between mere usurpation and a new creation. Quoted in http://www.artinamericamagazine.com/news-features/news/richard-prince-wins-major-victory-in-landmark-copyright-suit/. Accessed October 10, 2017.

[41] Arthur Danto, "The Art world," *Journal of Philosophy* 61, no. 19 (1964): 580.

member of Prince's audience, or of Cariou's, both, or neither. Even where the original and the secondary work appear visually indistinguishable, the audience familiar with the aims and practices of appropriation art will treat them very differently, and in many cases, they are likely to find something new—a new meaning, a fundamentally different aesthetic. And much of this will turn *precisely* on what the artist says about his work.[42]

The conflicting decisions of the courts in *Cariou v. Prince* show that the question of how much authority to accord authors over the meaning of their artworks remains an open, unresolved problem. While the district court's initial ruling on *Cariou v. Prince* resulted in a judgment that was unfavorable to Prince, ironically, its guiding hermeneutic principles were in fact more congruent with the theoretical demands of appropriation art than was the appellate court's aesthetic empiricism.[43] Whereas the appellate court relied on the visual appearance of Prince's paintings to make its judgment, the basic premise of appropriation art is that the meaning of an artwork is not simply visible to the eye. Under the right circumstances, what seems to be merely a copy can in fact result in a new artwork with a different meaning than its source. Despite Prince's victory in the appellate court, the ruling does not really inform us about the compatibility of appropriation art as such with copyright law. In the final section, I discuss recent theoretical attempts to align appropriation art with fair use, and I offer my own proposal for a solution.

IV. A Fair Solution

There have been many attempts in the past twenty years to articulate a fair use standard that would accommodate appropriation art and yet avoid the slippery slope leading to 'copyright anarchy,' in which anyone could claim that their act of copying was in fact a transformative use, and therefore a legitimate form of taking. Before I discuss the details of these proposals, we should first consider what motivates these attempts. The underlying assumption seems to be that since appropriation art is a culturally signifi-cant artistic strategy, and both copyright and fair use were designed precisely to encourage the production of culturally significant authored

---

[42] Hick, "Appropriation and Transformation," 128.
[43] "The assumption here is that whether a work is a new expression, has a new message, or is invested with new meaning, is something that the work will wear on its face," ibid., 117.

works, we must therefore find a way to provide legal sanction to works of appropriation art so as to encourage, rather than punish, artistic production in this arena.

The different rulings in *Cariou v. Prince* reveal what a difficult if not impossible task it is to find a legal standard that can differentiate between transformative or meaningful appropriation and illegitimate forms of taking. By design, appropriation art shares what we might call the formal conditions of a copyright violation: it is formally similar to a preexisting work because it is copied from it. (A work that by chance just happens to look like an already existing work is not a violation, because it does not share a causal history with that work—it did not copy.) The difference, at least in theory, is that this fact of having taken a preexisting work is folded into the meaning of the new work; the overt act of appropriating an existing work thereby transforms the old work into something new. But since we cannot necessarily rely on a visible difference between the original and the appropriation, as the appellate court in *Cariou v. Prince* would clearly prefer, then this requires the courts to take on the role of art critic and interpreter. There are a number of copyright cases in which the court has expressed hesitation about being forced into such a role. This idea was articulated by the Supreme Court in the 1903 case *Bleistein v. Donaldson Lithographing Co.*: "it would be a dangerous undertaking for persons trained only to the law to constitute themselves final judges of the worth of pictorial illustrations, outside of the narrowest and most obvious limits."[44] This concern was echoed by the dissenting appellate court Judge Wallace, who asked, if twenty-five of the *Canal Zone* paintings are clear cases of transformative fair use in the eyes of a hypothetical "reasonable viewer," why can't this viewer make a determination about the remaining five, rather than remanding them to the district court for a decision according to its revised standard? He objected to the notion that the court could simply compare the original and secondary works and "employ its own artistic judgment."[45] It is particularly difficult for the

---

[44] *Bleistein v. Donaldson Lithographing Co.*, 188 U.S. 239, 251 (1903). It might be objected that pictorial worth is not the same as pictorial status, which is neutral with respect to aesthetic value. But in cases such as these, it is nearly impossible to distinguish in practice what is very easy to keep separate conceptually. See Amy Cohen, "Copyright Law and the Myth of Objectivity: The Idea-Expression Dichotomy and the Inevitability of Artistic Value Judgments," *Indiana Law Review* 66 (1990).

[45] *Cariou v. Prince*, No. 11-1197-cv (2d. Cir. April 25, 2013).

court to make such a judgment when the difference between the appropriating work and its source is not visual, but conceptual. While this is a distinction that philosophers and art critics make quite comfortably in theory, it is more difficult to ask judges to do so with particular cases. This is not because judges make unreliable art critics, but because they are being asked to make a decision largely based on the intentions and motivations of the artist in doing the appropriation. If the appropriation is done out of laziness or in order to usurp the market for the original work, then it is an infringement, but if the copying is done for a higher artistic purpose, in order to make an assertion about the nature of originality, or the banality of consumer culture, then it is transformative and presumably fair.

While he acknowledges that such a standard would require "a fairly high degree of sensitivity on the part of the courts," this is the essence of Hick's proposed solution to appropriation art's fair use problem.[46] Since the purpose of copyright is to encourage the proliferation of ideas, he suggests that a secondary use should be presumptively fair whenever it expresses an idea that is distinct from that of the original. In other words, Hick also relies on the notion of "transformation" as the benchmark for separating fair appropriations from those that infringe. Hick points out that a finding of fair use does not itself guarantee a copyright to that use, and accordingly he suggests that artists who engage in acts of appropriation should only be given copyright ownership over the material in an artwork, if any, that was not copied.[47] Under Hick's proposal, Prince's *Canal Zone* paintings would be considered instances of fair use, but he would not be able to copy the parts of his paintings that involve Cariou's photographs, nor produce derivative works based on them.[48] His idea has the advantage of forging a middle path for appropriation art between total refusal and total permission, by separating an instance of fair use from a copyright ownership of that use. Nevertheless, it places too high of a burden on the courts to make nuanced interpretations of artworks that may, both in look and in etiology, bear all the marks of a copyright

---

[46] Hick, "Appropriation and Transformation," 138.   [47] Ibid., 137.

[48] Some of the *Canal Zone* paintings use other presumably appropriated images not taken from Cariou's work, in particular the many photographs of naked women that appear in the collages. It was not mentioned in the trial whether these, too, were copyrighted images.

violation.[49] In ambiguous cases such as the *Canal Zone* paintings, the decision may likely come to down to what Barbour calls "the secret consideration present in every appropriation art case: the court's value of the secondary use's aesthetics."[50] Remember that even the appellate court in *Cariou v. Prince* found five of his paintings too close to call.

While the appeal to a "reasonable observer" worked in Prince's favor this time, it is easy to imagine how this device could be used to mask judicial bias when it comes to subjective aesthetic judgments. For this reason, some legal scholars have suggested that the courts should rely on experts on aesthetic theory, rather than risk allowing cognitive bias to color their judgment.[51] As Christine Farley puts it:

> There is no excuse for courts to act as if questions of artistic value and classification have not already been theorized. It is time for these courts to begin to take advantage of that work. The law here should be better theoretically informed. Engagement in aesthetic discourse would reduce the mismatch of legal and artistic developments.[52]

Pace Barnett Newman, perhaps birds need ornithologists after all! While the idea that courts might make use of philosophers' expertise on such matters is gratifying, I do not share Farley's optimism that it would reduce the uncertainty surrounding the status of appropriation art vis-à-vis fair use. After all, philosophers are known for their spirited disagreements with one another, as we see in the intentionalism debate itself. There is no reason to assume that the use of philosophers or art critics as expert witnesses will yield a consistent standard of judgment. Furthermore, one can be well versed in the historical and theoretical foundations of appropriation as an artistic trope—and even be very sympathetic to it—and yet

---

[49] Elsewhere, Hick has offered a different solution, using another piece of appropriation art by Prince as his case study: Darren Hudson Hick, "Toward an Ontology of Authored Works," *British Journal of Aesthetics* 51, no. 2 (2011). There he argues that we should treat the source and the appropriation as two different artworks, but for the purposes of copyright as the same authored work. The problem with this solution is that it makes the work of appropriation art into an effective orphan: it is a new and different artwork, but it has no author, since the author of the source material cannot be said to have authored the appropriation of his own work. See Christy Mag Uidhir, *Art and Art-Attempts* (Oxford University Press, 2013), 45–6.

[50] Adrianne Barbour, "Yes, Rasta 2.0: Cariou v. Prince and the Fair Use Test of Transformative Use in Appropriation Art Cases," *Tulane Journal of Technology & Intellectual Property* 14 (2011): 382.

[51] McKenzie, "Drawing Lines: Addressing Cognitive Bias in Art Appropriation Cases."

[52] Christine Haight Farley, "Judging Art," *Tulane Law Review* 79 (2005): 857.

find it difficult to say definitively whether an artist's attempt at meaningful appropriation falls into the category of fair use. One example of a difficult case of appropriation involved the then thirty-one-year-old sculptor Lauren Clay, who in 2013 was accused by David Smith's estate of copyright infringement. She had created a collection of sculptures to be exhibited at Grounds For Sculpture, a sculpture garden and museum in New Jersey, which closely re-created at a different scale and material the forms of several of Smith's works. Clay argued that the allegedly infringing work was appropriation art and hence fair use. The two parties reached an agreement before the case was litigated.[53] While one critic may find Clay's sculptures to be meaningfully transformative, another may see her act of appropriation as lazy and uncreative. It is not as though philosophers are uniquely able to see the otherwise invisible line that marks the point where an act of infringement is transfigured into an artwork with new meaning. In a way, it is absurd to expect one, since the very point of appropriation art, as many theorists have articulated, is precisely to challenge the dichotomy between original and derivative works. And yet such a line is essentially what the law would need in order for fair use cases to be adjudicated consistently.

Another proposal, by Michael Carroll, would establish an advisory board to which potential fair users could petition before a potentially infringing act. This would help combat the uncertainty and self-censorship that authors and artists experience by providing them with an expert evaluation of their use in advance of any potential litigation.[54] However, given the inconsistency of the rulings on appropriation art cases, I do not see how an advisory board would be able to use past decisions to advise artists about future instances of secondary use. In addition to its impracticality, it seems to me that such a proposal moves in the wrong direction: away from clearer guidelines that authors can follow themselves, and instead adding an extra layer of bureaucracy and legal oversight. It is unclear to me how this will save us from the "clearance culture" of permissions seeking that Carroll decries.

---

[53] See https://itsartlaw.com/2013/10/07/david-smith-estates-recent-allegations-of-copy right-infringement-highlights-ongoing-debate-on-fair-use-and-appropriation-art/. Accessed September 15, 2016.

[54] Michael Carroll, "Fixing Fair Use," *North Carolina Law Review* 85 (2007).

As for the use of artists' testimony in such cases, I think it is inappropriate to treat their statements about the meaning of their work as dispositive.[55] Prince's straightforward, unapologetic demeanor during his deposition makes for a fascinating portrait of the artist and his ideas. It also contained conflicting statements about the intended message behind the *Canal Zone* paintings, a point that the prosecution tried to use to its advantage. But why should the artist have a coherent, consistent story about the meaning of his work that he can produce on demand? Under copyright law, the authored work is the expression of an idea, and copyright protects the expressions, not the ideas. To demand that an artist then explain his expression in a way that will satisfy a court of law (as opposed to an artist's statement published in a catalogue essay or press release) is unreasonable. It not only expects artists to have a logically consistent message behind their work, it requires them to articulate verbally what they have already expressed visually—something that may be an impossible task.[56] This is not to say that Richard Prince is incapable of speaking clearly about his own work—far from it. My point, rather, is that if artists are in the business of trying to make compelling images, which they may do for any number of reasons, their primary focus may not be in communicating "core truths" that can then be translated into a coherent set of propositions.

I propose that we ought to treat works of appropriation art as derivative works, and therefore as presumptively *unfair*. This may seem to make me an enemy of appropriation art. But it is a mistake to assume that one must find legal sanction for an art form simply because it is culturally important. Graffiti artists such as Banksy, for example, have been embraced both by the upper echelons of the artworld and popular culture; nevertheless, they perform illegal acts of vandalism when they paint their works on public buildings without permission. Just because we find Banksy's art compelling, attractive, and meaningful does not

---

[55] See also Monica Isia Jasiewicz, "A Dangerous Undertaking: The Promise of Intentionalism and Promise of Expert Testimony in Appropriation Art Infringement Cases," *Yale Journal of Law & the Humanities* 26, no. 1 (2015).

[56] Speaking of the dance works that he and Merce Cunningham created, composer John Cage was quoted in a lecture as follows: "We are not, in these dances, saying something. We are simple-minded enough to think that if we were saying something we would use words." Cited in Julie Van Camp, "Non-Verbal Metaphor: A Non-Explanation of Meaning in Dance," *British Journal of Aesthetics* 36, no. 2 (1996): fn 41, 187.

mean that we should revise the law so that graffiti artists can have their way with other peoples' buildings. (Indeed, its illicit character may be, in part, what we find significant).[57]

Appropriation has been and continues to be one of the most significant artistic strategies of the past century; but this is not reason enough to sanction it as prima facie fair use. In fact, part of the conceptual interest that appropriation art generates is its transgressive, potentially illicit nature. By taking, often without asking, it confounds our expectations about what it means to own an image. As Carlin, in his detailed defense of the art form puts it: "Appropriation is one of the most important conceptual strategies in late 20th century art because it underscores the role of the artist as the manipulator or modifier of existing material, rather than as the inventor or creator of new forms."[58] It would be much more consistent with the conceptual premises of appropriation art, and would nevertheless enable its proliferation, if we recognized it as derivative. This is an accurate description of its nature: in deliberately taking objects or images already found in the world, the appropriator makes a work that derives from the taken material. I may regard Prince's *Untitled (Cowboy)* (1989) as a different (and quite meaningful) work from the Marlboro ad that was its source. But it is still, by its very design, derivative. This is in fact a key component of its meaning. In other words, if one does not know that a work of appropriation art is an appropriation, then one cannot understand the work correctly.

It seems strange that appropriation art's defenders consistently articulate its significance as a means of rejecting the concept of absolute originality, and yet they nevertheless want to defend its importance as a new and original form of art-making that results in new and different works of art. One would think that appropriation artists might embrace the status of their works as "derivative," since the loftier philosophical aim of their approach is to suggest that all authored works are, in a sense.

There are two main reasons, I think, why this point of view has not gained traction: one is normative; the other, conceptual. First, some advocates of appropriation art seem to assume that being derivative

---

[57] Tony Chackal "Of Materiality and Meaning: The Illegality Condition in Street Art," *Journal of Aesthetics and Art Criticism* 74, no. 4 (2017).

[58] Carlin, "Culture Vultures: Artistic Appropriation and Intellectual Property Law," 129 fn 106. Cited in Hick, "Appropriation and Transformation," 124 fn 159.

implies some kind of inferiority.[59] It is true that the term 'derivative', when applied to artworks, is often used as a reproach. We think, for example, of the stylistic followers of an artistic innovator, and we regard them as epigones of the master. But since appropriation art, by its own terms, sets out to undermine the ideal of the original, the masterpiece, the creative genius, shouldn't we use it as an occasion to rethink the pejorative connotation that we assign to a 'derivative' work? In this case, it becomes merely a descriptor for the process by which the work came to be. Perhaps it is even a badge of honor for those who adhere to the orthodox theory behind it.

The second mistake consists in treating 'derivative' and 'transformative' as mutually exclusive, as the courts have. These terms have taken on a legal significance in fair use litigation because it marks the theoretical line between infringement and innovation. And yet it seems clear to me that the reason why appropriation art has been treated so inconsistently by the courts—we have seen contradictory rulings in *Cariou v. Prince*—is that it aims precisely to blur the boundary between the derivative and the transformative.

The important thing to note here is that recognizing appropriation art as derivative would not then prevent artists from making such works. It would require them, however, to seek permission from the copyright owners of the source material. Just as artists must purchase the physical materials that they use to create their works—the paint, clay, software, and so on—it seems reasonable to require appropriation artists to purchase the right to use the intellectual property of others when it serves as material for their works. This may be as simple as seeking permission from the copyright owner, or it may mean paying hefty licensing fees. But artistic freedom does not imply that one's art materials come for free.

---

[59] Carlin, "Culture Vultures: Artistic Appropriation and Intellectual Property Law," 129: "Appropriation is, by design, the conceptual equal of its source. Appropriation transcends parody because it is a well-grounded and conscious attack on traditional notions of originality and authorship in art."

7

Conclusion

BROOKS: Do you agree that you've redefined the concept of authorship?

PRINCE: I would hope that I've had some hand in redefining the issues that have to do with authorship.

BROOKS: How so?

PRINCE: It has to do with that concept that people really believe artists are special and they have something special to say. There was a time in the late '70s when I didn't go along with that concept. And there was that essay by Roland Barthes called Death of an Author, and it was just an issue that was going around town. And I think that I got caught up in it and I got involved in it and I sort of decided to do something about it in my own particular little way. And hopefully, yes, I hope that—you know, I would have called it the death of the ego, but I guess authorship is a fairly accurate and it's an okay word. I mean it's very—all it is is philosophical. And, you know, it's sort of like someone writing a term paper, you know, it's academic. You know, it's something that takes place in October Magazine, which I don't particularly like and Columbia University and you know, it's—I'm much more of a—well, I'm much more interested in trying to make art that stands up next to Picasso, De Kooning, and Warhol. That's what I'm interested in.[1]

With my dual-intention theory I have sought to refine and clarify our understanding of artistic authorship. My basic insight can be summarized as follows: we assume that authorship names the person (or people) responsible for having made a work. And indeed it does. But we overlook

---

[1] Prince Dep. 298–9. Reproduced in Greg Allen, ed. *Canal Zone Richard Prince Yes Rasta: Selected Court Documents from Cariou v. Prince Et Al* (greg.org, 2011).

the fact that our understanding of artistic authorship also entails endorsement. Artists author works in the fullest sense of the term not just by producing them, but by choosing which to sign and put into the world as their own. Of course, there are exceptions: we sometimes encounter sketches, drafts, rejects, or unauthorized artworks, usually published posthumously, and usually because the author's works are so valued by the public that even the unendorsed pieces are objects of fascination. Nevertheless, we respect the difference in status between those that the artist considers as truly 'his' and those that were merely found lying around his studio.

The robust conception of authorship, which is the (often unarticulated and unexamined) norm, entails the first-order intention to generate an artwork and the second-order intention to accept the artwork that was made as good enough. I have linked this necessary second moment of ratification or endorsement to the concept of artistic freedom. Artistic freedom can mean different things depending on the context in which it is invoked. I maintain, however, that the most fundamental form of artistic freedom involves the artist's authority to accept or disavow the works she produces, to curate the works that bear her name and come to represent her artistic oeuvre. Our very concept of what an artwork is—the intentional expression of the artist, for its own sake—depends on this second-order endorsement by the artist of what he or she has made. I have argued that the leading accounts of artistic authorship, which I call the emotivist and responsibility accounts, have overlooked the significance of this moment.

My dual-intention theory developed out of an attempt to understand the conceptual justification behind moral rights legislation, which protects an artist's personal and reputational interests in her work and affords her some degree of control over the work even when it is owned by another. In the United States this includes the right of integrity, which enjoins against the mutilation, distortion, and in some cases destruction of a work; and the right of attribution, which gives the artist the right to claim authorship of the work, or to use a pseudonym. These rights, I maintain, follow logically from the idea that what is important about the authorship of an artwork is not just that it was made by the author, but that the author gets to control which works bear her name. The "presumed intimate bond" between artist and artwork that grounds moral rights legislation cannot be accounted for, as it often is in the legal scholarship, by the claim that artworks are the personal and emotional expressions of their authors.[2] I think what the proponents of those theories are actually trying to capture with the emotivist account is the fact that, in our culture, authorship is particularly salient with respect to art because we understand and appreciate artworks primarily as the expressions of their authors. A beautifully designed smartphone may embody just as much of its designer's talent, skill, and vision as any work of art, but we value the phone for what it can do for us, first, and think about the intentions of its author, if at all, only secondarily. Artworks, on the other hand, put the expressive intentions of their authors up front and center as their primary raison d'être. Thus, when we encounter an artwork as appreciators and interpreters it is especially important to ascertain whether the work in question is the work that the artist intended. Moral rights are designed to ensure precisely this. They protect artists from misrepresentations of their work and its authorship after it has left their immediate control.

Another aim of this book has been to understand what I see as a performative contradiction between the rhetoric surrounding authorship in contemporary art theory and the way in which authorship actually functions in the art world. On the one hand, advanced art practice in the past century often presents itself as a sustained challenge to the traditional understanding of authorship and a demystification of artistic genius. The Duchampian readymade, Pop Art, Appropriation Art, Minimalism's anti-expressive objects, the rise of site-specific works, 'relational' art: each of these movements can be seen as part of a larger project to reject the Romantic ideal of the artwork as a unique, self-contained, self-sufficient product of an artist's singular vision and an inalienable expression of the artist's inner self. As Arthur Danto remarks, the consequence of these movements on our conception of the artist was profound: "Art no longer needed to be made by some specially gifted individual—the Artist—nor did it require any particular set of skills. It no longer needed to be difficult to make."[3] Thus, the changes to the artistic landscape in the past century can be seen as repeated challenges not only to the question "What is an artwork?" but also "What is an

---

[2] Cyrill Rigamonti, "Deconstructing Moral Rights," *Harvard International Law Journal* 47, no. 2 (2006): 355.

[3] Arthur Danto, *Unnatural Wonders* (New York: Farrar, Straus, Giroux, 2005), 14–15.

artist?" Danto's text implies that the most salient art movements of the twentieth century involved a self-imposed downgrade in status for the artist (who was formerly the 'Artist'). We can see echoes of this idea in Prince's statement, quoted at the beginning of this chapter, that he didn't go along with the belief that artists were special people who had something special to say.

On the other hand, however, it seems clear to me that these theoretical gestures at the demystification and diminishment of the artist's status do not carry over to the practical sphere of art authorship. Internationally, moral rights legislation for artists has been strengthened, not diminished, over the past few decades.[4] In many if not most respects, the Romantic ideology of authorship seems just as firmly in place as ever, even if our understanding of the possible forms that art can take has been enlarged.[5] I do not think this is a bad thing; what I find puzzling is the dissonance between the theoretical disavowals of the importance and meaning of artistic authorship and the evident commitment that artists, viewers, collectors, and institutions maintain toward it.

Richard Prince may not be responsible for making the images that he chooses to feature in his artworks, but he is widely recognized in the art world as their author. In the quote above, he identifies himself as a player in the artistic movement to "redefine" the concept of authorship in just the way that Danto describes. As I pointed out in Chapter Six, however, that is only partially true. Prince has certainly achieved fame and fortune by successfully appropriating mass-produced advertising imagery as the source material for his art. While this may subvert the expectation that artists be the source of their works' imagery, Prince is just as much the author of his artworks as the canonical artists he mentions hoping his work "stands up next to." He claims responsibility and credit for selecting certain images from the vast ocean of available material; he alters their scale; sometimes he adds painterly touches or collages them. By using advertisements as the source material for his art he was original in one way by refusing to be original in another. The fact that his work is

---

[4] Cyrill Rigamonti, "The Conceptual Transformation of Moral Rights," *The American Journal of Comparative Law* 55 (2007). See also Martha Buskirk, *The Contingent Object of Contemporary Art* (Cambridge, MA: MIT Press, 2005), 49.

[5] K. E. Gover, "The Solitary Author as Collective Fiction," in *Collaborative Art in the Twenty-First Century*, ed. Sondra Bacharach, Jeremy Neil Booth, and Siv B. Fjaerestad (New York: Routledge, 2016). A few sentences in the present chapter originally appeared here.

collected in major museums around the world suggests that at least some very influential people do believe that as an artist he is someone special with "something special to say," even and perhaps because his work is designed, on one level, to contravene precisely that ideal.

Perhaps one will see this not as a contradiction but as merely a clever irony: Prince and his peers in appropriation art author works that challenge the concept of authorship as such. But I think the tension between theory and practice sometimes goes beyond irony. The point is not to bemoan postmodernism and the current 'deskilled' artistic climate. That ship sailed long ago. Rather, my intention is to point out a peril of reducing the artwork to the idea that it represents at the expense of the social reality it inhabits and circulates in. By focusing only on what makes certain artworks—or entire art forms—distinctively different from what has come before them, we run the risk of ignoring the fundamental stability of the concepts within which these variations take place and have meaning. In other words, the movements that Danto points to as so conceptually innovative take place within a system that simultaneously encourages and absorbs the new and 'contra-standard' while preserving the basic concepts of artwork and artist that govern it. As Larry Shiner puts it:

the modern system of art has retained its most general features even in the gestures and writings of those who challenge it. When critics like Rosalind Krauss expose the 'myth of the avant-garde' or artists like Sherrie Levine exhibit photographic copies of Walker Evans's works as a parody of 'originality,' they pay tribute to the norms of the modern system of art even as they challenge them.[6]

Shiner is not the only observer to notice this tension in contemporary art between, on the one hand, the gestures of defiance and challenge to the ideology of authorship, and, on the other hand the practical dependence on those norms and concepts.[7] As Richard Prince says, "all it is is philosophical . . . its academic." I take him here to be using "philosophical" and "academic" in the derogatory sense that these ideas are purely theoretical and do not necessarily have any real consequence. He seems to be saying that while his art does engage with some of the ideas surrounding the demystification of artistic authorship, his primary

---

[6] Larry Shiner, *The Invention of Art* (Chicago: University of Chicago Press, 2001), 8.

[7] Martha Buskirk, for example, articulates this dynamic as well. Buskirk, *The Contingent Object of Contemporary Art.*

concern is not to provide a comprehensive redefinition of the term, but to make great works of art that will enable him to stand as a peer next to his artistic heroes. I find this to be a touchingly honest admission of his fundamental aim as an artist, and one that in my experience many other artists share: they aspire to make artworks that live up to the standard set by those who most inspire them.

As an academic philosopher, however, my question is actually about the relation between the ideal and the real in contemporary art. As someone who takes both art and theory seriously, I find it puzzling that the social reality of art authorship so often belies the claims made by artists and their artworks about the nature of their own activity. Since a third aim of this book has been to show that real-world cases and controversies are valuable sources for philosophical reflection, I would like to offer three final examples that will illuminate my query before I bring this book-length essay on artistic freedom and authority to a close.

1. In the 1960s and 70s Minimalist sculptor Donald Judd sold work to collectors that sometimes consisted of nothing more than a document with instructions and authorization for the construction of a sculpture. This disrupted the usual expectation that an artwork be a finished artifact. It was also seen as a refutation of the notion that an authentic artwork must issue directly from the hand of its artist. Count Giuseppe Panza di Bruno was a leading collector of Minimalist and Conceptual art who owned some of Judd's certificates. In Panza's words:

They were not objects. They were works of the intellect that could become a reality at any time, in the near or distant future, just like a plan for erecting a building or making a machine. They were works of intelligence in the real sense of the word. The artists were fully aware of this fact. They sold the certificate with all the instructions for making the work: they were not selling an existing sculpture made with their own hands from wood or stone, or cast in bronze from a model. The artists were not only conscious of this special trait of their work but, on the contrary, they were proud of having been the first to create a new approach to art, free from the slavery of the market or money. In a period when everything, above all the merchandizing of art, was being disputed, this characteristic was acclaimed as the beginning of a new freedom and a new age.[8]

---

[8] Giuseppe Panza, *Memories of a Collector*, trans. Michael Haggerty (New York: Abbeville Press, 2007), 137.

Some years later, Panza attempted to have some of the Judds fabricated because he was selling his collection to the Guggenheim and the museum wanted objects and not just sets of instructions. Judd angrily denounced the fabrications as fakes because he claimed that Panza did not faithfully follow his instructions or consult him.[9] To this day, the Guggenheim owns certificates from Panza's collection that it will not fabricate because of the uncertainty surrounding the conditions for authenticity.[10]

2. The composer John Cage is a major figure of the postwar avant-garde. He is famous for his unusual instrumentation, the use of chance elements in his compositions, and most of all for his piece 4'33", which consists of the ambient sounds of the music hall while a musician sits in silence for three movements totaling four minutes and thirty-three seconds at the piano. Cage deliberately defied the usual standards and expectations for musical works, often shocking or annoying his audiences so as to expand their understanding of what music could or should be.

And yet, as the scholar and critic Richard Taruskin points out, Cage's avant-garde gestures often had the opposite effect from their ostensible intent. The piece 4'33", for example, was supposed to bring art down to the level of 'life,' and to liberate the musical work from the aesthetic attitude. And yet

the audience is invited—no, commanded—to listen to ambient or natural sounds with the same attitude of reverent contemplation they would assume if they were listening to Beethoven's Ninth. This is an attitude that is born not of nature, but of Beethoven. By the act of triggering it, art is not brought down to earth; "life" is brought up for the duration into the empyrean. 4'33" is thus the ultimate aesthetic aggrandizement, an act of transcendental empyrialism.[11]

Taruskin goes on to point out that 4'33" also has a published, copyrighted score. The radical gesture of making a musical work that consists of the *absence* of composed, performed music simultaneously challenges the standard concept of 'musical work' and at the same time remains utterly dependent on it. 4'33" gains its significance as a radical work from the fact that it takes place in the same context (the concert hall), with

---

[9] Randy Kennedy, "Tricky Business: Defining Authenticity: Guggenheim Project Confronts Conceptual Art's Nature," *New York Times*, December 20, 2013.

[10] See https://www.guggenheim.org/conservation/the-panza-collection-initiative/donald-judd. Accessed September 10, 2017.

[11] Richard Taruskin, "No Ear for Music: The Scary Purity of John Cage," *The New Republic*, March 15, 1993, 33–4.

the same attitudes and practices (reverent attention) that have been developed for the appreciation of standard musical works. In much the same way that works of appropriation art highlight the fact of authorship rather than undermine it, 4'33" does not succeed in bringing art down to the level of life, but instead has the effect of throwing into high relief the conditions in which musical appreciation occurs and is made possible.

Taruskin also observes that Cage's aleatory compositions consisted in a similarly paradoxical dynamic concerning the composer's status and power. His compositions involving chance operations were ostensibly a form of artistic ego-effacement because it marked an absence of artistic control. The *I Ching* determined the order in which the parts were played, rather than the artist. However, this compositional device that aimed at a renunciation of artistic agency and responsibility had in many respects the opposite effect. Cage is unable to fully hand over authorship of his compositions to chance, because he is the one who chose to use the *I Ching*.

3. Wim Delvoye's *Cloaca*. "Cloaca" is Latin for "sewer." And yet Delvoye's sculpture does not imitate or represent a sewer, but rather reproduces what the human body puts *into* one. Delvoye's giant contraption, which in one version looks like a series of vertically stacked washing machines, seeks to replicate the human digestive system. Food is added at the top, and, when all goes well, something resembling human fecal matter exits at the bottom. The excretions are then dried, vacuum-sealed in plastic, and sold to collectors. In an interview, Delvoye describes the somewhat surprising turn of events in which the price for Cloaca's output doubled after it was exhibited in Paris.[12]

Cloaca's products are not only surprisingly popular, but some of it is in higher demand than others. The artist explains that there is a waiting list for the New York shit. (Despite its ungainly size, *Cloaca* is a travelling digestive tract). As Delvoye somewhat forlornly explains in the interview, this difference in demand "in itself contradicts what my intentions were, because it's all about being equal. Art is always about enhancing your status, so I'm very interested in shit because shit somehow is so anti-status. It's an equalizer. We are all much more closer together if we think of our arse."[13] The artist claims that his intention was to make an

---

[12] Ben Lewis, "Art Safari" (Brooklyn, NY: Icarus Films Home Video, 2009).
[13] Ibid.

artwork that challenges our obsession with status, that offers a democratizing gesture in the face of art world fetishism, and yet by his own admission he has failed to do so: his manufactured shit is selling like hotcakes.

In all three of these examples, the artworks provocatively challenge the boundary between art and life. In daily life, we have abundant access to mass-produced plywood shelves, to four-and-a-half-minute stretches of silence, and to genuine shit. But to encounter a work of art that consists of these disposable features of everydayness is something else entirely. Among other things, these works exemplify artistic freedom in one of its derivative senses—the negative freedom from ideological constraint or custom. The artists have succeeded in making art out of shockingly mundane materials. (And if these displays of artistic derring-do serve to *épater la bourgeoisie*, so much the better.) In each case, however, there is a conflict between what the artist intends or purports to accomplish in the work, and the actual effect it has as an authored work of art. I do not think these are isolated examples. I see them as emblematic of the tension between the modern art system and the expectation, borne of the nineteenth-century avant-garde, that art will somehow, per impossibile, dismantle that system from within.

It may be tempting to read these examples simply as illustrations of the mendacity, pomposity, and Tartuffery that surround contemporary art and its attendant rhetoric. The popular notion that cutting-edge artists are frauds and charlatans is as old as the positive view that they are visionaries and prophets.[14] A softer version of the hypocrisy charge would be to say that these artists have simply failed to realize their intentions for their artworks. Just as a traditional portrait painter may try and fail to produce an adequate likeness of his model, conceptual artists may try and fail to accomplish something particular with their works. According to this line of argument, artists such as Judd, Cage, and Delvoye simply lack the integrity to follow through in practice with what their artworks tacitly assert in theory. The cognitive dissonance that arises from the tension between their attempts to challenge artistic norms and the concomitant reinforcement of those norms is just an indication of their artistic failings. If Delvoye, for example, truly believed

---

[14] Shiner, *The Invention of Art*, 201–6.

that his artwork were about democracy and equality, then he would choose not to profit from the high prices that his *Cloaca* is able to command. If Cage truly wanted to efface the distinction between art and life, music and noise, he would not make works that rely so heavily on the norms and conventions of musical appreciation.[15] And if Judd really believed that authorship consists in the design of an artwork and not its execution, he would not have been so concerned about controlling the details of his work's fabrication, especially since this is precisely the aspect of the work that he had renounced in the first place by choosing not to make it himself. Perhaps, if Barthes really wanted to be consistent with his own message, he should have refused to sign his influential "Death of the Author" polemic. And yet he did.

But personal and artistic failings cannot account for the conflicts and tensions that these cases contain. While the portrait of the artist as a divinely inspired madman is an ancient one, the examples I offered above are not instances of artists behaving badly, or even disingenuously, with respect to their work. Of course, artists (like anyone else) are capable of breaking promises or contradicting themselves. In Chapter Two, I discussed one of the first lawsuits to invoke an artist's 'moral right': James McNeill Whistler refused to deliver a portrait of Lady Eden that had been commissioned by Lord Eden. Whistler had initially agreed to a possible price of 100 guineas for the picture, but he evidently changed his mind once the minimum payment was made. While we can ask whether the principle of artistic freedom authorizes an artist to change the terms of a commission, there is no question that he breached the initial agreement. Similarly, one could ask whether Donald Judd failed to honor the language of his original contract with Count Panza when he acrimoniously objected to the fabrication of his plywood boxes decades later.[16]

Aside from the perhaps irresolvable questions of whether Panza deliberately disregarded Judd's wishes, or whether Judd changed his mind or

---

[15] Stephen Davies uses the language of failed intentions when he says "Cage failed with 4'33" if his prime intention was to draw our attention to the naked aesthetic potential of ordinary sounds. He failed because he intended to create an artwork and succeeded in doing so, thereby transforming the qualities of the sounds to which that work directs our attention." Stephen Davies, "John Cage's 4'33": Is It Music?," *Australasian Journal of Philosophy* 75, no. 4 (1997): 453.

[16] For a detailed discussion of Panza and Judd's struggles over authorship and authorization, see Buskirk, *The Contingent Object of Contemporary Art*, 34–48.

was merely acting out of pique at Panza for selling his work to a major museum at a very high price, this case is emblematic of a deeper conflict that supersedes the particular circumstances surrounding the personalities involved. These examples all demonstrate the persistence of the norms and concepts surrounding artistic authorship even in those artworks that seek to undermine it. In the case of Judd's sculptures that he designs but does not assemble himself, they are only significant as a challenge to the norms of artistic production if they maintain their status as *his* authored artworks. Otherwise they risk misrecognition as some other kind of artifact—perhaps as recipes for a rather simplistic set of shelves. Judd's anxiety that his sculptures might not look exactly the way he wanted, despite his having ceded at least some degree of control over this very aspect of his work, reflects the fact that they were first and foremost authored works. As presumptive extensions and representatives of Judd the Artist, he would be seen as responsible for their three-dimensional manifestations. If Judd thinks they look bad, then they might make *him* look bad.

Thus, Danto's description of the effects that postwar American art has had on the concept of the artist only tells part of the story. His observation captures something important about the ways in which movements like Pop Art, Minimalism, and appropriation art have expanded our understanding of what it can mean to author an artwork and what forms that authorship can take. However, his account focuses so narrowly on the philosophical dimension of these gestures—the ways in which these innovative art forms have expanded and challenged the limits of what we consider to be art, and how we expect it to be made—that it ignores the basic stability of the system in which these works circulate and obtain recognition. Indeed, one might respond to his story about artists having undergone a self-imposed diminution in status by objecting that the effect is just the contrary: the ability of artists in the past century to transfigure just about anything into a work of art, be it a urinal, random noises, or even their own anxiety, serves to further mystify the artist's special powers of transformation, not to unmask them.[17] The fact that

---

[17] Cf. Steven Goldsmith, "The Readymades of Marcel Duchamp: The Ambiguities of an Artistic Revolution," *Journal of Aesthetics and Art Criticism* (1983). Becker points out that "Moulin (1978) and many others suggest that contemporary visual art, following the lead of Marcel Duchamp, has increasingly emphasized the artist over the work, insisting in effect

making art appears not to require special skills and no longer has to be difficult to make has not in fact resulted in a concomitant decline in the status, prestige, or power of the artist. Danto claims that the artist no longer needs to be a gifted individual, but one might see their ability to transfigure the most unlikely of objects into works of art as a special gift, indeed. It would be more precise to say that making art requires skill, but the artistic movements of the past century have had a significant impact on what kinds of skills are seen as important.[18]

The much-maligned and misunderstood Romantic artist is an entrenched feature of our culture, even in so-called postmodern art that claims to rebel against precisely this idea. Part of the problem, as I have argued elsewhere, is that we do not have an accurate understanding of what the Romantic conception of art authorship is, which was far more limited and pragmatic than its antagonists portray it as.[19] The ideal of artistic freedom is part of that cultural heritage, and it has come to have a variety of concatenated but disparate meanings: freedom from rules or constraints; freedom of expression; freedom from contracts or commissions; and, most fundamentally, I have argued, freedom to claim or disavow authorship of the works that one has made.

One might reply that Judd is so invested in the public face of his work because his name had by that time become a brand, and he was simply trying to protect the value of his name and his work. This indicates another possible response to the problem posed by the foregoing examples: blame the market. One might argue that the demands of the art market require artists to behave in ways that contravene the loftier ideals that their artworks might express, but that this is not a philosophical problem. For example, Delvoye's *Cloaca* is an artwork that produces manufactured human excrement so as to make a statement about our

---

that anything an artist does thereby becomes art." Howard S. Becker, *Art Worlds*, 25th Anniversary ed. (Berkeley: University of California Press, 2008), 355.

[18] See Paisley Livingston, *Art and Intention: A Philosophical Study* (Oxford: Oxford University Press, 2005), 41. As another author puts it, "other guarantees are necessary to convince audiences that art, even in its most radical and nihilistic expressions, is still a serious matter of skill, knowledge, and involvement, an expert activity over which the artist and his coworkers justifiably claim jurisdictional control." Pierre-Michel Menger, "Profiles of the Unfinished: Rodin's Work and the Varieties of Incompleteness," in *Art from Start to Finish*, ed. Howard S. Becker, Robert R. Faulkner, and Barbara Kirshenblatt-Gimblett (Chicago: University of Chicago Press, 2006), 61.

[19] Gover, "The Solitary Author as Collective Fiction."

shared, common humanity. But it will be no surprise (at least to some) that the value of *Cloaca's* output has grown, and that the shit produced in some cities has become more desirable, and hence more expensive, than that produced in others. People are irrational; they fetishize all kinds of strange things and are willing to pay exorbitant prices for them. One might also point out that Delvoye deserves to make a living from his artistic labors. Most importantly, however, it could be replied that whatever value the market attaches to his artwork as a commodity has nothing to do with its meaning—the meaning communicated by the work belongs to an entirely different order than the contingent value it acquires as an artifact circulating (however ironically) as a marker of prestige. It may be the case, as Delvoye himself suggests, that the meaning of the work contravenes its value on the art market, but there is no necessary connection between the work's meaning *qua* artwork and its value *qua* commodity.

I find it difficult to insist on such a rigorous conceptual separation between the work's meaning and its value as an object, however, when so much of the art of the past century has been devoted to a self-referential critique of its own nature, value, and position in society. Count Panza himself said that Judd's artwork-instructions were supposed to constitute a liberation from the artist's "slavery" to the art market. (Though Panza subsequently sold his collection to the Guggenheim for millions.) It seems to me that the explanation for this strange discrepancy can be found in the tacit expectation that we overlook the inherently utopian character of art's attempts to dismantle its governing concepts from within. If art were to truly succeed in effacing the boundary between art and life, or in denying that artists are the effective cause of the works they author, then the works in question would risk being unrecognizable as works of art. And it is only by virtue of being first of all artworks that their radical gestures gain interest or meaning.

It seems that we are being asked to regard these works with a kind of double-vision, in which we agree that nothing that the artist or artwork says about itself has any bearing on the practical transactions in which that work appears and circulates. But if, as philosophers of art, we only consider the work in abstraction from its actual habitat, we will misunderstand our subject. Some things will seem clear that are not in fact so simple, and others will appear puzzling when in fact the answers can be found by taking praxis seriously.

In this sense, the relation between artists and philosophers of art is asymmetrical in precisely the way that Barnett Newman supposedly said in his famous quip that "Aesthetics is for painting as Ornithology is for the birds." Richard Prince does not need to consult any theoretical treatises on art authorship (not even this one) in order to make his artworks, even artworks that meaningfully engage with ideas about the nature of authorship. Philosophers of art, however, can only understand their subject if they attend to the practices and norms that inform artistic production. And it is often in the midst of messy real-world controversies that they will find those norms being both challenged and at the same time made explicit.

Acknowledgments

This book would not have been possible without the generous assistance and influence of many people and institutions. I owe my home institution, Bennington College, and in particular Isabel Roche, a large debt of gratitude for support of this project in all of its stages. My colleagues there have been a tremendous source of inspiration and support. Peter Momtchiloff at Oxford University Press has been a patient and steadfast supporter. The *Journal of Aesthetics and Art Criticism* originally published my essay on the Mass MoCA case in 2011, which became the seed of this book. Chapter Four is a revised version of that article. The following people have been indispensable in providing their support, advice, feedback, and encouragement during the many stages of this work's development: Larry Shiner, Paul Voice, Christy Mag Uidhir, Darren Hudson Hick, Sherri Irvin, Dom Lopes, and the anonymous reviewers of this manuscript. Finally, I would like to thank Jon Isherwood for all of his personal and professional support, and to whom I dedicate this work with love, admiration, and respect.

Works Cited

Adeney, Elizabeth. *The Moral Rights of Artists and Performers*. Oxford: Oxford University Press, 2006.

Adorno, Theodor. *Aesthetic Theory*. Translated by Robert Hullot-Kentor. Minneapolis: University of Minnesota, 1997.

Allen, Greg, ed. *Canal Zone Richard Prince Yes Rasta: Selected Court Documents from Cariou V. Prince Et Al*: greg.org, 2011.

Auden, W.H. *The Collected Poetry of W.H. Auden*. New York: Random House, 1945.

Bach, Steven. *Final Cut: Art, Money, and Ego in the Making of Heaven's Gate, the Film That Sank United Artists*. Updated ed. New York: Newmarket Press, 1999.

Baldwin, Carl. "Art & the Law: Property Right vs. 'Moral Right'." *Art in America*, September/October 1974, 33–4.

Barbour, Adrianne. "Yes, Rasta 2.0: Cariou v. Prince and the Fair Use Test of Transformative Use in Appropriation Art Cases." *Tulane Journal of Technology & Intellectual Property* 14 (2011): 365–84.

Barker, Ian. *Anthony Caro: Quest for the New Sculpture*. Hampshire: Lund Humphries, 2004.

Barron, Anne. "Kant, Copyright, and Communicative Freedom." *Law and Philosophy* 31 (2012): 1–48.

Baum, Kelly, Andrea Bayer, and Sheena Wagstaff. "Unfinished: Thoughts Left Visible." edited by The Metropolitan Museum of Art. New Haven: Yale University Press, 2016.

Baxandall, Michael. *Painting and Experience in Fifteenth-Century Italy*. Oxford: Oxford University Press, 1988.

Baxandall, Michael. *Patterns of Intention: On the Historical Explanation of Pictures*. New Haven: Yale University Press, 1985.

Becker, Howard S. "The Work Itself." In *Art from Start to Finish*, edited by Howard S. Becker, Robert R. Faulkner, and Barbara Kirshenblatt-Gimblett. Chicago: University of Chicago Press, 2006.

Becker, Howard S. *Writing for Social Scientists*. Second ed. Chicago: University of Chicago Press, 2007.

Becker, Howard S. *Art Worlds*. 25th Anniversary ed. Berkeley: University of California Press, 2008.

Beitz, Charles R. "The Moral Rights of Creators of Artistic and Literary Works." *The Journal of Political Philosophy* 13, no. 3 (2005): 330–58.

Binkley, Timothy. "Piece: Contra Aesthetics." *Journal of Aesthetics and Art Criticism* 35, no. 3 (1977): 265–77.

Blume, Dieter, ed. *Anthony Caro. A Catalogue Raisonné. Steel Sculptures 1960–1980.* 14 vols. Vol. 3. Cologne, Germany: Galerie Wentzel, 1981.

Brain, David. "Material Agency and the Art of Artifacts." *The Sociology of Art: A Reader*, ed. Jeremy Tanner. London: Routledge, 2003.

Buskirk, Martha. *The Contingent Object of Contemporary Art*. Cambridge, MA: MIT Press, 2005.

Camp, Julie Van. "Freedom of Expression at the National Endowment for the Arts: An Opportunity for Interdisciplinary Education." *Journal of Aesthetic Education* 30, no. 3 (1996): 43–65.

Camp, Julie Van. "Non-Verbal Metaphor: A Non-Explanation of Meaning in Dance." *British Journal of Aesthetics* 36, no. 2 (1996): 177–87.

Carlin, John. "Culture Vultures: Artistic Appropriation and Intellectual Property Law." *Columbia VLA Journal of Law and the Arts* 13 (1988): 103–43.

Caro, Anthony, and Toby Glanville. *Caro by Anthony Caro*. London: Phaidon, 2014.

Carroll, Michael. "Fixing Fair Use." *North Carolina Law Review* 85 (2007): 1089–154.

Carroll, Noël. "Cage and Philosophy." *Journal of Aesthetics and Art Criticism* 52, no. 1 (1994): 93–8.

Chackal, Tony. "Of Materiality and Meaning: The Illegality Condition in Street Art." *Journal of Aesthetics and Art Criticism* 74, no. 4 (2017): 359–370.

Cohen, Amy. "Copyright Law and the Myth of Objectivity: The Idea-Expression Dichotomy and the Inevitability of Artistic Value Judgments." *Indiana Law Review* 66 (1990): 175–232.

Cohen, Patricia. "Ruling on Artistic Authenticity: The Market vs. The Law." *New York Times*, August 5, 2012.

Crowther, Paul. "Art and Autonomy." *British Journal of Aesthetics* 21 (1981): 12–21.

Danto, Arthur. "The Artworld." *Journal of Philosophy* 61, no. 19 (1964): 571–84.

Danto, Arthur. *Unnatural Wonders*. New York: Farrar, Straus, Giroux, 2005.

Davies, David. *Art as Performance*. Malden, MA: Blackwell, 2004.

Davies, David. "The Primacy of Practice in the Ontology of Art." *Journal of Aesthetics and Art Criticism* 67, no. 2 (2009): 159–70.

Davies, Stephen. "John Cage's 4'33": Is It Music?" *Australasian Journal of Philosophy* 75, no. 4 (1997): 448–62.

de la Fuente, Eduardo. "The 'New Sociology of Art': Putting Art Back into Social Science Approaches to the Arts." *Cultural Sociology* 1, no. 3 (2007): 409–25.

Derrida, Jacques. *Limited Inc.* Translated by Jeffrey Mehlman and Samuel Weber. Evanston: Northwestern University Press, 1988.

Dewey, John. *Art as Experience.* New York: Minton, Balch, & Co., 1934.

Dutton, Dennis. "Why Intentionalism Won't Go Away." In *Literature and the Question of Philosophy*, edited by Anthony J. Cascardi. Baltimore: Johns Hopkins University Press, 1987.

Editorial. "Issues and Commentary." *Art in America*, September/October 1974, 32.

Farley, Christine Haight. "Judging Art." *Tulane Law Review* 79 (2005): 806–58.

Fenner, David E. W. "Why Modifying (Some) Works of Art Is Wrong." *American Philosophical Quarterly* 43, no. 4 (2006): 329–41.

Finney, Henry. "Mediating Claims to Artistry: Social Stratification in a Local Visual Arts Community." *Sociological Forum* 8, no. 3 (1993): 403–31.

Freeland, Cynthia. *Portraits and Persons.* New York: Oxford University Press, 2010.

Fromer, Jeanne. "A Psychology of Intellectual Property." *Northwestern University Law Review* 104, no. 4 (2010): 1441–509.

Gaiger, Jason. "Dismantling the Frame: Site-Specific Art and Aesthetic Autonomy." *British Journal of Aesthetics* 49, no. 1 (2009): 43–58.

Garson, Francesca. "Before the Artist Came Along, It Was Just a Bridge." *Cornell Journal of Legal and Public Policy* 11 (2001): 203–244.

Gaskell, Ivan. "Being True to Artists." *Journal of Aesthetics and Art Criticism* 61, no. 1 (2003): 53–60.

Goehr, Lydia. *The Imaginary Museum of Musical Works.* Revised ed. New York: Oxford University Press, 2007.

Goldsmith, Steven. "The Readymades of Marcel Duchamp: The Ambiguities of an Artistic Revolution." *Journal of Aesthetics and Art Criticism* 42, no. 2 (1983): 197–208.

Gover, K. E. "Ambivalent Agency: A Response to Trogdon and Livingston on Artwork Completion." *Journal of Aesthetics and Art Criticism* 73, no. 4 (2015): 457–60.

Gover, K. E. "The Solitary Author as Collective Fiction." In *Collaborative Art in the Twenty-First Century*, edited by Sondra Bacharach, Jeremy Neil Booth, and Siv B. Fjaerestad. New York: Routledge, 2016, 65–76.

Gover, K. E. "What Is Humpty Dumptyism in Contemporary Visual Art? A Reply to Maes." *British Journal of Aesthetics* 52, no. 2 (2012): 169–181.

Greenberg, Clement. "Letter to the Editor," *Art in America*, May/June 1978, 20–2.

Greenberg, Clement. "P.S." *Art in America*, March/April 1978.

Hammill, Sarah. "Polychrome in the Sixties: David Smith and Anthony Caro at Bennington." In *Anglo-American Exchange in Post-War Sculpture, 1945–1970*, edited by R. Peabody. Getty Online Publications, 2011.

Heinich, Natalie. "The Van Gogh Effect." In *The Sociology of Art: A Reader*, edited by Jeremy Tanner. London: Routledge, 2003, 122–31.

Hick, Darren Hudson. "A Reply to Paisley Livingston." *Journal of Aesthetics and Art Criticism* 66, no. 4 (2008): 395–8.

Hick, Darren Hudson. "When Is a Work of Art Finished?" *Journal of Aesthetics and Art Criticism* 66, no. 1 (2008): 67–76.

Hick, Darren Hudson. "Expressing Ideas: A Reply to Roger Shiner." *Journal of Aesthetics and Art Criticism* 68, no. 4 (2010): 405–8.

Hick, Darren Hudson. "Toward an Ontology of Authored Works." *British Journal of Aesthetics* 51, no. 2 (2011): 185–99.

Hick, Darren Hudson. "Appropriation and Transformation." *Fordham Intellectual Property Media & Entertainment Law Journal* 23 (2013): 101–40.

Hick, Darren Hudson. "Authorship, Co-Authorship, and Multiple Authorship." *Journal of Aesthetics and Art Criticism* 72, no. 2 (2014): 147–56.

Hilpinen, Risto. "Authors and Artifacts." *Proceedings of the Aristotelian Society* 93 (1993): 155–78.

Irvin, Sherri. "Appropriation and Authorship in Contemporary Art." *British Journal of Aesthetics* 45, no. 2 (2005): 124–37.

Irvin, Sherri. "The Artist's Sanction in Contemporary Art." *Journal of Aesthetics and Art Criticism* 63, no. 4 (2005): 315–26.

Irvin, Sherri. "Authors, Intentions, and Literary Meaning." *Philosophy Compass* 1, no. 2 (2006): 114–28.

Irvin, Sherri. "The Ontological Diversity of Visual Artworks." In *New Waves in Aesthetics*, edited by K. Stock and K. Thomson-Jones, 1–19. Basingstoke, UK: Palgrave Macmillan, 2008.

Jasiewicz, Monica Isia. "A Dangerous Undertaking: The Promise of Intentionalism and Promise of Expert Testimony in Appropriation Art Infringement Cases." *Yale Journal of Law & the Humanities* 26, no. 1 (2015): 143–83.

Joyce, Michael. "How Do I Know I Am Finnish?" In *Art from Start to Finish*, edited by Howard S. Becker, Robert R. Faulkner, and Barbara Kirshenblatt-Gimblett. Chicago: University of Chicago Press, 2006, 69–90.

Kant, Immanuel. *Critique of the Power of Judgment*. Translated by Paul Guyer and Eric Matthews. The Cambridge Edition of the Works of Immanuel Kant. Cambridge: Cambridge University Press, 2000.

Kaplan, Justin. *Walt Whitman: A Life*. New York: Simon and Schuster, 1979.

Kelly, Michael. "Public Art Controversy: The Serra and Lin Cases." *Journal of Aesthetics and Art Criticism* 54, no. 1 (1996): 15–22.

Kennedy, Randy. "Tricky Business: Defining Authenticity: Guggenheim Project Confronts Conceptual Art's Nature." *New York Times*, December 20, 2013, AR22.

Khatchadourian, Haig. "Artistic Freedom and Social Control." *Journal of Aesthetic Education* 12, no. 1 (1978): 23–32.

Kolker, Robert. "The Betrayal of Jasper Johns." *New York*, November 17–23, 2014.

Krauss, Rosalind. "Changing the Work of David Smith." *Art in America*, September/October 1974, 30–4.

Krauss, Rosalind. "Rosalind Krauss Replies." *Art in America*, March/April 1978.

Krauss, Rosalind. "The Cultural Logic of the Late Capitalist Museum." *October* 54 (1990): 3–17.

Kwall, Roberta Rosenthal. *The Soul of Creativity: Forging a Moral Rights Law for the United States*. Stanford: Stanford University Press, 2009.

Laermans, Rudi. "Deconstructing Individual Authorship: Artworks as Collective Products of Art Worlds." In *Art & Law*, edited by Bert Demarsin, Eltjo J.H. Schrage, Bernard Tilleman, and Alain Verbeke. Belgium: die Keure, 2008, 50–61.

Lamarque, Peter. "The Death of the Author: An Analytical Autopsy." *British Journal of Aesthetics* 30, no. 4 (1990): 319–31.

Lamarque, Peter. "Object, Work, and Interpretation." *Philosophy in the Contemporary World* 12, no. 1 (2005): 1–7.

Lamarque, Peter. "On Bringing a Work into Existence." In *Work and Object*. Oxford: Oxford University Press, 2010.

Lamarque, Peter. "The Uselessness of Art." *Journal of Aesthetics and Art Criticism* 68, no. 3 (2010): 205–14.

Lange-Berndt, Petra. "Replication and Decay in Damien Hirst's *Natural History*." Short Discussion Document, *Tate Papers*, no. 8 (2007). http://www.tate.org.uk/research/publications/tate-papers/08.

Lankford, E. Louis. "Artistic Freedom: An Artworld Paradox." *Journal of Aesthetic Education* 24, no. 3 (1990): 15–28.

Lee, Brian A. "Making Sense of 'Moral Rights' in Intellectual Property." *Temple Law Review* 84 (2007): 71–118.

Lerner, Ben. "The Custodians: How the Whitney Is Transforming the Art of Museum Conservation." *The New Yorker*, January 11, 2016.

Leval, Pierre N. "Toward a Fair Use Standard." *Harvard Law Review* 103 (1990): 1105–36.

Levinson, Jerrold. "Intention and Interpretation: A Last Look." In *Intention and Interpretation*, edited by Gary Iseminger. Philadelphia: Temple University Press, 1992, 221–56.

Lewis, Ben. "Art Safari." Brooklyn, NY: Icarus Films Home Video, 2009.

Liemer, Susan. "Understanding Artists' Moral Rights: A Primer." *Boston University Public Interest Law Journal* 41 (1998): 41–57.

Livingston, Paisley. "Counting Fragments, and Frenhofer's Paradox." *British Journal of Aesthetics* 39, no. 1 (1999): 14–23.

Livingston, Paisley. "Pentimento." In *The Creation of Art*, edited by Berys Gaut and Paisley Livingston. Cambridge: Cambridge University Press, 2003, 89–115.

Livingston, Paisley. *Art and Intention: A Philosophical Study*. Oxford: Oxford University Press, 2005.

Livingston, Paisley. "When a Work Is Finished: A Response to Darren Hudson Hick." *Journal of Aesthetics and Art Criticism* 66, no. 4 (2008): 393–5.

Livingston, Paisely, and Carol Archer. "Artistic Collaboration and the Completion of Works of Art." *British Journal of Aesthetics* 50 (2010): 439–55.

Maes, Hans. "Intention, Interpretation, and Contemporary Visual Art." *British Journal of Aesthetics* 50, no. 2 (2010): 121–38.

Mag Uidhir, Christy. *Art and Art-Attempts*. Oxford: Oxford University Press, 2013.

McKenzie, Liz. "Drawing Lines: Addressing Cognitive Bias in Art Appropriation Cases." *UCLA Entertainment Law Review* 20, no. 1 (2013): 83–105.

McLean, Willajeane. "All's Not Fair in Art and War: A Look at the Fair Use Defense after Rogers V. Koons." *Brooklyn Law Review* 59 (1993): 373–422.

Menger, Pierre-Michel. "Profiles of the Unfinished: Rodin's Work and the Varieties of Incompleteness." In *Art from Start to Finish*, edited by Howard S. Becker, Robert R. Faulkner, and Barbara Kirshenblatt-Gimblett. Chicago: University of Chicago Press, 2006, 31–68.

Merryman, John Henry. "The Refrigerator of Bernard Buffet." In *Thinking About the Elgin Marbles: Critical Essays on Cultural Property, Art, and Law*, 406–30. Alphen aan den Rijn, the Netherlands: Kluwer Law International, 2009.

Merryman, John Henry, Albert E. Elsen, and Stephen K. Urice. *Law, Ethics, and the Visual Arts*. Fifth ed. Alphen aan den Rijn, the Netherlands: Kluwer Law International, 2007.

Micchelli, Thomas. "Purgatory Lost: Mass Moca Trashes *Democracy*." *Brooklyn Rail*, 2007.

Neill, Alex, and Aaron Ridley, eds. *Arguing About Art: Contemporary Philosophical Debates*: New York: Routledge, 2007.

Newman, G. E., and Paul Bloom. "Art and Authenticity: The Importance of Originals in Judgments of Value." *Journal of Experimental Psychology: General* (November 2011): 1–12.

Ng, Alina. "The Author's Rights in Literary and Artistic Works." *J. Marshall Review of Intellectual Property Law* 9 (2009): 453–99.

Ong, Burton. "Why Moral Rights Matter: Recognizing the Intrinsic Value of Integrity Rights." *The Columbia Journal of Law & the Arts* (2003): 297–312.

Panza, Giuseppe. *Memories of a Collector*. Translated by Michael Haggerty. New York: Abbeville Press, 2007.

Rigamonti, Cyrill. "Deconstructing Moral Rights." *Harvard International Law Journal* 47, no. 2 (2006): 353–412.

Rigamonti, Cyrill. "The Conceptual Transformation of Moral Rights." *The American Journal of Comparative Law* 55 (2007): 67–122.

Rose, Mark. *Authors and Owners: The Invention of Copyright*. Cambridge: Harvard University Press, 1993.

Rubin, William. "More on David Smith." *Art in America*, May/June 1978, 5.

Sax, Joseph. *Playing Darts with a Rembrandt*. Ann Arbor: University of Michigan Press, 1999.

Schjeldahl, Peter. "When It Pours: Works by Helen Frankenthaler and Morris Louis." *The New Yorker*, September 22, 2014, 110–11.

Shiner, Larry. *The Invention of Art*. Chicago: University of Chicago Press, 2001.

Shiner, Roger. "Ideas, Expressions, and Plots." *Journal of Aesthetics and Art Criticism* 68, no. 4 (2010): 401–5.

Sibley, Frank. *Approach to Aesthetics: Collected Papers on Philosophical Aesthetics*, edited by John Benson, Betty Redfern, and Jeremy Roxbee Cox. Oxford: Clarendon Press, 2001.

Smith, Roberta. "Is It Art Yet? And Who Decides?" *New York Times*, September 16, 2007.

Sparshott, Francis. "Why Works of Art Have No Right to Have Rights." *Journal of Aesthetics and Art Criticism* 42, no. 1 (1983): 5–15.

Stecker, Robert. *Interpretation and Construction: Art, Speech, and Law*. Malden, MA: Blackwell, 2003.

Stecker, Robert. "Moderate Actual Intentionalism Defended." *Journal of Aesthetics and Art Criticism* 64, no. 4 (2006): 429–38.

Sturgis, Alexander, Rupert Christiansen, Lois Oliver, and Michael Wilson. *Rebels and Martyrs: The Image of the Artist in the Nineteenth Century*, edited by National Gallery. London: Yale University Press, 2006.

Sundara Rajan, Mira. *Moral Rights: Principles, Practice and New Technology*. Oxford: Oxford University Press, 2011.

Taruskin, Richard. "No Ear for Music: The Scary Purity of John Cage." *The New Republic*, March 15, 1993, 26–35.

Temkin, Ann. "Strange Fruit." In *Mortality/Immortality? The Legacy of 20th Century Art*, edited by Miguel Corzo. Los Angeles: Getty Conservation Institute, 1999, 45–50.

Thomasson, Amie. "Ontological Innovation in Art." *Journal of Aesthetics and Art Criticism* 68, no. 2 (2010): 119–30.

Tormey, Alan. "Aesthetic Rights." *Journal of Aesthetics and Art Criticism* 32, no. 2 (1973): 163–70.

Trogdon, Kelly, and Paisley Livingston. "The Complete Work." *Journal of Aesthetics and Art Criticism* 72, no. 3 (2014): 225–33.

Trogdon, Kelly, and Paisely Livingston. "Artwork Completion: A Response to Gover." *Journal of Aesthetics and Art Criticism* 73, no. 4 (2015): 460–2.

Vogel, Carol. "When Modern Art Shows Its Age, Conservators Struggle to Reconstruct the Fragile and Ephemeral." *New York Times*, April 5, 2001.

Waterfield, Giles. "The Artist's Studio." In *The Artist's Studio*, edited by Giles Waterfield. London: Paul Holberton Publishing, 2009.

"Whistler's Paris Suit Ended: He May Keep the Picture of Lady Eden and Declares His Triumph." *The New York Times*, December 18, 1897.

Wolterstorff, Nicholas. "Philosophy of Art after Analysis and Romanticism." *Journal of Aesthetics and Art Criticism* 46 (1987): 151–67.

Woodmansee, Martha. *The Author, Art, and the Market: Rereading the History of Aesthetics*. New York: Columbia University Press, 1994.

Young, James. "Destroying Works of Art." *Journal of Aesthetics and Art Criticism* 47, no. 4 (1989): 367–73.

Zemer, Lior. "Moral Rights: Limited Edition." *Boston University Law Review* 91 (2011): 1519–68.

Index

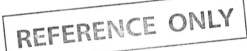